Essays on Skepticism, Relativism, and Ethics in the *Zhuangzi*

SUNY Series in Chinese Philosophy and Culture

David L. Hall, Editor

Essays on Skepticism, Relativism, and Ethics in the *Zhuangzi*

Edited by
Paul Kjellberg
and Philip J. Ivanhoe

State University of New York Press

Published by
State University of New York Press, Albany

© 1996 State University of New York

For information, address State University of New York Press,
90 State Street, Suite 700, Albany, NY 12207

Production by Laura Starrett
Marketing by Dana Yanulavich

Library of Congress Cataloging-in-Publication Data

Essays on skepticism, relativisim, and ethics in the Zhuangzi / edited
    by Paul Kjellberg and Philip J. Ivanhoe
        p.   cm. — (SUNY series in Chinese philosophy and culture)
    Includes bibliographical references and index.
    ISBN 0-7914-2891-5. — ISBN 0-7914-2892-3 (pbk.)
    1. Chuang-tzu.   2. Skepticism.   I. Kjellberg, Paul.   II. Ivanhoe,
P. J.   III. Series.
BL1900.C576E77   1996
181'.114—dc20   95-19688
                                                              CIP

10 9 8 7 6 5 4 3 2 1

Contents

Acknowledgments [vii]

Note on Conventions [xi]

Introduction [xiii]

One   Sextus Empiricus, Zhuangzi, and Xunzi
           on "Why Be Skeptical?" [1]
                 Paul Kjellberg

Two   Skeptical Strategies in the *Zhuangzi* and *Theaetetus* [26]
                 Lisa Raphals

Three   Zhuangzi and Nāgārjuna on the Truth of No Truth [50]
                 David Loy

Four   Zhuangzi's Attitude Toward Language and His Skepticism [68]
                 Eric Schwitzgebel

Five   Language: The Guest of Reality—Zhuangzi and Derrida
           on Language, Reality, and Skillfulness [97]
                 Mark Berkson

Six   Cook Ding's Dao and the Limits of Philosophy [127]
                 Robert Eno

Seven   Zhuangzi's Understanding of Skillfulness and
           the Ultimate Spiritual State [152]
                 Lee H. Yearley

Eight   Spontaneity and Education of the Emotions
           in the *Zhuangzi* [183]
                 Joel Kupperman

Nine   Was Zhuangzi a Relativist? [196]
                 Philip J. Ivanhoe

Bibliography [215]

Contributors [227]

Name Index [229]

Subject Index [235]

Acknowledgments

We thank the contributors to the present volume for their work and for their patience with us as editors and Roger T. Ames, editor of *Philosophy East & West*, for permission to print the essays by Kjellberg and Raphals, earlier versions of which appeared in this journal.

We also would like to acknowledge the generous support of the School of Humanities and Sciences and the departments of Philosophy and Religious Studies of Stanford University, who provided funds to help in the preparation of this manuscript for publication. Our special thanks goes to Margaret Weatherford for her careful reading and helpful comments on these essays.

—Paul Kjellberg
Whittier, California
—Philip J. Ivanhoe
Stanford, California

We dedicate this volume to the memory of Angus Charles Graham, whose pioneering excursions into Chinese thought—in particular the *Zhuangzi*—opened up the fields so many of us now cultivate. His scholarship broke new ground and set the standards across a broad spectrum of disciplines.

In addition to being a brilliant scholar he was also a strange and remarkable person who left in his trail a collection of stories and anecdotes—"like vapor condensing into mushrooms"—which enliven his scholarship and no doubt will continue to proliferate unabated in his absence. Graham's work was more than just sinology and more than just philosophy: it was a personal exploration into the richness of existence that continues to inspire us not just in our scholarship but in our lives. We hope that something of his spirit lives on in the present volume.

Note on Conventions

The articles in the present volume employ the *Pinyin* system of romanization. Chinese names or terms in quotations from other works have been converted to *Pinyin* whenever they appear in the essays or in their subsequent notes. To facilitate location, however, the names of works and their authors have been left in their original romanization. Works listed in the bibliography at the end of the volume are cited in the text by author and date. Works not listed in the bibliography receive, on their first appearance in each chapter, a full citation in the endnotes; subsequent appearances in the same chapter are cited in the text by author and date. Although the 子 *zi* at the end of names like 莊子 *Zhuangzi* technically constitutes a title, "Master Zhuang," we have treated it as part of a whole name in deference to common usage. For similar reasons, we have chosen to treat "dao" as a word now accepted into the English language, like "karma." Unless otherwise specified, references in the editors' footnotes are to page numbers in this volume. References to the Chinese text of the *Zhuangzi* are by chapter and line according to the Harvard-Yenching Sinological Index Series.

Introduction

The *Zhuangzi* is a delightful book to read,[1] containing a dizzying array of dialogues, fables, and allegories, all written in a lively and engaging style. But it is also a profoundly serious book, some of its most memorable characters being people who have suffered mutilating punishments, crippling diseases, or horrible deformities. It is a treatise on how to survive, both physically and spiritually, in a dangerous and confusing world; yet it also emphasizes reconciliation with the inevitable fact of death, both our own and those of the people we love. Part of the book's allure lies in its ability to raise such dreadful and disturbing issues without being weighed down by them. Zhuangzi confronts his readers with some of life's most painful and difficult problems, problems which for the most part they would rather avoid thinking about; but he does so with a confidence and good humor that holds the promise of some solution.

Just as philosophers often miss the literary aspects of the texts they study and how these contribute to the thought of a given author, the style and unparalleled beauty of the *Zhuangzi* can easily lead one to overlook its philosophical profundity. Indeed, one of the greatest challenges facing any interpreter of the *Zhuangzi* is that its protean nature and literary subtlety are inseparable from its philosophical message: one cannot understand its content without careful attention to its multifarious and moving form. The very difficulty of the text is one of the ways the *Zhuangzi* uses literary style to make its philosophical point. On the level of individual characters, technical terms like 明 *ming* "clarity" and 道 *dao* "way" are obviously of central importance though they are never precisely defined. On the level of whole stories, even when the sequence of events is more or less straightforward, the overarching moral often remains unclear. Is the hermit Xu You, for instance, a hero or a fool? Are we supposed to reject the cicada or reconcile ourselves to being one? The *Zhuangzi* presents us with interpretive challenges at every turn. It does not seem possible to read the text without relying on a host of assumptions; and yet there is no way to verify those assumptions except on the basis of some reading, all of which leaves readers wondering whether or not they know what the text is really about. But these are exactly the issues that Zhuangzi is trying to raise: the impact that interpretive assumptions make on our everyday experience and the consequent difficulty of figuring out what human life is "really about." Thus the text presents us stylistically with an example of the problem it examines philosophically.

In spite of this close interconnection between theory and style in the *Zhuangzi*, a given study can focus more on the work's philosophical content than on its literary form. Such is the case with the present volume. In particular, the following essays are concerned with reconciling Zhuangzi's skepticism with his normative vision. Zhuangzi mounts powerful arguments questioning our ability to know that we have interpreted the world correctly, especially regarding our evaluative judgments of good and bad, right and wrong, etc. But the simple fact he wrote a book indicates that he has *some* ideas on how people ought to live. One place we see this positive vision given form is in a series of vignettes known collectively as the "skill stories." These stories, which depict people involved in activities the principles of which remain inexpressible and inexplicable even to themselves, represent the convergence of Zhuangzi's skepticism concerning knowledge and language and his confidence that there is a better way for people to live. It is no accident that almost every contributor to this volume makes reference to the most famous of these stories, that of the Cook in the third chapter, *Yang Sheng Zhu*. The task of reconciling the skeptical and the visionary strands in the *Zhuangzi* is of course an interpretive problem for the reader; but it is also Zhuangzi's way of raising the practical problem of figuring out how to act amid the inevitable uncertainties of ordinary life.

The first two essays focus attention on Zhuangzi's skepticism by juxtaposing it to forms of classical Greek skepticism. In the lead essay, "Sextus Empiricus, Zhuangzi, and Xunzi on 'Why be skeptical?'," Paul Kjellberg compares Zhuangzi to Sextus in order to establish the nature and limits of skeptical arguments. None of the arguments that Sextus or Zhuangzi deploys proves that knowledge is impossible, nor, Kjellberg argues, does either philosopher intend for them to. The purpose of the skeptical arguments is not to disprove knowledge but to draw it into question, and to produce a state of uncertainty—referred to by Sextus as *epochē* "suspension of judgment"— which is quite a different thing from the conviction that nothing can be known. In spite of this similarity, however, the two philosophers value uncertainty for notably different reasons, prompting Kjellberg to distinguish skeptical arguments, which question knowledge, from justifications for skepticism, which explain why the process of questioning is worthwhile. Sextus is quite explicit in identifying the goal of his skepticism as *ataraxia* "peace of mind," or relief from the anxiety caused by the commitment to unverifiable assumptions. Zhuangzi is less obvious. And while all the essays in this volume generally concur on his skepticism, each of them offers a somewhat different version of the motivation lying behind it. Kjellberg argues that Zhuangzi prescribes skepticism as a means of living in accord with nature and uses a consideration of Xunzi's objection to clarify precisely what this natural life entails, with the disturbing conclusion that Zhuangzi's arguments presuppose the value of such a life without providing any ultimate justification for it.

In "Skeptical Strategies in the *Zhuangzi* and *Theaetetus*," Lisa Raphals uses a similar comparison between the arguments in Zhuangzi's *Qi Wu Lun* and Plato's *Theaetetus* to distinguish three versions of skepticism. By "skepticism" one can mean, first, a thesis or doctrine denying the possibility of true knowledge. Such a thesis, if it entails a categorical denial of all knowledge, is generally acknowledged as self-refuting since, if knowledge is impossible, we cannot know even that we know nothing. Second, skepticism can be a recommendation to live with a certain attitude of doubt, as Sextus Empiricus recommended suspension of judgment so as to arrive at peace of mind. Finally, skepticism can be a method of questioning and inquiry that leads the practitioner to doubt. Raphals argues that Zhuangzi and Plato alike employ skeptical methods and implicitly recommend skeptical attitudes but that they carefully refrain from committing themselves to skeptical theses and thus avoid self-refutation. With her fine-grained analysis Raphals is able to define more clearly what we see in the *Zhuangzi* while simultaneously dispelling the common myth that casts Greek and Chinese thought as polar opposites with nothing in common.

The next three essays all focus on language and its relationship to truth as the particular object of Zhuangzi's skeptical attack. David Loy's contribution, "Zhuangzi and Nāgārjuna on the Truth of No Truth," presents an analysis of both these thinkers as anti-rationalists[2] who use rational arguments to demonstrate the untenability of reason, particularly the rationalist attempt to analyze the world into discrete self-existing entities and binary oppositions. We try to distinguish between things like dreaming and waking, self and other, life and death, pursuing one and avoiding the other; but in practice we cannot tell which is which and so are in constant anxiety. Loy argues that both authors borrow or temporarily "lodge" in ordinary, dualistic language in order to turn it back onto itself in a negative or self-deconstructing dialectic. In the process of undermining our confidence in language and logic, these authors dismantle our everyday conceptions both of the self and of things, thus releasing us from oppositional notions such as truth versus nontruth and revealing "nonduality [as] the great dream which we awaken not from but to."

In "Zhuangzi's Attitude Toward Language and His Skepticism," Eric Schwitzgebel offers a different reading of the text based on a careful study of Zhuangzi's view of language and the particular form of skepticism that results from it. A central concern of Schwitzgebel's essay is reconciling the apparent tension between those passages in the text that seem to argue either for a skeptical denial that we could ever know the truth or for a relativistic denial that there is any truth to know, on the one side, and those that clearly advocate some positive position, on the other. Schwitzgebel focuses on the question of skepticism, though he suggests that much the same argument can be made for Zhuangzi's relativism as well, and offers a simple solution: "Although Zhuangzi argues for radical skepticism, he does not sincerely subscribe to it." In other words, Schwitzgebel contends that Zhuangzi does not always mean what he says and that his statements of more radical forms of skepticism are designed as a kind of therapy, the aim of which is to bring us to what Schwitzgebel calls "everyday skepticism . . . a willingness to concede that we probably do put more stock in our beliefs then they truly deserve," which Schwitzgebel describes as "both an epistemic and a moral boon." For Schwitzgebel, then, what concerns Zhuangzi is not the inability of analytic reason to comprehend a unified reality, as it was for Loy, but rather the tendency of entrenched views to insulate themselves from justified criticism. Zhuangzi's motivation for doubting, on this reading, is not to release people from the torments of a dualistic metaphysics but simply to render them more willing to admit their mistakes and to learn from experience.

In "Language: The Guest of Reality," Mark Berkson reviews some of Ferdinand de Saussure's and Jacques Derrida's central views on the nature and function of language and its relationship to truth. Berkson is careful to point out, as many are not, some of the important differences between Saussure and Derrida and then goes on to show that there are genuine and significant similarities between certain of their views and those of Zhuangzi. In opposition to certain recent studies, however, Berkson argues that reading Zhuangzi as a postmodern thinker ignores essential elements in his thought and distorts his over all philosophy. In particular, while Zhuangzi shares with Saussure and Derrida a deep appreciation of the role language plays in shaping experience, he does not go so far as they do in denying that there is any reality outside of language, which then allows him to go beyond them in supplementing the negative, deconstructive project with a positive, constructive one. Zhuangzi believes that there is a way that the world is, a dao, that imposes limitations on language's proper use. By breaking people of their dependence on language, then, his skepticism returns them to a set of prelinguistic intuitions that offer an alternative source of knowledge to those skillful enough to tap into them.

The next three essays all focus attention on the consequences of Zhuangzi's philosophical position, offering three distinct interpretations of the form of life that Zhuangzi's skepticism is meant to produce. Robert Eno, in his "Cook Ding's Dao and the Limits of Philosophy," argues that Zhuangzi identifies two kinds of "knowing," skill knowing and fact knowing, which are reminiscent of if not identical to Gilbert Ryle's notions of "knowing how" and "knowing that".[3] Fact knowing is essentially linguistic and lies in the ability to name and describe things correctly according to some rule. Skill knowing, by contrast, is practical and is manifested in the ability to perform an activity successfully rather than simply to describe it correctly. Real knowing is skill knowing, according to Eno, but this was being increasingly overshadowed in Zhuangzi's time by the sophistries of the later Confucians and the Mohists who, in effect, put more emphasis on talking about how to live than in actually living. By invalidating fact knowing, Zhuangzi's skepticism functioned to restore skill knowing to its rightful place. Eno characterizes skill learning as "dao-learning" and says that it "provides a conduit away from the human perspective and into a holistic engagement with nature." Beyond its being nonlinguistic, however, Eno sees no limitations to what may constitute dao-learning. In particular, he contends that there are no ethical requirements governing it and concludes that Zhuangzi's dao is wholly amoral; "the dao of butchering people might provide much the same spiritual spontaneity as the dao of butchering oxen—as many a samurai might testify." The goal is simply a direct interaction with nature unmediated by concepts, in whatever form that interaction might take.

In "Zhuangzi's Understanding of Skillfulness and the Ultimate Spiritual State," Lee H. Yearley begins with an analysis of Zhuangzi's notion of the self into three kinds of "drives": dispositional drives, involving either instinctive or habitual responses to circumstances; reflective drives, consisting of intentional preferences that may or may not conflict with dispositions; and finally transcendent drives, which combine the spontaneity of dispositions with the intelligence of reflection. Arguing that Zhuangzi has a complex and subtle picture of the self and its potential deformations, Yearley sees him as outlining a course of spiritual training designed to bring people to the point where they are "animated by transcendent drives." Skillfulness points to this highest state, he argues, but only points to it. People who come to be moved by transcendent drives attain a state Yearley describes as "intra-worldly mysticism." Having been mediated by reflection, these transcendent drives manifest none of the stupidity of unreflected dispositions. But having become, as it were, second nature, they entail none of the internal conflict of reflective drives. The result is a state of tranquility, ease, power, and attentiveness in which individuals feel a joyful connection to transcendent spiritual patterns and processes. In this regard, Yearley's claims seem similar to Eno's regarding dao-learning. While it is not clear whether he would agree with Eno that *any* skillful activity can lead one to this desired state, Yearley does concur that Zhuangzi's dao is amoral, at least when judged by the normal standards of morality.

In his essay "Spontaneity and Education of the Emotions in the *Zhuangzi*," Joel Kupperman describes an ideal of "educated emotions" that is similar in many respects to Yearley's notion of "transcendent drives." Kupperman understands Zhuangzi's underlying project as "self-transformation" and argues that, far from being relativistic, the text clearly implies, "that one would be better off if one approximated the free and spontaneous life that is presented as a possibility." At the same time, Zhuangzi does not believe in or advocate any single type of life and Kupperman suggests that the fluid and humorous nature of the text itself reflects this broad and flexible ideal. For this and other reasons, Kupperman thinks it is wrong to see the self-transformation described by Zhuangzi in the overly narrow terms of moral improvement, by which he seems to mean the conscious adherence to and cultivation of a particular set of principles. Instead, he describes the goal as a renegotiation of the relation between people's feelings and their actions. Kupperman speaks in terms of a continuum between spontaneous urges and desires at one extreme, and self-conscious preferences at the other. The point of Zhuangzi's project is not to give the desires free rein, nor is it to eliminate them in favor of some externally imposed set of norms: "the Daoist sage is not someone who always acts on impulse . . . [but] will be someone whose preferences will not be at war with basic wishes or urges." The purpose of Zhuangzi's skepticism, on this account, is to bring people's spontaneous desires into harmony with the exigencies of the real world around us.

In the final essay, "Was Zhuangzi a Relativist?" Philip J. Ivanhoe takes up directly the question of the amorality or relativism of Zhuangzi's ultimate ideal. He reviews and criticizes two important interpretations of Zhuangzi as a relativist, those of Chad Hansen and David Wong, and argues first, that these authors have quite different notions of what relativism entails, and second, that neither seems appropriate as a description of Zhuangzi. Ivanhoe argues against any form of relativism as a viable reading of the text since Zhuangzi quite clearly advocates some ways of living and rejects others. He further suggests that neither of these interpretations is complete as a philosophical position in its own right since both rely on important yet suppressed premises. On Hansen's view, "no account of the world is any more accurate or valuable than any other." And yet if this were true, there would be no grounds for recommending any one form of life over another, and consequently no grounds even for arguing in favor of relativism. Since Hansen does argue in favor of relativism, however, he must be doing so for some reason, though he leaves it to his readers to speculate on what that reason is. Wong argues for relativism because he believes it can help us to realize the implications of the equal worth of individuals. Ivanhoe explores the ways in which this claim and other aspects of Wong's approach are similar to what we see in the *Zhuangzi*, and he points out that both Zhuangzi's and Wong's views rely upon implicit beliefs regarding the character of human nature. Ivanhoe goes on to argue that other parts of Wong's analysis find no clear parallels in the text and concludes his essay by examining some of the significant contributions Wong's interpretation of Zhuangzi's thought can make to contemporary ethics. Along the way, he outlines his own view of Zhuangzi's philosophical project according to which human nature is benign and "our suffering comes from our tendency to subvert our inherent nature by over-intellectualizing our lives." He regards Zhuangzi's skepticism as "a form of therapy, designed to curb our terrible tendency toward self-aggrandizement" so as to "enable us to accord with the nature of both ourselves as creatures—things among things in Nature's vast panorama—and Heaven's patterns and processes."

The volume concludes with a comprehensive and up to date bibliography of works on Zhuangzi in Western languages compiled by Ted Slingerland. Slingerland's bibliography lists every significant study of the *Zhuangzi* done over the last fifty years and provides a useful compendium of the wide variety of research on this most interesting text. As we have learned to expect with the *Zhuangzi*, no two readers see the text in quite the same way. There are, however, a few things that all the contributors to this volume agree on. All of them reject the interpretation of Zhuangzi as a relativist[4] and consequently they agree on the need for an account of his positive ethical project. They also agree in regarding Zhuangzi's project as therapeutic so that an understanding of the text involves not only an account of Zhuangzi's theories but also an analysis of the effect that the presentation of those theories is intended to have on the reader.[5] There are other issues, however, over which they part ways. They differ, for instance, in whether they see as the goal of Zhuangzi's philosophizing as spiritual fulfillment or practical success. Admittedly this may only be a difference in emphasis, but it manifests itself interestingly in their varying accounts of skillful behavior and in the aspects of skill that they point to as being particularly salient. Yearley and Kupperman focus primarily on the psychological aspects of skill—the spontaneous ease, confidence, and fulfillment of a skillful performance—while others put more weight on the practical effectiveness of skillful action. Similarly, though all of our authors agree that Zhuangzi is skeptical of the ability of knowledge and language to capture the way the world really is, they have different notions of precisely what it is about the world that so systematically resists our attempts to know it. Loy argues, for instance, that since language functions by distinguishing between things it is incapable of grasping a reality that is fundamentally unified and undifferentiated. According to Kjellberg, however, the problem with language lies not in distinguishing between things that are the same but in assimilating things that are different and thus losing sight of the subtle idiosyncrasies that need to be taken into account in order to live well. If there is one thing that the study of Zhuangzi teaches us, however, it is that no one has the last word. And if the essays in this volume have not provided definitive answers, we hope that they have at least raised provocative questions.

Notes

1. Here and throughout the introduction, when we refer to the *Zhuangzi* we mean primarily those sections, the seven Inner Chapters serving as their core, that are generally thought to be the work of a single author named Zhuangzi. However, we recognize that certain other parts of the text may represent genuine writings or at least writings that are consistent with or inspired by Zhuangzi. Scholars have long suspected that parts of the text were not genuine, and a considerable amount of work has been done on dating the text's different strata. The two most significant studies in English are Graham 1979 and Roth in Rosemont 1991.

2. Loy adopts the term "anti-rationalism" from Angus Graham, who used it throughout many of his works. Graham's most complete statements of this notion can be found in his *Reason and Spontaneity* (London: Curzon Press, 1985) and *Unreason Within Reason: Essays on the Outskirts of Rationality* (La Salle: Open Court, 1992).

3. See Gilbert Ryle, *The Concept of Mind* (London: Hutchinson's University Library, 1949), 25–61. Ryle distinguishes between knowledge *how* to do things and knowledge *that* certain state of affairs obtain. The traditional presupposition had been that all knowledge *how* could be reduced to knowledge *that*, that is knowledge that a certain set of rules needed to be followed in order to perform the task successfully. Ryle uses a reductio ad absurdum to overturn this assumption, arguing that even if one knows *that* a certain rule holds true, one still needs to know *how* to apply it. Thus, he concludes, knowledge *that* is really a species of knowledge *how*, rather than vice versa. Zhuangzi can be seen as making a similar point, not as rejecting articulable, linguistic knowledge, but as arguing that such knowledge relies on non-linguistic and inarticulable skills in order to be effectively employed.

4. This view has been argued for most influentially by Chad Hansen, concisely and compellingly in his "A Tao of Taos in Chuang Tzu" in Victor Mair 1983 and then in greater detail in his *Daoist Theory of Chinese Thought* (New York: Oxford University Press, 1992).

5. Wu Kwang-ming has made this point eloquently, arguing that the point of the Zhuangzi lies not in what the book says but in what it does. See Wu 1982, xiii and Wu 1990, 367. Robert Allinson argues at length for a similar reading in Allinson 1989.

ONE

Sextus Empiricus, Zhuangzi, and Xunzi on "Why Be Skeptical?"

Paul Kjellberg

Most philosophers look for answers. But the search seems ill-omened from the start given the incalculable number of assumptions that go not only into our conclusions but also into our methods and even into our choices of the issues to explore. After all, we might simply have made a mistake in our reasoning: it would not be the first time. Or we may not even have the right approach: the language we use in conducting our inquiries, for instance, may create more problems than it solves. Perhaps we have not even asked the right question: we could be looking in the wrong places, fixating on irrelevant details while ignoring—or avoiding—the things that really matter. In light of all these possibilities, it seems that the only thing we can say with any confidence is that we are not really sure what is going on.

But while most philosophers have struggled to escape uncertainty, a few have turned around to embrace it. These skeptics see doubt not as a problem but rather as the solution. Uncertainty, even about the things most important to us, far from being an impediment, is for them the first step on the path toward a good life. But how is this possible? How can people live in utter uncertainty? And even if they can, why should they? In what follows we will compare two skeptics, Sextus Empiricus and Zhuangzi, and one nonskeptic, Xunzi, each of whom offers different answers to these questions. In the process we will gain some insight into doubt and the possibilities, if we cannot rid ourselves of it, for living with it.

Sextus Empiricus

Although there were skeptical tendencies in the classical period, the most famous being Socrates' claim to know only his own ignorance,[1] the particular branch of Greek skepticism we will examine here traces its origins to Pyrrho of Elis. Pyrrho lived between 360 and 275 B.C.E. and traveled to India with Alexander, where he encountered the *gymnosophs,* or "naked philosophers," after which he was said to have exhibited a state of remarkable peace of mind through his refusal to pronounce anything good or bad (Diogenes Laertius, "Life of Pyrrho," section II). Since he left no writings, it was largely on the strength of his personal example that he inspired the branch of Greek skepticism known as "pyrrhonism" in his name. Pyrrho's student Timon moved from Elis to Athens where various forms of skepticism thrived and competed with one another over the next century and a half. Aenesidemus carried skepticism from Athens to Alexandria in Egypt, where it was adopted by the medical empiricists, who sought to conduct their science purely by reference to observable phenomena, without appealing to hidden or invisible causes such as the humors or the four elements. Pyrrhonian skepticism received its paradigmatic expression in the writings of Sextus Empiricus (160–210 C.E.).[2]

Sextus, whose name suggests that he may have been a trained physician, compiled the works of his predecessors and marshalled skepticism's attack against opposing schools. In his principal work, *Outlines of Pyrrhonism,* he describes skepticism as;

> the ability to oppose appearances and ideas to one another in any way whatever, by means of which, on account of the counterbalancing of examples and arguments, we arrive first at *epochē,* the suspension of judgment, and after this at *ataraxia,* peace of mind (OP 1.8).[3] . . . The originating cause of skepticism is, we say, the hope of attaining peace. Talented people who were disturbed by the inconsistencies in things and at a loss as to which of them they should accept embarked on the search for what is true in things and what is false, in order that by deciding this they might attain peace of mind (OP 1.12). . . . (But) having begun to philosophize in order to decide about appearances and to judge which of them are true and which false so as to attain peace, they fell into equally balanced contradictions, and being unable to decide they suspended judgment; and for those who had suspended their judgment, there followed at the same time, as it happened, peace with respect to the way things seem. (OP 1.26)

The goal of philosophy for Sextus is *ataraxia,* "peace" or "peace of mind", which is attained through *epochē,* the "suspension" of dogmatic judgments.

Dogmatic judgments concern "things non-evident," the most important of which being any alleged truth about things beyond or behind their appearances (*OP* 1.13).

The pyrrhonian skeptic starts out making the natural assumption that things are the way they appear: that round-looking towers are round and that good-seeming actions are good. But his confidence is shaken by inconsistencies, such as the fact that the same tower looks square up close or that the same action seems reprehensible to someone else or considered in another light. The budding skeptic is torn between conflicting ways of looking at things and does not know which of them he should trust. So he turns to philosophy hoping that the discovery of truth will resolve his doubt and ease his mind. The more he considers these problems, however, the more intractable they seem. All he has access to are the ways things appear. Even if things actually were the way they seem, he would have no way of knowing this since he is not able to get beyond appearances to find anything to check them against. In the end the pyrrhonist despairs of truth and disclaims knowledge of anything at all beyond the way things appear. Once he relinquishes his demand for truth, however, he is no longer dissatisfied with appearance and he suddenly finds himself in possession of the very peace of mind he was looking for all along.

The implicit mechanics involved in this transformation are subtle but significant. On the surface, the skeptic may now simply preface everything he says with the phrase "it seems to me that" and continue on exactly as before (*OP* 1.15). But this seemingly inconsequential concession signals some far-reaching changes in the skeptic's underlying psychology. Plato had argued several centuries earlier that people are happy when they have what is good (see, for example, *Symposium* 204 d–e). Sextus, along with other Hellenistic thinkers, modified this claim to say that people are happy when they have what they *think* is good, and unhappy when they have what they think bad: "For the added opinion that something is of such a kind is worse than the actual suffering itself, just as sometimes the patients themselves bear a surgical operation, while the bystanders swoon away because of their opinion that it is a horrible experience" (*OP* 3.236–8).[4] The happiness and sadness that people experience in life are due to their opinions about what is good or bad. The skeptic's goal, then, is to lead a life that seems good to him. Whether it really is good in fact is a question that is beyond his knowledge and arguably does not even matter. It is not necessary, according to Sextus, to prove to people that, for instance, the pain of surgery is *not* a real evil; it is enough simply to shake their certainty that it *is* in order to deliver them from their trauma.

Sextus admits that some things seem bad inevitably whether or not we know if they are bad really.[5] The dogmatist, however, only makes matters worse with his belief that such things are not only bad-seeming but bad in fact: "He who assumes that there exists by nature something good or bad, or generally fit or unfit to be done, is disquieted in several ways. For when he experiences what he regards as naturally evil he deems himself beset by Furies, and when he possesses of what seems to him good he falls into no ordinary state of disquiet both through arrogance and through fear of losing it" (*OP* 3.237). The skeptic has to deal with these inevitable discomforts as best he can, "yet because he does not also opine that what he suffers is evil by nature, the emotion he suffers is moderate" (*OP* 3.238). *Ataraxia* is the skeptic's goal. But where some amount of disturbance is unavoidable, he will settle instead for *metriopatheia*, the "moderation" of feeling (*OP* 1.25). The skeptic pursues what seems good to him and avoids what seems bad, just like anyone else. But by suspending judgment over whether these things are really good or bad, he is able to do so with a calm unavailable to the dogmatist.

In addition to moderation with regard to life's inevitable unpleasantries, a second benefit stemming from the suspense of judgment is release from the tantalizing quest for truth. People are happy when they think they are happy, according to Sextus. The dogmatist thinks that in order to be happy he must know for certain that his life is good. But conflict of opinions makes this certainty impossible. Thus he is never completely happy in his own eyes, and consequently never happy at all. Because the skeptic is not committed to the belief that knowledge is necessary for happiness, he is not bothered by doubt and is content with what seems good. The fact that others disagree with him or even that he may later change his own mind and disagree with himself does not disturb him since it does not change the way things appear in the present. By demanding truth, the dogmatist sets a standard for happiness that he cannot achieve; by suspending judgment about the necessity of knowledge, the skeptic makes it possible to be happy in a world of appearances.

Peace, or *ataraxia*, is attained through *epochē*, the suspension of dogmatic judgments concerning the way things really are. The method Sextus uses to induce *epochē* is to dwell on precisely those inconsistencies in our experience that caused us to doubt in the first place. He systematizes this process by isolating various sets of *tropoi* "tropes", literally "turnings" or "moves", techniques for generating conflicting arguments and counterexamples that draw into question our access to any truth beyond appearances.

Sextus offers ten tropes to confute our intuitive judgments by comparing the way things appear to people with the way they appear to animals, to other people, to our ears as opposed to our eyes, in one context as opposed to another, etc. (*OP* 1.36–163). The point of these examples, Sextus emphasizes, is not to reject sense impressions altogether but simply to dispel the illusion that they provide us with anything more than evidence of the way things seem:

> When we question whether the underlying object is such as it
> appears, we grant the fact that it appears, and our doubt does not

concern the appearance itself but the account given of that appearance—and it is a different thing from questioning the appearance itself. For example, honey appears sweet (and this we grant, for we perceive sweetness through the senses), but whether it is also sweet in its essence is for us a matter of doubt, since this is not a matter of appearance but a judgment regarding appearance. And even if we do actually argue against appearances, we do not propound such arguments with the intention of abolishing appearances, but by way of pointing out the rashness of the dogmatist; for if reason is such a trickster as to all but snatch away the appearance from under our very eyes, surely we should view it with suspicion in the case of things non-evident. (OP 1.19–20)

Again, the phrase "things non-evident" refers here to any supposed way things really are, in contrast to the way they seem. His point is that if we demand that the senses give us insight into some truth about things beyond apearances we will always find their evidence unsatisfactory. Once we accept them instead as witnesses to the way things seem, however, we will find their testimony unimpeachable. Thus when we say that the skeptic is "without beliefs," we mean that he is without *dogmatic* beliefs. "Adhering to appearances," Sextus says, "we live in accordance with the normal rules of life, undogmatically" (OP 1.23). The skeptic still knows the way things seem to him: this seems like a cup, that seems like a good idea, etc. He simply does not take the additional step, which Sextus repeatedly describes as *propetes*, "rash", to postulate that things really are that way (OP 1.20, 177, 205, 3.280, etc.). Such a step is unjustified and so is the cause of anxiety; but it is also unnecessary and the skeptic can live perfectly well without taking it.

Sextus presents further sets of tropes designed to discredit demonstrative as well as intuitive judgments. We use reason to judge things true or false according to some criterion or standard, such as logical consistency, empirical evidence, the testimony of an impartial observer, etc. But how do we know that we have the right criterion, especially when people disagree about which one to use? "In order to decide the dispute that has arisen over the criterion, we must possess an accepted criterion by which we shall be able to judge the dispute: and in order to possess a criterion, the dispute must first be decided. And when the argument thus reduces itself to a form of circular reasoning, the discovery of the criterion becomes impracticable, since we do not allow them to adopt a criterion by assumption, while if they offer to judge the criterion by a criterion we shall force them into an infinite regress" (OP 2.20). Every argument, according to Sextus, can ultimately be reduced to either circular reasoning, truth by assumption, or an infinite regress (OP 1.164–7). Even if we proceed from axioms that seem indubitable, this still only tells us what *seems* necessarily true but provides no guarantee that these things are so in fact. Again, Sextus does not reject the use of reason any more than he rejects the use of the senses; both provide perfectly adequate information about the way things appear. What the tropes attack is the unsubstantiated claim that either reason or the senses give us any direct access into the way things really are.

It is important to be clear at this point on precisely what the tropes do. Generations of commentators have complained about the tropes' failure as proofs that knowledge is impossible, pointing out that the simple fact that people disagree does not entail that no answer can be found.[6] What these same commentators failed to notice, however, was that Sextus never intended to offer a proof of this kind. He attributes such a wholesale rejection of knowledge to the academic skepticism of Arcesilaus and Carneades but is careful to distinguish it from his own pyrrhonism: "The natural result of any investigation is that the investigators either discover the object of search or deny that it is discoverable and confess it to be inapprehensible or persist in their search. . . . Those who believe they have discovered it are the dogmatists, . . . academics treat it as inapprehensible, and the skeptics keep on searching" (OP 1.1–3). The pyrrhonian skeptics are not claiming that knowledge is impossible. Indeed, they are not *claiming* anything at all but are merely *asking*, as the name *skeptikoi*, "inquirers", suggests. Sextus emphasizes repeatedly that his goal in writing is not to establish and defend a position but rather simply "to describe the tropes by which suspension of judgment is brought about, but without making any positive assertion regarding either their number or validity, for it is possible that they may be unsound or that there may be more of them than I shall enumerate" (OP 1.35). Sextus is not writing about the truth but only about appearances, "simply record[ing] each fact, like a chronicler, as it appears to us at the moment" (OP 1.4 and passim, see, for example, 1.97). It appears to him as though we cannot be sure, and the purpose of the tropes is to make it appear that way to us as well.

The tropes do not disprove knowledge but induce *epochē*. Suspense of judgment is not the same thing as the belief that knowledge is impossible: we do not need to be shown that we cannot know something in order to be uncertain about it. Thus it is not necessary for the tropes to provide proofs in order to achieve their goal of *epochē*, as Sextus acknowledges in his chapter "Why the Skeptic Sometimes Purposely Propounds Arguments Which Are Lacking in the Power of Persuasion;"

> The skeptic, on account of being a lover of his fellow human beings, desires to cure by speech, as best he can, the rashness of the dogmatists. So, just as the physicians who cure bodily ailments have remedies that differ in strength, and apply the severe ones to those whose ailments are severe and the mild ones to those who are mildly affected, so too the skeptic propounds arguments which differ in strength. . . . Hence the adherent of skeptic principles does not scruple to propound at one time arguments that are weighty in

their persuasiveness, and at other times such as appear less impressive; and he does so on purpose, as the latter are frequently
sufficient to enable him to effect his object. (OP 3.280–1)

Skepticism is not theoretical but therapeutic.* Its purpose is not to establish
a truth but to bring about a change of mind in the reader from a state of
belief to one of suspense, which it can do perfectly well without resorting to
proofs. Even when the skeptic uses things that look like proofs, he does so
only provisionally, "such that they are able to cross themselves out on their
own," like a cathartic drug that purges itself along with the disease (OP
1.15).†

Suspension of judgment is not a decision, strictly speaking, but a spontaneous psychological event brought on by the conflict of impressions. Sextus
illustrates this with an analogy to the painter, Appelles:

The same thing is said to have happened to the painter Appelles.
Once, they say, when he was painting a horse and wished to represent in the painting the horse's foam, he was so unsuccessful that
he gave up the attempt and flung at the picture the sponge on
which he used to wipe the paints of his brush, and the mark of the
sponge produced the effect of the horse's foam. So too the skeptics
were in hope of gaining peace by means of a decision regarding the
disparity of objects of sense and thought, and being unable to do
this they suspended judgment; and they found that peace, as if by
chance, followed upon their suspension, even as a shadow follows
on its substance. (OP 1.28–9)

The tropes do not prove that knowledge is impossible; but they do not need
to and are not meant to. They *induce* the suspension of judgment much as a
lullaby induces sleep or a scary story induces panic.

And why is suspension of judgment valuable? Suspension of judgment
is valuable because it and only it provides peace of mind.[7] Certainty is
impossible; at least, no one has found it yet. So long as one believes anything, inevitably, one will be nagged by the fear of being wrong. Nor could
one even hold that knowledge is impossible without being haunted by the
possibility that it might be possible in some way one had not considered.
The only way to avoid worry is to avoid belief. And the only way to avoid
belief is to remain in the state of pristine uncertainty that skeptical practice
is designed to generate and preserve. Sextus says that peace of mind was
really everyone's goal all along. But he does not know this and cannot prove
it; he would compromise his project if he even tried. The purpose of
pyrrhonian skepticism is to *cause* peace, not to give us a *reason* for it. Its goal

* See the editors' note on page 90.—Eds.
† See the editors' note on page 110.—Eds.

is happiness, not truth.[8] And it achieves the first only by relinquishing all claim to the second.

Zhuangzi

Bearing all this in mind, let us turn to a passage from the fourth-century B.C.E. daoist, Zhuangzi:

Gaptooth asked Royal Relativity,[9] "Do you know what all things would agree upon as right?"

Royal Relativity said, "How could I know that?"

"Do you know that you don't know it?"

"How could I know that?"

"In this case, then, do things know nothing?"

"How could I know that? But even so, suppose I tried saying something. How could I possibly know that, when I say I know something, I don't not know it? How could I possibly know that, when I say I don't know something, I don't know it?

"But let me try asking you something. If people sleep in the damp, then their waists hurt and they wake half paralyzed; but is this true of an eel? If they live in trees they shudder with fear; but is this true of a monkey? Of these three then, which knows the right place to live? People eat the flesh of grass-fed and grain-fed beasts, deer eat fodder, maggots like snakes, and hawks enjoy mice. Of these four, which knows the right taste? Monkeys take baboons as partners, deer can relate to elk, and eels consort with fish. People say that Maoqiang and Lady Li are beautiful. But if fish saw them they would dive deep, if birds saw them they would fly high, and if deer saw them they would cut and run. Of these four, which knows beauty rightly? From where I see it, the principles of benevolence and righteousness and the path ways of right and wrong are all snarled and jumbled. How would I know the difference between them?"

Gaptooth said, "But if you do not know benefit and harm, then do Perfected People too not know benefit and harm?"

Royal Relativity said, "Perfected People are spiritual. Though the lowlands burn they are not hot. Though the Yellow River and the Han freeze they are not cold. When furious lightning splits the mountains and winds thrash the seas they are not scared. People like this mount the clouds and mists, straddle the sun and moon, and roam beyond the four seas. Death and life make no difference to them, how much less the principles of benefit and harm!" (2/64–73)

Sextus Empiricus and Zhuangzi are obviously worrying about similar problems, but in very different ways. Let us tease out the similarities and differences in their approaches and see what light, if any, these shed on the problem itself.

Despite marked differences in style, Zhuangzi and Sextus use similar types of arguments. Both, for instance, exploit the diversity of opinion. In the dialogue above, Zhuangzi has Relativity contrast the judgments of people with those of animals. Elsewhere, he challenges our intuitions by appealing to the differences between individual people, between cultures, between wakers and sleepers, etc., just as Sextus did with his ten tropes. And in the opening section above, too, he plays on the familiar problem of the criterion by having Royal Relativity ask repeatedly, "How could I know?"—literally, "By means of what?"—an argument Zhuangzi expands on in another passage: "Once you and I have started arguing . . . Who can we get to set us right? Shall we get someone who agrees with you to set us right? But if he already agrees with you how can he set us right? Shall we get someone who agrees with me to set us right? But if he already agrees with me how can he set us right? Shall we get someone who disagrees with both of us to set us right? But if he already disagrees with both of us how can he set us right? This being the case, you and I and others are all unable to understand one another. Shall we wait for someone else?" (2/84–91). The argument can only be settled by reference to some judge or criterion. But the choice of a judge or criterion depends in turn on one's initial standpoint, which is precisely the issue waiting to be resolved. Not only can the parties not reach an amicable solution, they cannot even be sure of being right themselves. Though Zhuangzi is less systematic than Sextus in his analysis of different types of arguments, throughout the text he employs similar techniques of reducing arguments to circles (see, for example, 2/22), regresses (see, for example, 2/49), and undefended hypotheses (see, for example, 2/2/31; see also 24/38).

But neither diversity of opinion nor the problem of establishing a criterion prove that knowledge is impossible for Zhuangzi any more than they did for Sextus Empiricus. And Royal Relativity's third iteration of his ignorance in the passage above indicates that Zhuangzi was aware of this fact, as well. The arguments would seem, therefore, to be performing much the same function for Zhuangzi that they were for Sextus, inducing uncertainty, which, as we noted earlier, is a very different thing from disproving knowledge. The enigmatic Perfected People at the end of the above passage make the most sense if interpreted as uncertain in this sense. At first sight, they appear to possess magical and mystical powers that allow them to walk through natural disasters unscathed. Charming though this reading may be, it has the distinct disadvantages that, first, it ascribes to Zhuangzi an implausible belief in magic and, second, it seems unconnected to the reasoning leading up to it or anywhere else in the text, for that matter. A more consistent reading has the Perfected People immune from harm not out of magic but because they are unsure of whether these things really count *as* harms. Thus Zhuangzi would share with Sextus the assumption that people need only be uncertain whether something is good or bad, rather than certain that it is neither, in order to remain unmoved. By the same token, other characters in the *Zhuangzi* such as the True Man, the various Friends, or any of the cast of misfits and outcasts, are best interpreted not as possessed of some secret wisdom but rather as paradigmatically uncertain. This suggests a different vision of the whole text not as providing solutions but rather as asking questions leading to uncertainty. If this is the case, then the question for interpreters is not what secret wisdom Zhuangzi is trying to divulge, but what effect his questions are meant to have on the reader and why.

Some commentators have suggested that, like Sextus, Zhuangzi recommends uncertainty as a means to the end of *ataraxia*.[10] But, although Zhuangzi may accept peace of mind as a fringe benefit, it cannot be all he is after, as a consideration of his negative examples proves. If peace of mind were Zhuangzi's primary goal, then his negative examples, the characters that he explicitly or implicitly counsels us *not* to be like, should consist of people who are needlessly distressed, like the bystanders at Sextus' surgical operation. And, in fact, Zhuangzi does provide us with some examples of this sort: "When the monkey trainer was distributing chestnuts he said, 'You get three in the morning and four at night.' The monkeys were furious. 'Alright,' he said, 'you get four in the morning and three at night.' The monkeys were delighted. Without any loss in either name or substance, he made use of their joy and anger" (2/38–39). Like the bystanders, the monkeys suffer not on account of things themselves but on account of their opinions about things: here Zhuangzi does seem to agree with Sextus.

But although some of Zhuangzi's negative examples do exhibit the monkeys' vice of pointless anxiety, the majority of them seem to illustrate a different flaw. Consider the following;

> Hui Shi said to Zhuangzi, "The king of Wei gave me the seeds of a big gourd. I planted them, and when they grew the fruit could hold five bushels. But when I filled them with liquid they were not firm enough to hold themselves up. And when I split them into ladles they were too big to dip into anything. It wasn't that they weren't fantastically large, but they were useless, so I smashed them."
>
> Zhuangzi said, "You, dear sir, are certainly stupid about using big things. There was a man in Song who was good at making an ointment to prevent chapped hands, and year after year he bleached silk in water for a living. A traveler heard about it and asked to buy the formula for a hundred pieces of gold. The man assembled his

clan and consulted with them, saying, 'Year after year we've bleached silk in water, and never made more than a few pieces of gold. Now in one morning we can sell the secret for a hundred pieces of gold. Let's give it to him!'

"The traveler got it and recommended it to the king of Wu. There was trouble with the state of Yue and the king of Wu made him general. That winter he met the men of Yue in a sea battle. [Because the salve enabled his men to maneuver their boats and handle their weapons more effectively] he greatly defeated the men of Yue and was enfiefed in a portion of the conquered territory. The ability to prevent chapped hands was the same, but one got a fief and the other never escaped bleaching silk because what they used it for was different. Now you had these five bushel gourds— why not lash them together like big buoys and go floating on the rivers and lakes? If you were worrying only that they were too big to dip into anything, you still must have a lot of weeds in your mind." (1/35–42)

There are two negative examples in this nest of stories: Hui Shi and the silk bleachers. But the fault of these characters is not that they are needlessly distressed. Quite the contrary, they seem rather smug. For Sextus, the problem in life that skepticism is meant to solve is *thinking* that one is living badly, which is inevitable if one thinks one must have knowledge in order to live well. For Zhuangzi, on the other hand, the problem is evidently *really* living badly, or at least not as well as one might, whether one is aware of it or not. If this is the problem he is trying to avoid, then the value of uncertainty for Zhuangzi must lie somehow in its facilitating good decisions and effective actions.

This diagnosis is confirmed if we turn our attention to the positive examples, such as the Cook:

The Cook was cutting up an ox for Lord Wenhui.[11]

> Wherever his hand touched,
> Wherever his shoulder leaned,
> Wherever his foot stepped,
> Wherever his knee pushed—
> With a "zip"! With a "whoosh"!—
> He handled his chopper with aplomb,
> And never skipped a beat.
> He moved in time to the Sanglin Dance,
> And harmonized with the Jingshou Symphony.[12]

Lord Wenhui said, "Ah, excellent, that technique can reach such heights!"

The Cook sheathed his chopper and responded, "What your servant values is the Way, which goes beyond technique. When I first began cutting up oxen, I did not see anything but oxen. Three years later, I never saw a whole ox. And now, I encounter them with my spirit and don't look with my eyes. Sensible knowledge stops and spiritual desires proceed. I rely on the 天理 tian li, "natural pattern", strike in the big gaps, am guided by the large fissures, and follow what is 固然 gu ran, "inherently so". I never even touch a ligament or tendon, much less do any heavy wrenching! A good cook changes his chopper every year because he chips it. An average cook changes it every month because he breaks it.[13] Those joints have spaces, and the blade of the chopper has no thickness. If you use what has no thickness to go where there is space, oh! there's plenty of extra room to play the blade about in. That's why after nineteen years the blade of my chopper is still as though just from the grindstone.

Even so, whenever I get to a hard place,[14] I see the difficulty and take breathless care—

> My gaze settles!
> My movements slow!
> I move the chopper slightly,
> And with a sigh it's done,
> Before the ox even knows he's dead,
> Crumbling to the ground like a clod of earth![15]

I stand holding my chopper, and glance all around, dwelling on my accomplishment. Then I clean my chopper and put it away."

Lord Wenhui said, "Excellent! I have heard the words of a cook and learned how to care for life!" (3/2–12)

If Zhuangzi's goal were *ataraxia*, then the Cook's virtue would lie in his ability to preserve his peace of mind: but surely a bad cook could do the same thing, provided he just not care how good a job he did. What is distinctive about the Cook, however, is not his apathy but his skill at cutting up oxen, which, at the lord's suggestion, should be taken as a metaphor for skillful living in general.* Similarly, the traveler is the hero in his story not just because he ends up content with his lot, which the silk bleachers also do, but because he has in fact gotten the better deal. And while the fault of the monkeys may be that they are distressed over nothing, the virtue of the trainer lies in his ability to resolve the situation to everyone's advantage. The implication of all this is that, while both Sextus and Zhuangzi administer skeptical arguments to induce uncertainty, they do so for different reasons:

---

* See the editors' note on page 76.—Eds.

Sextus for the psychological good of *ataraxia* and Zhuangzi for the practical good of what we shall call "skillful living."*

In order to understand what Zhuangzi's notion of skillful living entails and how uncertainty generates it, we need to look briefly at the respective objects of Sextus' and Zhuangzi's skepticisms. Sextus distinguishes *phainomena*, the "appearances" of things, and *phantasia*, the "impression" they make on us, from *alethia*, the "truth" about things, or the way they are *phusei*, "by nature". (For the equation of *phantasia* and *phainomena* see *OP* 1.19, and for the contrast of *alethia* and *phusei* with *phantasia* see *OP* 1.25–30.) Though Zhuangzi does not use terminology of this sort, he does draw a consistent distinction between 天 *tian*, "natural" and 人 *ren*, "human". (For instances of this contrast, see the story of the Commander of the Right at 3/12–14 and the description of the True Man at 6/1–9.) The word *tian* refers literally to the sky and is frequently translated as "heaven". Zhuangzi, however, uses it to refer to the way that things really, or as he says in the above passage, "inherently," are as opposed to the ways people think of them as being. Just as Sextus doubted our ability to distinguish truth from appearance, so Zhuangzi doubts our ability to distinguish the way the world really is from the human constructions we project upon it. In particular, he doubts our ability to capture nature effectively in language and thus questions the reliability of rational thought in figuring out what we ought to do.

But what does Zhuangzi mean by "nature"? What precisely does he doubt the ability of language or linguistic concepts to capture? We have seen several examples already. The possibility of being used as a float, for instance, is part of the real nature of a gourd even though it may not be part of our conception of what a gourd is for. Similarly, the *tian li* "natural patterns" of bones and muscles in an ox are inescapably real even if they are too variable or minute to be depicted on a butcher chart. The truth Zhuangzi is concerned with is not some elusive quality of things-in-themselves lurking behind their apearances, as it was for Sextus, but has to do with subtle details, unexpected idiosyncrasies, and surprising possibilities that people's preconceptions are liable to miss. His worry about knowledge is not that it is radically illusory so much as that it is partial and incomplete.†

In addition to these facts, nature for Zhuangzi has a normative component, as well. For any given creature, there is a fact of the matter about what course of action is best for it given its particular circumstances. The difficulty arises from the fact that what is good for one creature in one situation may not be good for another in a different one, as Zhuangzi illustrates: "Haven't you heard? Once a sea bird stopped in the neighborhood of Lu. The Duke of Lu received it and threw a party for it in the temple. He enter-

---

* See Raphals, page 39, for a different suggestion about the role *ataraxia* plays in Zhuangzi's thought.—Eds.

† See the editors' note on page 57.—Eds.

tained it with the Nine Shao music and feasted it with the Tailo sacrifice. But the bird only looked confused and sad, not daring to eat a slice or drink a glass. And in three days it was dead" (18/33–35).[16] Zhuangzi is what may be described as a "soft relativist," believing that values vary depending on the individual and the situation, though he quite clearly rejects the "hard relativism" that states that what is good for people is whatever they *think* is good for them: "Don't you know about the little boy from Shouling who went to learn the Handan walk? But before he could acquire the local ability he found he'd lost his old gait and had to crawl home" (17/79–80). If Zhuangzi were a hard relativist, then it would not be possible on his account for any-one to make a mistake. And yet clearly the boy from Shouling makes a mistake, as do Hui Shi and the silk-bleachers, the people who sleep in the damp, the Confucians, the Mohists, and the monkeys. Thus there is a true nature of things for Zhuangzi that involves both facts and values.

The connection between nature and skill is well illustrated in another story about a man named Woodcarver Qing, who is particularly famous for his bell stands. When asked how he does it, he says;

> I am only a craftsman. How could I have any method? There is one thing, however. When I am going to make a bell stand, I always fast in order to still my mind. When I have fasted for three days, I no longer have any thoughts of congratulations or reward, of titles or stipends. When I have fasted for five days I no longer have any thoughts of praise or blame, of skill or clumsiness. And when I have fasted for seven days, I am so still that I forget I have four limbs and a body. By that time, the ruler and the court no longer exist for me. My skill is concentrated and all outside distractions fade away. After that I go into the mountain forest and examine the heavenly nature of the trees. If I find one of superlative form, and I can see a bell stand there, I put my hand to the job of carving; if not I let it go. This way I am simply matching up nature with nature. (19/55–59)

The woodcarver's skill lies in his ability to integrate himself, including his own abilities and interests, as well as his unpredictable aesthetic responses, with the contours and capacities of the wood he is working with, a process he describes as "matching up nature with nature." Skill is the ability to har-monize ourselves with the world and consequently to live in accord with the facts of nature, that is, to fulfill one's own real needs as well as possible given one's own abilities and circumstances.

Zhuangzi doubts the ability of language to make people skillful for several reasons. Words are simply too crude either to capture subtle differences or to contain ambiguous possibilities. And since the best way to act in a situa-tion frequently depends on such possibilities and differences, Zhuangzi doubts the efficacy of language in communicating what is important about how to live. As one character, a wheelwright, puts it; "When I chisel a wheel, if I hit too softly then it slips and does not bite. If I hit too hard then it jams and will not move. Neither too soft nor too hard. I get it in my hand and respond from my mind. But my mouth cannot put it into words. There is a knack there. But I cannot teach it to my own son, and he cannot learn it from me" (13/71–73). But even if we created a language that was nuanced enough to communicate these subtle distinctions, there would still be the problem that different definitions of words like "good" and "right" will be appropriate in different circumstances: what is right for a fish is not right for a person, and what is right for a person from Handan is not right for someone from Shouling. Simple knowledge of the definitions themselves is not enough to determine which definitions apply in particular cases. Language alone is not enough; we need to know how to use it. And this is not something language can tell us. The humor of Zhuangzi's stories lies in his using language to point to something that language cannot capture, such as the fact that a gourd may also be a float, that an ox may not be the same as an ox, or that what is good may also be bad. Language is inadequate not only in communicating how to live but also in figuring it out in the first place. If people rely on language in making their decisions, therefore, they cannot help but live clumsily.

But in spite of Zhuangzi's skepticism concerning linguistic or "rational" knowledge, he has absolute faith in intuitive or "natural" knowledge.* However many examples Zhuangzi has illustrating the inadequacy of language, he has an equal number illustrating the adequacy of nature: "The walrus[17] said to the centipede, 'I go hopping around on this one leg and there's nothing like it! How can you manage with all those ten thousand legs of yours?' The centipede said, 'Not so. Haven't you seen a man spit? He just hawks and—drops big as pearls, fine as mist, mixing and falling!—you can't even count them all! Now I just put into motion my 天機 *tian ji*, 'natural mechanism'. I don't know how it works!'" (17/53–59). We are able to do things, like walk and digest, without knowing how we do them. By the same token, we know things, such as what objects are in front of us, without knowing how we know them. We simply open our eyes and see. Anything else that we are able to demonstrate or deduce all relies ultimately on these things that we just know. This much requires no explanation. What does require explanation is not how we succeed in knowing things but how we fail. And the reason we fail to know, according to Zhuangzi, is because of our conviction that we know already, that is, in effect, simply because of our refusal to open our eyes. The next ox may or may not be like the last one. No amount of meditating on the butcher chart in our minds will tell us the answer, but looking at the oxen will. A ladle is not a float; but the object in front of us

*See page xxi, note 3 in the Introduction.—Eds.

might be both. Words cloud our vision, tempting us to see the world not as it really is but only as we are predisposed to think of it as being. By undermining our faith in language, skepticism clears our vision and allows us to see things afresh as they naturally are. Certainty causes people to second guess nature and makes them clumsy. Uncertainty is valuable, for Zhuangzi, because it leaves people open-minded and attentive and thus enables them to live skillfully and well.

Zhuangzi's emphasis on uncertainty, however, should not be taken as denying the importance of education. Simply remaining open-minded would not automatically make someone a skillful surgeon or diplomat. The skill stories all emphasize the time required for people to master a craft: the Cook acknowledges spending nineteen years. Evidently Zhuangzi takes the need for education for granted. The open-minded attentiveness he advocates is not meant to replace learning so much as to complement it. Indeed, one of the finest examples of this combination is Zhuangzi himself who disparages the moribund logic of his adversaries, but uses it deftly against them when the situation demands. He denigrates book learning; and yet the wide variety of literary forms he incorporates into his writing and the infuriating number and obscurity of the characters he uses all evidence a familiarity with the Classics of which Confucius would have been proud.[18] What makes Zhuangzi so skillful is not simply his erudition but his ability to step outside of the tradition and to adapt it flexibly to his own situation. Evidently he recommends skepticism not as an alternative to learning but as a method by which to interpret and apply what one has learned.[19]

Both Zhuangzi and Sextus use skeptical arguments not to disprove knowledge but to induce in their listeners a feeling of uncertainty. But while the state of mind they advocate may be free from assumptions, their advocacy of it is not. Sextus makes the psychological assumption, for instance, that people worry only about what they believe to be really good or bad and so remain unaffected by uncertainties. He further presupposes the value of *ataraxia* that, as argued earlier, he does not and cannot prove. Zhuangzi makes his own recommendation of skepticism based on a different set of epistemological and evaluative assumptions, described above, that we can refer to collectively as his "naturalism". The precise nature of Zhuangzi's naturalism and the role that it plays in his thought come out more clearly if we consider his project in light of an objection raised against it by the Confucian philosopher Xunzi.

Xunzi

In his chapter 解蔽 *Jie Bi*, "Dispelling Obsessions," Xunzi criticizes Zhuangzi, saying "Zhuangzi was obsessed by *tian* 'nature' and did not know [the value of] 人 *ren*, the 'human'" (*Xunzi* 21/22). Xunzi uses the word "nature" here in the same sense that Zhuangzi used it, as the way things really are, including all their subtle variations, untapped ambiguities, and hidden potentials, as opposed to whatever ways people might be predisposed to think of them as being. In particular, Xunzi is talking about the natural state of people, with their intrinsic needs and often unrecognized capacities and limitations. By the "human" Xunzi means things that are man-made, artificial, and added to nature as the product of conscious thought, that is, culture.

There are several possible interpretations of Xunzi's objection, three of which we will consider in turn. The most obvious is that Xunzi is accusing Zhuangzi of being so narrow-mindedly fixated on the natural world that he fails to appreciate the values offered by the social one.[20] Such an objection is strongly suggested by the title of Xunzi's chapter and by its opening line, "The thing all men should fear is that they become obsessed by a small corner and lose sight of the larger pattern" (*Xunzi* 21/1). The problem with this reading, however, is that it does not really constitute an objection to Zhuangzi's skepticism at all. He seems to agree with Zhuangzi that what people *should* do is what they *would* do naturally if they paid open-minded attention to their situations. Rather than objecting to Zhuangzi's project, on this reading Xunzi would be agreeing with it and objecting only that Zhuangzi failed to prosecute it scrupulously enough.

On a second, more robust interpretation of Xunzi's objection, he continues to agree with Zhuangzi that what is natural for us is what is best, but he disagrees that skepticism reliably reveals the natural course. Zhuangzi assumes that if we simply respond open-mindedly and follow our natural inclinations we will be drawn toward the things that are naturally best. But is this true? There might well be things that fulfill very natural needs that we are not, however, in a position to appreciate ahead of time. We do not ask children, for instance, whether they feel naturally inclined to go to school; nor do we send sick people into drugstores to take whatever medicines appeal to them most after an open-minded consideration. People may well have real, natural needs that uncertainty will not reveal.

The thrust of Xunzi's objection, on this second interpretation, would be that skeptical open-mindedness must be supplemented by learning. He makes this point clearly in his chapter *Quan Xue*, "Encouraging Learning": "I once tried spending a whole day in thought, but found it of less value than a moment of study. I once tried standing on tiptoe and gazing into the distance, but found I could see much farther by climbing to a high place" (*Xunzi* 1/6–7). In fact, one anecdote in this chapter appears to be a direct parody of Zhuangzi: "In the Southern Region there is a bird. It's name is called 蒙鳩 *meng jiu*, 'stupid dove'. It makes a nest out of feathers woven together with hair and suspends it from the tips of reeds. But when the wind comes, the reeds break, the eggs are smashed, and the baby birds killed" (*Xunzi* 1/9).

The grammar of Xunzi's opening line here echoes the opening line of Zhuangzi's famous story about Kun and Peng: "In the Northern Obscurity there is a fish. It's name is called 'minnow'" (1/1). But the story itself makes the opposite point. Zhuangzi's tale of the fish swimming and then turning into a bird and flying away illustrates (at least on one interpretation) the reliability of our spontaneous responses in coping with changing situations. Xunzi's parable of the bird who builds her nest on too narrow a branch and so loses all her eggs in the high wind, by contrast, is a lesson about the inadequacy of our untutored intuitions and the necessity of forethought and study. The *meng jiu* "stupid dove" here may be a direct reply to Zhuangzi's 學鳩 *xue jiu*, "student dove", who illustrates the pointlessness of trying to learn from others (1/8). In any case, the story illustrates Xunzi's point that skeptical open-mindedness alone is not enough but that it must be supplemented by learning.[21]

The problem for us with this second interpretation of Xunzi's objection, however, is that it is based on a misinterpretation of Zhuangzi's actual position. This objection would make sense only if we attributed to Zhuangzi the belief that mere open-mindedness can replace learning, which, as we saw earlier, is clearly contradicted in the text as well as by common sense. Zhuangzi's actual belief is closer to the one that this objection ascribes to Xunzi, that one must take account of the way things actually are before deciding on a course of action. This is not to say that this second interpretation may not be an accurate reading of Xunzi. But since our purpose here is to consider the ways in which Xunzi might shed light on Zhuangzi, we should avoid attributing a misinterpretation of Zhuangzi to him so long as there is another alternative available.

There is a third interpretation according to which Xunzi's objection has some real teeth. On this interpretation, Xunzi objects not simply to skepticism as a means to the natural life but to the notion of the natural life itself as the proper goal of human existence. The purpose of education and training may not simply be to teach people new and unforeseen ways of fulfilling desires they already have but rather to cultivate in them new desires that they did not have before. Thus the goal of life, then, would lie not in the satisfaction of human nature so much as in its transformation. Not only would people in an untutored state be unable to appreciate the effectiveness of Xunzi's Confucianism in satisfying their needs, on this third interpretation they would not yet even *have* the needs that Confucianism so uniquely satisfies.

Xunzi suggests such an interpretation with his famous proclamation that "human nature is bad" (*Xunzi* 23/1 ff.) and with his vivid metaphors of humanity as, for instance, bent wood that has to be forced straight and dull metal that has to be ground against a stone (*Xunzi* 1–2, 23/5, cf. *Analects* 1.15). Good people, he says, train their eyes so that they do not desire to see what is not right, train their ears so that they do not desire to hear what is not right, train their mouths so that they do not desire to taste what is not right, train their minds so that they do not desire to choose what is not right. Once they have finally come to love [what is best], their eyes will love it more than the five colors; their ears will love it more than the five sounds; their mouths will love it more than the five flavors; and their minds will consider it more to their advantage than [dominion over] the empire. (*Xunzi* 1/47–50)

Xunzi does not think the natural desires can be gotten rid of, nor does he think they should be (*Xunzi* 22/56). Evidently, however, he does think they can be supplemented. And it is this supplementation of the natural desires with new ones that constitutes the transformation of human nature. The value of the best life, on this model, is measured by the satisfaction not of natural needs and desires but rather of artificial and constructed ones.

This reading of Xunzi as an advocate of artificial values is supported by several other aspects of his thought, such as, for instance, his choice of the word 偽 *wei* to refer to the activity of deliberately choosing a course of action rather than simply following one's inclinations. While *wei* certainly does mean this for Xunzi, it also has other overtones of which he was not unaware. Zhuangzi uses it to mean "false" in explicit contrast to 眞 *zhen*, "genuine" or "true" (2/25). Mencius uses it to mean something more like "hypocritical" or even "deceptive" (*Mencius* 3A4, 5A2). Although Xunzi does not think of *wei* as something bad, he no doubt chooses this particular term to emphasize that, to begin with at least, moral activity is *not* simply the sincere expression of one's true feelings. Quite the contrary, it is a self-conscious and deliberate effort to act contrary to one's natural and spontaneous inclinations. Rather than running away from the label "artificial," Xunzi embraces it as the hallmark of his system.

It is only on this third interpretation of Xunzi's position that we have a real disagreement with Zhuangzi and an adequate account of his criticism of Zhuangzi as "obsessed by nature and ignorant of the human." The most important things in life, according to Xunzi, are of artificial value and are not things toward which we are naturally inclined. Such carefully cultivated desires, among which Xunzi includes the social and moral desires, can become very deep-seated and sincere, but they will never be "natural" in Zhuangzi's sense; Xunzi compares the effort of the untrained person to appreciate them to that of "a blind man trying to distinguish colors or a deaf man tones" (*Xunzi* 2/39–40). Zhuangzi prosecutes his skepticism in the belief that it will lead to a natural life, "natural" as opposed to the "artificial" life advocated by Xunzi. But this naturalism is something Zhuangzi assumes in advancing his arguments, not something he proves by means of them.

Conclusions

So what have we learned from our comparison? First, the similarities between Sextus and Zhuangzi suggest that skepticism is not limited to any single culture or period. Forms of skepticism are frequently presented as being parasitic on particular epistemological theories; thus Hellenistic skepticism in general has been analyzed as an attack on stoicism[22] and daoist skepticism as a response to Neo-Mohism.[23] But while Sextus and Zhuangzi both deploy arguments against particular epistemological positions, their basic arguments take on an epistemology so widespread as to be almost universal. Simply put, so long as people admit that it is possible to be mistaken they are vulnerable to skeptical attack. This does not require a theory of mental images or even a correspondence theory of truth. The argument from diversity of opinion, of which the problem of the criterion is a special case, merely brings this situation out. Two people disagree, both of whom cannot be right, at least one of whom must therefore be wrong. People can be wrong even though they think they are right; so one cannot be sure one is not wrong at the present moment. This reasoning does not apply in all domains. Most people do not think that it is possible to be mistaken, strictly speaking, in matters of taste, for instance, though most agree that it is possible in matters of scientific fact. There is some dispute over whether it is possible to be mistaken over ethical issues, which only goes to show that the applicability of skeptical arguments to these issues is itself a fit subject for skepticism.

Second, the examples of Sextus and Zhuangzi show us that skeptical arguments do not necessarily deny knowledge but may merely question it. The goal of such arguments may not be to disprove knowledge but to lead the reader to a state of uncertainty; and, again, wondering whether one knows is a very different thing from concluding that one does not. Taking advantage of Sextus' terminology, we might distinguish between "dogmatic" skepticism, which denies knowledge, and "aporetic" skepticism, which merely questions it (OP 1.7).* Relativism, the denial that there is any truth outside of individual perspectives, would be dogmatic in this sense. Skeptical arguments might be thought of as "therapeutic" rather than as "conclusive," since their function is to cause a change in the listener rather than to prove a particular point.[24] Aporetic skepticism of this sort, which deploys therapeutic arguments designed to generate uncertainty, is better understood as a philosophical practice, analyzed in terms of its methods and goals, than as a position in the usual sense.

Third, our comparison has focused attention on the difference between skeptical arguments and what I will refer to interchangeably as the motivations or justifications behind those arguments. The two are easily confused

---

* See the editors' note to page 29.—Eds.

since both of them constitute responses to the question "Why be skeptical?" But in spite of this superficial similarity, the arguments for skepticism and the motivations behind those arguments are two entirely different and independent things, both of which we need to understand if we want to know what a particular skeptic is about. They are different in the sense that skeptical arguments question our beliefs and render us uncertain while skeptical justifications explain why uncertainty is a better state to be in: the first causes uncertainty, the second gives a reason for it. Any skeptical argument however, does need to have *some* motivation. The most ironclad argument does not make itself. We need a reason to make the argument, and that reason has inevitably to come from somewhere outside of the argument itself.

This leaves us in a bit of an awkward position, however, since the justifications for skepticism are vulnerable to attack by their own arguments. Anyone who admits the possibility of being wrong will find the diversity of opinion unsettling and uncertainty the inevitable result. The question at issue is not whether skeptical arguments are compelling but whether they ought even to be made. Sextus says they should, because suspension of judgment gives rise to peace of mind. Zhuangzi agrees, but for the different reason that uncertainty leads to a skillful and natural life. Xunzi disagrees entirely, however, attacking not the skeptical arguments but the motivations lying behind them. Who is right? What do we even mean by "right" here? Is the right answer the one that brings us peace or the one that accords with our natural intuitions? Is it right according to some set of acquired standards, and if so, which ones? One is tempted to respond that what one means by "right" depends on certain fundamental personal commitments. But unless one is willing to commit to a complete relativism, there will still have to be some "right" right, though there is no obvious noncircular way of determining what that is. We said in the beginning that the only thing we can say with confidence is that we are not really sure what the answer is. If our reasoning here is correct, however, then the unfortunate conclusion is that we cannot even say that.

Notes

1. Plato, *Apology*, 21d. Among the pre-Socratics, Heraclitus (c. 500 B.C.E.) is often cited as a skeptic. His claim that "it is not possible to step twice into the same river," however, though it does question conventionally accepted knowledge, simultaneously lays claim to a special insight into the constantly changing nature of all things. Xenophanes (c. 530 B.C.E.) also exhibits skeptical tendencies, though he does not integrate them systematically into his thought, either: "and as for certain truth, no man has seen it, . . . For if he succeeds to the full in saying what is completely true, he

himself is nevertheless unaware of it; and Opinion (seeming) is fixed by fate upon all things." (See Kathleen Freeman, *Ancilla to the Pre-Socratic Philosophers* (Cambridge: Harvard University Press, 1948), 31 and 24.)

2. Most of our information on the history of early skepticism stems from Diogenes Laertius' *Lives and Opinions of Eminent Philosophers*, from Cicero's *Academica*, and from Sextus' own account. A detailed history can be found in Mary Mills Patrick, *The Greek Skeptics* (New York: Columbia University Press, 1929) and a convenient summary in R. G. Bury's introduction to the 1955 Loeb Classical Library edition. Questions both of lineage and of directions of influence are debated. Slightly different versions can be found in Anthony Long and David Sedley, *The Hellenistic Philosophers* (Cambridge: Cambridge University Press, 1987) and in Philip Hallie's "A Polemical Introduction" to Hallie, ed., *Sextus Empiricus: Selections from the Major Writings on Scepticism, Man, & God*, tr. Sanford G. Etheridge (Indianapolis: Hackett Publishing Company, 1985).

3. Translations from Sextus are Bury's with a few emendations of my own. References to Sextus will be either *OP* (*Outlines of Pyrrhonism*) or *AE* (*Against the Ethicists*), followed by the book and section number as listed in the Loeb edition. This passage, for instance, is *OP* I 8, that is *Outlines of Pyrrhonism*, book one, section eight.

4. The stoics are quite explicit on this point. As Epictetus puts it in chapter five of his *Encheiridion*, "What upsets people is not things themselves but their judgments about the things" (Nicholas White, tr., *The Handbook of Epictetus* (Indianapolis: Hackett Publishing Company, 1983), 13.) Compare book four, chapter thirty-nine of Marcus Aurelius' *Meditations*: "For you, evil comes not from the mind of another; nor yet from any of the phases or changes of your own bodily frame. Then whence? From that part of yourself which acts as your assessor of evil. Refuse its assessment, and all is well" (Maxwell Staniforth, tr., *Marcus Aurelius: Meditations* (London: Penguin Classics, 1964), 72.) Such reasoning is implicit in Epicureanism, as well, as in the assumption motivating Lucretius' *De Rerum Naturae* that people will be made happy by dispelling their fear of death. See Rolfe Humphries, tr., *Lucretius: The Way Things Are* (Bloomington: Indiana University Press, 1968).

5. This is an important point differentiating the skeptics from the stoics, who think that we always have the power to decide whether something seems good or bad to us. Compare Marcus Aurelius, book seven, chapter fourteen: "If I do not view a thing as an evil, I take no hurt. And nothing compels me to view it so" (Staniforth 1964, 107).

6. Gisela Striker explores this issue in "The Ten Tropes of Aenesidemus" in Myles Burnyeat, ed., *The Skeptical Tradition* (Berkeley: University of California Press, 1983), 95–115.

7. David Sedley explores the role of *ataraxia* in pyrrhonian skepticism in "The Motivation of Greek Skepticism" in Burnyeat 1983, 9–29.

8. For a discussion of eudaimonism, the belief that truth is secondary in importance to happiness, see Hallie 1985, 6–9.

9. The translations of these names are tentative. But since they are clearly meant to be allegorical in Chinese I saw fit to maintain this quality in English. The name *Nie Que*, "Gaptooth", could refer to a gap between the front teeth, a missing tooth, or an overbite; in any case, the name clearly signals some kind of imperfection. The name 王倪 *Wang Ni*, "Royal Relativity", is a little more involved. 17/21–27 argues that the small is small only from the point of view of the large and vice-versa, and that therefore the small and the large cannot be *ni* "contrasted" or "considered different", except relative to one another. Here it echoes the phrase 天倪 *tian ni* at 2/90 and presumably describes someone who is good at the technique described there of "harmonizing things by means of the natural relativity [of their judgments]," for which reason he is described as "royal." A more detailed analysis of these names and this passage is included in Kjellberg 1993, 132–6.

10. Commentators who have taken a position like this include Fung 1953, 221–245, Waley 1939, 3–79, Watson 1968, 1–28, and Herrlee Creel, *What Is Taoism?* (Chicago: University of Chicago Press, 1970), 37–47. David Nivison refers explicitly to *ataraxia* as a "supreme personal religious goal" for Zhuangzi in Rosemont 1991, 136.

11. Commentators and translators have traditionally taken 包丁 *baoding* as the Cook's name. *Bao* means "kitchen." The character *ding* can be a proper name but can also mean "fellow" or "guy." Lord Wenhui's concluding remark, that he "has heard the words of *bao ding* and learned how to care for life," suggests this latter reading. If *bao ding*, is translated as a proper name, "Cook Ding," all the line tells us is that what the Cook has said has applications wider than just butchery, which we already knew. But if it is translated as an indication of his rank, then the line makes the ironic point that Wenhui has listened to someone as lowly as a cook and learned something as lofty as how to care for life. Zhuangzi typically chooses characters from downtrodden groups to cast as heros: outcasts, the handicapped, and women. Most of these characters, too, are known only by description, as is the Cook here and arguably Gaptooth in the previous passage. Lacking as they do proper names as well as social distinction, they are literal examples of the "nameless sage" referred to at 1/22. Commentators identify Lord Wenhui as King Hui of Liang, with whom Mencius converses in *Mencius* 1A1–5. It is possible that here and elsewhere Zhuangzi is intentionally parodying stories found in the *Mencius*. In *Mencius* 1A7, Mencius demonstrates that King Xuan of Qi is capable of compassion by reminding him of an incident in which he spared

an ox from sacrifice because he could not bear to see its innocent suffering. This passage may be poking fun at that story, with a cook lecturing the ruler on how to butcher oxen most effectively. David Nivison was the first to suggest to me that several passages in the *Zhuangzi* may represent parodies of the *Mencius*.

12. These nine lines are in meter and full of onomatopoeia. Zhuangzi is unique among early Chinese philosophers for his extensive use of this stylistic device, which may be related to his suggestion that, in the absence of agreed upon definitions, human discourse might in the end be nothing more than empty sounds.

13. The interpretation of these lines is disputed. I follow Guo Xiang (in Guo Qingfan 1988, 122). At issue is whether *gu* is a verb meaning "to pry" or a noun meaning "large bone", and also whether the verbs in the following two sentences describe what other cooks do *to* their choppers or what they do *with* them. An alternate reading is "I never touch a ligament or tendon, much less a big bone! A good cook changes his knife every year, because he cuts. An average cook changes it every month, because he hacks."

14. I follow the commentators in reading *zu* as "crowded" or "complex" (Guo Qingfan 1988, 123). The same character has occured only a few lines previously, however, where it clearly meant "average". This leads Arthur Waley to read this whole section as a description of clumisness of ordinary cooks in contrast to the dexterity of the protagonist (Waley 1939, 47–8).

15. These six lines also appear to be in verse. The fifth is absent from most versions but preserved in the *Wenruhai* manuscript (Guo Qingfan 1988, 124). I choose to include it because of its implication that the Cook kills the ox as well as cutting it up, which is particularly significant if the passage is read as a response to *Mencius* 1A7.

16. This and the following anecdote are both in chapters that modern scholars attribute to Zhuangzi's disciples (Graham 1981, Graham 1986, Liu 1987). Both are imbedded in larger stories, the plot structure and narrative style of which diverges significantly from that of the Inner Chapters. The two anecdotes themselves, however, have the compact style and the relent-less but humorous irony characteristic of the Inner Chapters. This, along with the fact that both are introduced by the phrase "Have you alone not heard?" suggests that they may derive from an oral tradition, perhaps stem-ming from Zhuangzi himself, which was then incorporated into these contexts by later disciples. This style of quoting a characteristically Zhuangzi-esque story as though it were a piece of common lore is also present in the Inner Chapters (see, for example, 2/38, 4/59, 4/61), which has caused the German sinologist Alfred Forke to suggest that the the Inner Chapters, too, may have been composed in this manner (Forke 1927, 303–328).

17. The 夔 *kui* was a mythic one-legged beast that commentary suggests may have been based on the walrus (Guo Qingfan 1988, 592).

18. In *Analects* 17.9 Confucius recommends study of the *Odes* for "a broad knowledge of the names of birds, animals, grasses and trees." No writer that I am aware of in the classical tradition took this advice more to heart than Zhuangzi.

19. A similar tension existed in the Confucian tradition itself between introspection and study. See Philip J. Ivanhoe, "Thinking and Learning in Early Confucianism," *Journal of Chinese Philosophy* 17 (1990), 473–493.

20. David Nivison presents an interpretation much like this, describing Xunzi's Confucianism as the "logical outcome of Chuang Tzu's Taoism" in Rosemont 1991, 138.

21. Ivanhoe presents a reading of Xunzi as making roughly this point in "A Happy Symmetry: Xunzi's Ethical Thought," *Journal of the American Academy of Religions* 59.2 (1991), 309–322.

22. Pierre Coussin makes this point about the skepticism of the new Academy and also about pyrrhonism, though not at the same length, in "The Stoicism of the New Academy" in Burnyeat 1983, 31–63.

23. Hansen argues that the *Zhuangzi* is a "skeptical relativistic response to the philosophy of language of the Neo-Mohists," though he does not mean to imply that its relevence is restricted to a refutation of the Neo-Mohists (Mair 1983:27).

24. Many of my reflections on the nature of therapeutic arguments has been informed by Martha Nussbaum, "Therapeutic Arguments: Epicurus and Aristotle," in Malcolm Schofield and Gisela Striker, eds., *The Norms of Nature: Studies in Hellenistic Ethics* (Cambridge: Cambridge University Press, 1986).

TWO

Skeptical Strategies
in the Zhuangzi and Theaetetus

Lisa Raphals

The *Qi wu lun* or "Sorting that Evens Things Out" chapter of the *Zhuangzi* ends with a famous story about Zhuangzi: "Last night Zhuang Zhou dreamed he was a butterfly, spirits soaring he was a butterfly . . . and did not know about [Zhuang] Zhou. When all of a sudden he awoke, he was Zhou with all his wits about him. He does not know whether he is Zhou who dreams he is a butterfly or a butterfly who dreams he is Zhou" (2/94).[1] Against this, we might counterpose a question that the young Theaetetus asks Socrates in the first section of Plato's dialogue of that name: "But I really shouldn't know how to dispute the suggestion that a dreamer [believes what is false] . . . when he imagines he has wings and is flying in his sleep" (*Theaetetus* 158b).[2] Zhuangzi might have answered Theaetetus: "While we dream we do not know that we are dreaming, and in the middle of a dream interpret a dream within it; not until we wake do we know that we were dreaming. Only at the ultimate awakening shall we know that this is the ultimate dream" (2/81–82). Socrates replies: "You see, then, it is not difficult to find matter for dispute, when it is disputed even whether this is real life or a dream. Indeed, we may say that, as our periods of sleeping and waking are of equal length, and as in each period the soul contends that the beliefs of the moment are pre-eminently true, the result is that for half our lives we assert the reality of the one set of objects, and for half that of the other set. And we make our assertions with equal conviction in both cases" (*Theaetetus* 158d). Both passages use the example of dreams to question or doubt our ability to know in two of the most important epistemological inquiries within their respective traditions. *Theaetetus* 158 is the first of many examples within the Western tradition of the use of dreams to frame skeptical claims or counterarguments.[3] Zhuangzi's dream has become a *locus classicus* for articulating a variety of views about the unknowable, or impermanent, nature of things.[4] Both the *Qi wu lun* and *Theaetetus* engage in extended discussions of the nature of knowing, language, explanation, perception, and perceptual judgment. Paul Woodruff asks a question about Plato that can also be applied to Zhuangzi: "Which came first, the skeptic or the epistemologist?"[5] The epistemologist asks what knowledge is and how it can be acquired; the skeptic tries to detach her from that project. Zhuangzi, like Plato, may be doing something different from either of these, though it smacks of both. The *Qi wu lun* is the major consideration of epistemology in Warring States writings; the *Theaetetus* is the only Platonic dialogue devoted to a discussion of *epistēme*, "knowing". Yet we may observe that Zhuangzi never offers his own theory of knowing, and Socrates never reaches a definition of *epistēme*. In this paper I compare several ostensibly skeptical elements in the *Qi wu lun* chapter of the *Zhuangzi* and the *Theaetetus* of Plato. I argue that the *Zhuangzi* and the *Theaetetus* use remarkably similar skeptical methods to explore epistemological problems in ways that are unique within their respective traditions. My purpose in making this case is twofold. One, I want to show that methods of argument in China and Greece may have more in common than we may be predisposed to suppose. Two, the comparison allows us to reexamine our own understanding of what skepticism is and does.

The term skepticism generally refers to viewpoints that doubt the possibility of real knowledge, or that claim that there are no adequate grounds for certainty as to the truth of any proposition (OED). Skepticism has shaped many of the questions and answers of several areas of the Western philosophical tradition, whether as a serious view or as an object of continual attack and refutation.

In Greek philosophy, the term generally refers to two Hellenistic schools. The skeptics of Plato's Academy, Arcesilaus and Carneades, claimed the legacy of Plato, especially Socrates' claims to "know nothing." Pyrrhonian skepticism was associated with Pyrrho of Elis and Sextus Empiricus.[6] Skepticism had a constitutive role in the development of modern philosophy through the study of works of Pyrrhonian skepticism, beginning in the sixteenth century, and through the efforts of such philosophers as Descartes, Berkeley, Hume, and Kant to address skeptical challenges.[7] Some claim that it has been dismissed and undervalued because skeptics reject (or doubt) a commitment to reason that is central to the history of Western thought.[8] Hostile accounts of skepticism have even gone so far as to describe it as "oriental indifference" or "systematic negation."[9]

Three Kinds of Skepticism

For purposes of this discussion, I want to distinguish between three kinds of skepticism: skepticism as a thesis, skepticism as a recommendation, and skepticism as a method. As a thesis or doctrine, skepticism is the proposition, explicit or tacit, that nothing can be known.[10] The so-called "skeptic's circle," the logically self-refuting claim that nothing can be known (including the claim that nothing can be known) refers to, and tends to undermine, skepticism as a doctrine.

As a recommendation, skepticism is an imperative to suspend judgment. According to Sextus, the result of this attitude of mind is "mental suspense" or suspension of judgment, *epoche*, followed by "unperturbedness", tranquility or quietude, *ataraxia* (*OP* 8). As a recommendation, skepticism does not risk self-refutation, since it makes no positive claim to, or denial of, knowledge or belief.

As a method, skepticism is a question or inquiry that leads to doubt. Its form tends to reject, or ignore, a skeptical thesis, and tends to advocate, or at least suggest, a skeptical recommendation. Skeptical methods refute existing claims to knowledge, including their own. Some methods work by direct argument, for example, Socrates' technique of refuting, first, the theses of a dogmatic opponent, and then, his own.[11] Direct approaches of this kind may be attempts to steer a path between a skeptical thesis and the skeptic's circle; the systematic and regular method of the *elenchus* itself suggests a skeptical thesis, the latter by never formulating one in so many words. Other, less direct techniques include humor, complex narrative structures, and what Gregory Vlastos has called complex irony.[12] These indirect methods avoid the risks of the skeptic's circle by never articulating a skeptical thesis. Yet they take more risks than a passive suspension of judgment. They lead the inquirer to a state of mind that questions claims to knowledge, but in doing so they also evoke complex emotional registers: for example, the power of complex narrative structures to create momentary disorientations as they shift perspectives; or the power of humor to evoke the tensions of misplaced (if tacit) expectation.

Skeptical doctrines, methods, and recommendations are all logically independent.[13] Each is susceptible to multiple interpretations. As Gisela Striker points out, modern debates have concentrated on skepticism as a doctrine, while ancient debates were more concerned with skepticism as a recommendation. This emphasis would severely limit the scope of an investigation of skepticism since a skeptical thesis seems incommensurable with skeptical recommendations and methods. The follower of a skeptical recommendation suspends judgment about everything, including a skeptical thesis. And if she proceeds by skeptical methods, she is likely to prefer something more subtle than a skeptical thesis, which, in any event, remains vulnerable to the charge of self-refutation, the classical argument against skeptical doctrines.

In the case of the *Zhuangzi*, I begin by showing the noteworthy absence of a skeptical doctrine in the *Qi wu lun*, a text pervaded by a skeptical flavor. I go on to show how skeptical methods create that flavor. My discussion of the *Theaetetus* focuses on 151d–186e, in which Socrates argues that knowledge is perception. I elucidate the skeptical methods of the *Theaetetus* by comparing them with the skeptical theses of Sextus Empiricus. Finally I compare the skeptical methods used in both texts.*

Skeptical Doctrines

In the *Zhuangzi*, the dream passage concludes the *Qi wu lun*.[14] This chapter mingles dream journeys and logical attacks on the philosophies of the day. Opinions divide over the nature and extent of rationalism, skepticism, and relativism in the *Zhuangzi*, and in the *Qi wu lun* in particular.[15] Angus Graham has presented Zhuangzi as a "great anti-rationalist" who had his own reasons for not listening to reason.[16] Chad Hansen reads the *Zhuangzi* as "a skeptical, relativistic reaction to the philosophy of language of the Neo-Mohists" in which the *Qi wu lun* is a coherent exposition of a relativist (as opposed to an absolutist) position.[17] Robert Allinson argues that Zhuangzi was not a relativist,[18] and P. J. Ivanhoe goes further, to claim that Zhuangzi was not only not a relativist but, at least in some senses, not a skeptic.[19]

Much of that debate is not apt for our purpose for two reasons. First, most of these discussions do not distinguish skeptical doctrines from skeptical methods or recommendations.[20] Second, some of this debate is not about skepticism, however defined, but about relativism, with a certain tendency to conflate the two by attributing a position of "skeptical relativism" to Zhuangzi.[21] Skeptical theses and relativist doctrines are both self-referential, and as such are open to the charge of self-contradiction.[22] Otherwise, they are mutually exclusive in that, strictly speaking, skepticism precludes relativism. A skeptical thesis holds that we cannot know anything; a relativist thesis holds that we can know, but that knowing is relative to our (individual, cultural, etc.) perspective. To put it another way, if we doubt our ability to recognize truth (the skeptical position), we must also doubt our ability to know that there isn't any (the relativist position).

The *Zhuangzi*

I divide the *Qi wu lun* into three sections. At the beginning and end, vivid narratives frame and reframe, but do not necessarily resolve, the problem of

---

*The reader may want to compare Raphals' distinction between skeptical theses and skeptical recommendations with Kjellberg's distinction between dogmatic and aporetic skepticisms (p. 20) and Schwitzgebel's between philosophical and everyday skepticism (p. 85). —Eds.

knowing. The central section consists of a series of arguments against a variety of doctrines and methods.

The Introductory Narratives: Ziqi's Trance

Ziqi of Nanguo reclines on a cushion, sighs, loses himself in a trance: "The reclining man here now is not the reclining man of yesterday" (2/1). 吾喪我 *wu sang wo*, "I lost 'me'," he adds,[23] and elaborates with a metaphor of the "pipes" of earth, humanity, and heaven. The pipes of earth are the hollows and valleys through which the wind blows. The pipes of humanity are the hollow tubes that comprise the human body. The pipes of heaven "puff out the ten thousand distinctions."[24]

A short poem introduces distinctions between great and small perspectives about 知 *zhi*, "wisdom", and 言 *yan*, "language":[25]

大知 *da zhi*, "great knowledge", is free and easy,

小知 *xiao zhi*, "petty knowledge", picks holes.

大言 *da yan*, "great speech", has a mild taste,

小言 *xiao yan*, "petty speech", is all rant. (2/9–10, Graham 1969–
70, 151)

The poem sets up a hierarchy between "great" and "small" knowledge, language, fear, and awakening but proffers no theory or recommendation as to which is which. Small knowledge is associated with 是非 *shi-fei*, the language and practice of moral judgment.[26] Great knowledge is associated with 明 *ming*, "illumination", 道 *dao*, and 覺 *jue*, "awakening".The *Zhuangzi* does not describe it directly but uses a variety of formal devices to illustrate it. These include paradox, perspective shifts, and thumbnail sketches of the behavior and skills of sages; these devices go a long way to produce the unique humor and flavor of the *Zhuangzi*.[27]

Together, the narrative and the poem question what we can know. The suggestion that Ziqi, in "losing himself," experienced a profound reorientation toward the world calls into question all his previous perceptions of external reality. But is this skepticism? We may ask where Zhuangzi places himself in his own hierarchy of great and small knowledge. What is his experience of, and attitude toward, great knowing? Our answer to this question will have important implications for our reading of the text. Which reading we prefer will affect our interpretation of many individual passages in the *Qi wu lun*.

Let us consider three possibilities: (1) Zhuangzi writes as a seeker of great knowledge who has not yet experienced it, but is sure it exists; (2) he doesn't have great knowledge, seeks it, but questions whether knowing is possible; (3) unitive mystical experience is the source of the knowing Zhuangzi refers to as "great"; he has great knowledge but writes as if he didn't. In these three interpretive standpoints, Zhuangzi respectively seeks great knowing, questions whether it is possible, and claims to have it but declines to talk about it. This last position may go hand-in-hand with skepticism about the "knowing" of mundane life, be it *shi-fei* distinctions or the cognitive systematic "knowledge" of contemporary political and cultural elites.[28] For the purposes of this discussion, I adopt a skeptical reading, but one that does not preclude the third, mystical approach.[29]

The Arguments

The central section attacks claims for an innate (and knowable) criterion for epistemological and moral judgments. These include claims for an innate authority for *shi-fei* judgments and claims for an innate natural order expressed in language and susceptible to 辯 *bian*, "discrimination".[30] The discussion begins with the analogy of the parts of the body. The question is: "Who's in charge?" "It seems that there is something genuinely in command, and that the only trouble is we cannot find a sign of it. . . . Of the hundred joints, nine openings, six viscera all present and complete, which should I recognize [as a source of authority]?" (2/15–17, Graham 1981, 51).

Most of the central section is taken up with a series of arguments, which call into question a series of tacit or explicit claims, namely:

1. Subjective certainty of the correctness of one's judgments is sufficient to grant them moral authority.

2. *Shi* and *fei* exist independently of or prior to the cultured heart-minds that make *shi-fei* judgments.

3. Language has fixed meaning.

4. The *shi-fei* judgments of Confucians and Mohists lead to knowledge.

5. (Sophist) discrimination provides an adequate basis for judgment.

6. Language is meaningless.

(1) questions Mencian claims for the 成心 *cheng xin*, "cultivated heart-mind" as a source of authoritative judgment:[31] "But if you go by the complete heart and take it as your authority, who is without such an authority? Why should it be only the man who knows how things alternate and whose heart approves its own judgments who has such an authority? The fool has one just as he has" (2/21–22, Graham 1981, 51). Here the *Zhuangzi* uses skeptical methods to question claims for the inherent authority of cultivated minds. If everyone's judgment has authority, no one's has. (This is the argument Socrates uses in his first refutation of Protagoras.) The passage does not, however, explicitly reject the possibility of authoritative moral judgments, as would a skeptical doctrine, nor does it make a clear recommendation on how to act.

The force of the next claim (2) is to question the a priori existence of *shi-fei* moral judgments. "For *shi* and *fei* to exist before a completed mind would be to 'go to Yue today and arrive yesterday'. This would be to take what doesn't [yet] exist as existing" (2/22). Hui Shi's paradox uses humor to make the indirect claim that *shi-fei* judgments have no existence prior to that of completed heart-mind, *cheng xin*; therefore Mencius is wrong to claim authority for them. Any claim for the authority of *cheng xin* presupposes the prior existence of *shi-fei*, which would be to put the cart before the horse.[32] It also suggests that there is nothing innate about *shi-fei*, and that *shi-fei* judgments are conventional, a view rejected by Mencius.[33] The method is to use humor and analogy to induce doubt about the possibility of authoritative moral judgments. There is no assertion that they are groundless (a skeptical doctrine) and no claim that they should be rejected in practice (a skeptical recommendation). The ground shifts to a consideration of whether the distinctions of language reflect an inherent order of nature.

The next passage (3) seems to claim that there is no fixed meaning in language: "Saying is not blowing breath. When someone speaks, there is something said, but *what* is said is never fixed. Is there truly something said? Or has there never been anything said? If you think it different than the sounds of fledglings, is there a *bian* 'distinction' or is there no distinction?" (2/23–24, Graham 1981, 52). The force of this passage is to question the possibility of fixed meaning or the existence (or intelligibility) of an external standard. It uses a series of rhetorical questions to ridicule the distinctions of the Neo-Mohists and Sophists. Yet it does not offer a skeptical doctrine that there is no difference between human language and bird calls, or a skeptical recommendation that conventional meanings or language be ignored.

The next passage (4) introduces the claim that language is the source of Confucian and Mohist discriminatory judgments. What obscures both dao and language, and leads to artificial notions of real and false and of *shi-fei*? The answer is: *xiao* "small" speech and knowledge: "Thus we have the *shi-fei* of Confucians and Mohists, by which what one *shi*s the other *fei*s, and what one *fei*s the other *shi*s. You may want to *shi* what they *fei* or *fei* what they *shi*, but this is not as good as using illumination" (2/26–27). Here we have what seems to be an unambiguous statement that *ming* "illumination" is better than the *bian* "discriminations" of the Confucians and Mohists, which are interchangeable, depending on perspective. This argument broadens into a general comment on evaluative judgments.

At this point Zhuangzi introduces a historical perspective, within which he locates distinctions as an intermediary stage in the history of knowledge: "The knowledge of the ancients had arrived at something, but at what? There were some who thought there had not yet begun to be things—the utmost, the exhaustive, there is no more to add. The next thought there were things, but there had not yet begun to be borders. The next thought there were borders, but there had not yet begun to be *shi-fei* [judgments]. The lighting up of *shi-fei* is the reason the dao is flawed" (2/40–42, based on Graham 1981, 54). These four stages seem to describe: (1) the ancients who had arrived at the utmost in knowledge, (2) earlier monistic Daoism, (3) the Sophists or Neo-Mohists, and (4) the *shi-fei* judgments of Mencius.[34]

In the next section (5) Zhuangzi uses a series of temporal and existential distinctions to question, or ridicule, Sophist dialectic. "Trying to put it into words," Zhuangzi makes a string of discriminations of the form 有 X 也 者 *you* X *ye zhe*, "there exists X." Each move makes a new distinction from the previous one. He distinguishes the existence of:

1. "Beginning".

2. A time before "beginning" existed.

3. A time before the time before "beginning" existed.

4. "Something" and "nothing".[35]

5. A time before "nothing" existed.

6. A time before the time before "nothing" existed.

"All of a sudden, there is 'nothing', yet we don't yet know of 'something' and 'nothing' which truly *is* and which truly isn't. Now, I have already referred to 'something', yet I don't yet know whether my reference really refers to 'something' or whether it refers to 'nothing'" (2/50–51). The argument seems to be that the categories of something and nothing are meaningless because they are mutually pervasive and mutually contradictory; therefore we cannot use these categories to make discriminatory judgments. But is this a joke, or does he make this argument in earnest? In a skeptical reading, the *reductio ad absurdum* is at least partially serious. We can, of course, make temporal and ontological discriminations in practice, yet the discriminations of *language* are conventional, and, if pushed to the extreme, ridiculous and unverifiable.[36] Avoiding skeptical doctrines, the passage never asserts that there is no such thing as 有無 *you wu*, "being" and "not-being", or that words are meaningless, only that referents are not fixed, and therefore, not verifiable.

These discriminations are posed as questions, not as assertions. Zhuangzi never answers these questions, and never directly claims that we cannot make distinctions, whether as perceptual judgments or in language. Were he to make the skeptical claim that language is meaningless, Zhuangzi would be open to the charge of self-refutation. The Neo-Mohists, whose arguments Zhuangzi presumably knew, make exactly this charge against the monistic Daoist Shen Dao.[37]

Thus Zhuangzi uses discrimination to attack discrimination. He induces doubt of the very method he uses to induce doubt. Several of Hui Shi's paradoxes bring the reader to the question of (6) whether it is possible to *say* something:[38] "Now that we are one, can I still say something? Already, having called us one, did I succeed in not saying something? One and the saying makes two, two and one makes three. Proceeding from here even an expert calculator cannot get to the end of it, much less a plain man. Therefore if we take the step from nothing to something we arrive at three, and how much worse if we take the step from something to something! Take no step at all, and the *shi* that works by circumstance will come to an end" (2/53–55, Graham 1981, 56).[39] The skeptical methods in this passage rely on the humor of *reductio ad absurdum*. Skeptical doctrines (or even recommendations) would have no place in it.

The final note is to relegate *bian* to the realm of *xiao yan* "small talk" without quite articulating the position that all language was meaningless:

> The greatest dao does not usurp.
> Great *bian* does not *yan* "speak".
> Great 仁 *ren*, "benevolence" is not *ren*.
> Great integrity does not make itself awkward.
> Great courage is not excessive. (2/5859)

The Closing Narratives of Dream and Waking

The *Qi wu lun* closes as it began, with a series of stories in which quasi-"idiotic" characters question our ability to know. In the first, "Gaptooth" questions Wang Ni:

> G: Would you know something of which all things agreed *shi*?
>
> W: How would I know that?
>
> G: Would you know what you did not know?
>
> W: How would I know that?
>
> G: Then does no thing know anything?
>
> W: How would I know that? However, let me try to say it [put it into words]: How do I know that what I call knowing is not ignorance? How do I know that what I call ignorance is not knowing? (2/64–66, Graham 1981, 58)

Next, the passage questions the human tendency to love life and fear death. Another series of perspective-shifts contrast imagination and "reality," 大 蒙 *da meng*, "the ultimate dream", and the 大覺 *da jue*, "the ultimate awakening" (2/82), and even, self-referentially, "you and I arguing over alternatives" (2/84–85). The *Qi wu lun* closes with Zhuangzi's dream of the butterfly.

Is Zhuangzi a skeptic by doctrine? The evidence seems to refute this possibility. Only two statements in the *Qi wu lun* even suggest a skeptical doctrine. We are asked whether it differs from the twittering of birds (A negative answer might count as a skeptical doctrine.), but the question is never answered. While Zhuangzi does state unambiguously that language is the source of the false distinctions of the Ruists and Mohists, that statement is not in itself a skeptical doctrine. In most of the other sections of the chapter, there is a striking refusal to state a skeptical doctrine, but considerable evidence for skepticism as a method.

The Question of Socratic Skepticism

Before turning from the *Zhuangzi* to the *Theaetetus*, I want to contextualize the problem of skepticism in the *Theaetetus* in a long-standing debate about the origins of skepticism.[40] At issue was whether Plato and Socrates were skeptics. Arcesilaus (ca. 315–241 B.C.E.), the founder of the skeptical Academy, claimed Plato and the Platonic Socrates as his source.[41] This claim for the legacy of Plato's Academy became a focus of a variety of attacks, both ancient and modern. Cicero (106–43 B.C.E.) defends the claim,[42] and describes the methods of Socrates at some length. Socrates affirmed nothing, but refuted others; he asserted that he knew nothing except that he knew nothing.[43] According to Cicero, Plato's followers in both the Academy and the Lyceum abandoned this Socratic practice of doubt and restraint from making positive statements.[44] Yet less than three hundred years later, Sextus Empiricus (ca. 200 C.E.) distinguishes skepticism from the "dogmatism" of Socrates and Plato, despite their didactic methods,[45] and rejects a skeptical interpretation of Plato.[46]

One difficulty with this historical argument is that neither side specifies what kind of "skepticism" it means when it applies, or denies, the name of skeptic to Plato and Socrates. It is noteworthy that the arguments that Plato and Socrates were not skeptics focus on the question of skeptical doctrines and recommendations, while Cicero's defense focuses on skeptical methods. Paul Woodruff argues that much of the subsequent study of Plato has emphasized his doctrines at the expense of his methods, and that this emphasis has taken attention away from the aspects of his work that made him an ancestor of skepticism, specifically his methods.[47]

Skeptical Doctrines in *Theaetetus*

Bearing in mind this debate, we may ask whether the style of argument of *Theaetetus* 151–184 is skeptical, and if so, in what way. To answer this question, I begin by asking whether this section of the *Theaetetus* contains skeptical doctrines.

The *Theaetetus* Argument on Knowledge as Perception

In the *Theaetetus*, Plato proposes and rejects four definitions of knowledge. He rejects several proposed branches of knowledge (for example, geometry and astronomy) as descriptions of objects of knowledge, rather than of knowledge itself (146c–e). He rejects definitions of knowledge as perception or sensation (151d–186e), true opinion (187a–201c), and true opinion justified by an account or *logos* (201c–210a). The dream passage occurs within the attempt to define knowledge as sense perception. This discussion is concentrated at 151d–186e, and occupies over half the dialogue.

The *Theaetetus*, like the *Zhuangzi*, has been subject to divergent interpretations. Bishop Berkeley read the *Theaetetus* as anticipating and supporting his own empiricist theory of knowledge. Yet the eighteenth-century philosopher Richard Price considered the dialogue to effectively refute the empiricist epistemologies of Berkeley and Hume.[48] These two interpretations take very different views of 151d–184a, the consideration of sense perception. At issue are two approximately parallel questions: whether Plato agrees with the arguments of Protagoras and Heraclitus; and whether the epistemology of the *Theaetetus* is consistent with the Theory of Forms as presented in the *Phaedo* and *Republic*. A positive answer to both questions supports Berkeley's empiricist reading. Here Plato believes that Protagoras and Heraclitus give a true account of perception, but that perception is not knowledge. A negative answer to both questions supports Price's antiempiricist interpretation. In this view, *Theaetetus* 151d–184a presents a self-sufficient critique of empiricism in which Plato changes his mind from earlier work. His treatment of Protagoras is then ironic, and he is not committed to the arguments of Protagoras and Heraclitus.[49]

The Exposition

The first section introduces three doctrines and the example of dreams and madness.[50] The Measure Doctrine of Protagoras is a theory of general relativism in which "man is the measure of all things" (151e–152c). The Flux Theory of Heraclitus states that nothing is just one thing and that everything is its opposite, because nothing "is" but everything "becomes" (152d–155e). Next, a Heraclitean explanation of Protagorean relativism reformulates Protagorean "being" as Heraclitean "becoming" (157b). After the presentation of the three theses to Theaetetus, Socrates disavows knowledge by claiming to be a midwife who is barren of theories, and who is attending the labor of Theaetetus. Only after he has brought Theaetetus' own beliefs (*dogma*) into light will it become clear whether they are a live birth or a wind-egg (157d).[51] At this point we may speculate as to what a "live birth" would be. If we emphasize that Socrates is not a skeptic by doctrine, we might expect him to eventually guide Theaetetus through his own objections to some correct definition. If, on the other hand, we emphasize his skeptical methods, a live birth might be guiding Theaetetus to ask the right questions, not to formulate the right answers.

When Theaetetus seems satisfied with this account, Socrates challenges

it with the evidence of dreams and madness, arguing that dreams and madness are indeed false perception. However, if nothing remains the same over
time because being and becoming are always relative to somebody or something, which are also in flux, a false perception may be true for the person
who made it at the time it was made. Thus the argument from dreams provides the challenge that forces Socrates to refute the combined argument of
Protagoras and Heraclitus, which do not admit the possibility of false perception, whether it be dreams, madness, or mistaken judgments about the future.

The Refutations of Protagoras

The trivial refutation of Protagoras raises the problem of expertise (161c–
163a) as a new challenge to the Measure Doctrine, which seems to deny the
possibility of differences in wisdom. If knowledge is perception, how can
expertise exist? How can Protagoras teach? It accuses Protagoras of self-
contradiction (163a–165e) by means of arguments that show that "know"
and "perceive" are not interchangeable. In a "Defense of Protagoras" Socrates
takes on the role of Protagoras (166a–170a) and argues that the charge of
self-contradiction against Protagoras rests on trivial semantic distinctions.
Socrates makes the pragmatic argument that experts, for example, doctors
or politicians, know how to make the perceptions of others better, but not
truer. Socrates restates the Relativism doctrine as: for each person and each
city, things are what they seem to them to be (168b).
    The serious refutation of Protagoras reintroduces the issue of expertise,
restates the self-refutation argument against Protagoras on a more serious
level, and reformulates the Defense of Protagoras, allowing for some objective judgments. In arguing that the Pythagorean Measure Doctrine is self-
contradictory (170a–171d), it reformulates the question of what expertise is
as what people think it is. It introduces the claim that people think that
experts make true judgments and that other people make false ones. It argues
that Protagoras is caught in the dilemma of averring the possibility of false
judgment, which the Measure Doctrine denies. Next Plato argues that completely general relativism is self-refuting (170e–171c). If Protagoras believes
his own theory, he must admit the contrary of his own view, the Measure
Doctrine, since all judgments are true. Thus Protagoras' doctrine is not true
for anyone, even for Protagoras. Socrates reformulates the Defense of
Protagoras and offers a new version of the Measure Doctrine (171d–172b).
Since complete relativism undermines itself, we must determine in what
areas objectivity and expertise prevail. A certain class of objective judgments
are possible: judgments about what benefits an individual or city. An apparent
digression on justice and prudence contrasts the philosopher and the worldly
person (172c–177c). Finally, Socrates claims to refute Protagoras on the
grounds that the Measure Doctrine does not admit judgments about the
future, a large class of objective judgments (177c–179b).

The Refutation of Heraclitus

The refutation of Heraclitus introduces a new distinction, between *paron* "immediate perception" and *doxa* "perceptual judgment". It also introduces an Extended Flux Doctrine, which distinguishes two kinds of flux: spatial motion and alteration. The argument moves from the claim that there is no stability to the perceived properties of objects to the generalization that language has no meaning, because there is nothing left for perceptual judgment to be right about, so any statement is as right or wrong as any other. Therefore the claim that knowledge is perception, a statement in language, is no more true than false. Socrates claims that this refutation encompasses not only Heracliteans, but Protagoras and Theaetetus.

Socrates' answer to the argument for sense perception based on the case of dreams and madness takes up the first part of Woodruff's "definition-testing *elenchus*," wherein he undermines the premises of his interlocutor, in this case the definition of Theaetetus, based on the theories of Protagoras and Heraclitus. However, at this point, any number of questions can be raised about Socrates' disproof of the definition of *epistēme* as *aisthēsis*. These include ironic elements in Socrates' impersonation of Protagoras[52] and questions about whether Socrates has really refuted Heraclitus.[53]

The Direct Proof

In the second part of the *elenchus*, Plato begins again, this time from his own premises, in an entirely new demonstration (184e–186e). Socrates begins by asking whether we perceive with or through the eyes and ears to raise the philosophical issue of whether there is one perceiving consciousness (through) or a plurality of perceivers (with), whom Plato compares to the soldiers hidden in the Trojan horse. Plato rejects the "Trojan horse" model of perception in favor of the unity of consciousness. He argues that there are qualities that are grasped, not through the senses, but through the mind's activity of thought. These include existence, number, and likeness. The argument concludes with the observation that, if perception cannot grasp being, it cannot grasp truth, a necessary condition of knowledge. Therefore, Plato argues, perception is not knowledge.

Is Plato's argument from dreams a skeptical doctrine? If so, it is clearly not the doctrine of Socrates, but rather follows from the combined position of Heraclitus and Protagoras. Socrates not only refutes it; he refutes it twice. Does this mean that we are to side with Sextus and judge that the Platonic Socrates is not a skeptic? Not necessarily. We may still decide that Socrates takes seriously the skeptical recommendation to suspend judgment, without explicitly affirming the skeptical doctrine that one cannot aver or deny knowledge about knowledge. Socrates constantly disavows knowledge. We may also decide that he is a skeptic by method, a possibility that even Sextus leaves open.

Skepticism as a Recommendation

Both the *Qi wu lun* and *Theaetetus* seem to encourage doubt by advocating skepticism in its second sense, as a recommendation. Like Sextus, Zhuangzi is clearly concerned with problems of equanimity amidst the difficulties of a vexed age,*[54] and traditional interpretations of the *Zhuangzi* tend to emphasize this aspect.[55]

We can go one step further, and give this method a name: *ming* "illumination". Zhuangzi consistently states that various formulations of "small knowing" 莫若以明 *mo ruo yi ming*, "are not as good as using *ming*" (see, for example, 2/27). In the case of great knowing, the typical formulation is 此之謂以明 *ci zhi wei yi ming*, "it is this that is meant by 'using *ming*'" (see, for example, 2/47, Graham 1981, 55). The characters who have great knowing consistently refrain from dogmatic judgments, although their equanimity never prevents them from acting .[56]

In the case of the *Theaetetus*, the skeptical recommendation is made through the force of the persona of Socrates and his methods of inquiry, to which he gives the name of midwifery. In comparing his own questioning of Theaetetus to the activity of the midwife, Socrates claims to be himself a midwife, and the son of a midwife, Phaenarete, "she who brings virtue to light" (149a), a phrase that might pass as a literal translation of 明德 *ming de*, the traditional activity of the sage-kings. There follows an extended description of the skills of the midwife/enlightener (149a–151d). At the end of the last section of the dialogue, Socrates and Theaetetus seem to conclude that Theaetetus has finished giving birth, but has produced only wind-eggs (210b–c). Socrates concludes that, while he himself "does not know what other men know," the inquiry itself will improve the subsequent theories of Theaetetus (210c), if he has any. This is all the midwife's art can hope to achieve (210d). Here Socrates' *elenchus* seems to collapse. He denies that his method can define knowing, but continues to recommend his method of inquiry. This would appear to be skepticism as a recommendation.

Skeptical Methods

Next I want to discuss several of the skeptical methods that I consider to be operating in the *Qi wu lun* and *Theaetetus*. Skeptical methods produce a state of uncertainty by appearing either to affirm nothing, or to affirm what they concurrently deny. Skeptical methods in these texts include the alternate pursuit and abandonment of *reductio ad absurdum* arguments, humor, complex narrative structures, and complex irony. Overall, they use narra-

---

* Compare Kjellberg's analysis of the role of *ataraxia* in Zhuangzi (p. 13).—Eds.

tive and dramatic techniques to create a textual situation that invites the reader to question whether the meaning of the whole is precisely equal to the sum of its philosophical parts.

Reductio Ad Absurdum

Both dialogues use *reductio ad absurdum* arguments to attack the views of predecessors or contemporaries. Zhuangzi uses them to attack quasi-Mencian claims for the supremacy of the complete heart-mind, to show the limitations of *shi-fei* judgments, and to ridicule Sophist, Neo-Mohist, and Daoist prede- cessors and near-contemporaries. In the *Theaetetus*, Plato uses elaborate (and arguably unnecessary) *reductio ad absurdum* arguments to refute Protagoras and Heraclitus, before introducing his own premises. Both sets of polemics deal with the serious problem of self-refutation, but in very different ways. The *Zhuangzi* manages to avoid it entirely by never articulating a skeptical doctrine directly, and never risking an inherently self-refuting statement of the limitations of language. Plato takes on the problem of self-refutation directly. His second refutation of Protagoras (170a–171d) provides a classic formulation of the self-refutation argument against skepticism.[57]

Narrative Techniques

Both texts seem to say one thing and do another. They use the arguments they appear to refute, or don't use the arguments they appear to advance. In the end, each admits of interpretations that are so divergent as to be contra- dictory, and the reader is led to suspect that this is not an accident. There is, in both texts, a curious lacuna between the questions they ask and the lack, or complexity, of the answers they provide. Jokes, puns, poetry, and charac- ter sketches provide commentary or "stage directions" about the explicit arguments, which are digressive and indirect.

The *Qi wu lun* emphasizes the limitations of Neo-Mohist dialectic, yet it makes extensive *use* of the very form of argument it appears to attack. The *Theaetetus* seems to seek a positive definition by *elenctic* argument, yet none of the *elenctic* argument leads to a positive definition. Over half the dialogue concerns the first definition of knowledge as sense perception. Most of that consists of indirect proofs and a substantial digression. The direct proof used to reject the first definition is very brief. All four proposed definitions of knowledge are ultimately rejected.

The *Qi wu lun* is easily accused of "not quite making sense," of being disjointed and disjunctive. Are these breaks in the narrative an artifact of textual corruption, a demonstration of Zhuangzi's disregard for, disinterest in, or hostility toward rationality?* Or is it part of the "mysticism" of the

---

*Graham (1981, 48) suggests that the chapter was assembled by a later and unsympa- thetic editor he calls the "Syncretist." Hansen (1983, 38–50) and Wu (1990, 171–277) assume

text? The *Qi wu lun* uses humor to demonstrate the relative and arbitrary nature of the *xiao zhi* "small knowing" of Confucians and Mohists: quasi-Mencian *shi-fei* judgments and Neo-Mohist *bian*. It surrounds arguments with images: Ziqi reclining in reverie, Gaptooth, and the dream of the butterfly.

The *Theaetetus* uses a variety of jokes and puns in such incidents as the critical portrayal of the materialists (as opposed to the Heracliteans) and in its sketches of Heraclitean "Flux" extremists. Plato may have banished the poets from the Republic, but they are very much present in the *Theaetetus*. Homer appears at the head of the Heracliteans and in the "Trojan horse model" of a nonunified consciousness. Lines of Pindar appear for dramatic effect (for example, at 173e). Later portions of the *Theaetetus* rely not only on logical argument but on detailed similes to represent theories of knowledge, for example, the wax block (19la–195b) and the aviary (196d–199c). It has even been argued that *Theaetetus* 161–171 has the structure of a comedy, in which Plato "turns the tables" (*peritrope*) on Protagoras. He does so by embroiling Protagoras in a philosophical farce, that not only lends dramatic flair to the arguments under discussion, but also allows Plato to "show up," as well as refute, Progratoras.[58]

Like Socrates, Zhuangzi asks more questions than he answers, and repeatedly formulates ideas in order to revise and attack them.[59] He asks, and never answers questions of the form "Is it X, or is it not X?"[60] Yet Zhuangzi and Plato each presents a hierarchy of knowing that contrasts a kind of superior knowing, which is never precisely defined, with inferior "knowledges" that are discussed at great length. In the *Theaetetus*, this "true knowledge" is *epistēme*. In the Zhuangzi, the superior knowledge is *da zhi* "great knowing" and is identified with *ming* and dao.

The argument from dreams does very different things in these two texts. For Zhuangzi, it challenges our ability to know the truth of our perceptions. For Plato, it demonstrates the existence of false, and thence of true, perceptions (although it does not specify which perceptions are true or how we would identify them).[61]

Skeptical Methods and Styles of Reasoning

Because of the similarities between the skeptical methods used in these works, we should abandon the bias that Greek thought is analytic or rational and Chinese thought is holistic or intuitionist. But how do we understand those similarities?

One explanatory device that will *not* work is the vexed, but still pervasive notion of mentalities. The term was given currency by the French sociologist

the chapter's integrity. In the absence of external evidence, the justification for this assumption depends on our ability to provide a convincing interpretation of the chapter as a unified and continuous whole.—Eds.

Lucien Levy-Bruhl, who used it to explain the thought processes and/or belief systems of groups of peoples, especially peoples whose thought processes he characterized as prelogical and mystical.[62] These terms have been widely applied to Chinese thought in general and to the Zhuangzi in particular, but they might not find ready acceptance as descriptive of Plato, Socrates, or the Theaetetus. An alternative would be to frame the question of skeptical methods within the broader problem of styles of reasoning in China and Greece.[63]

Conclusion

In this paper I have perhaps artificially emphasized a distinction between skeptical doctrines, recommendations, and methods, in a manner that Zhuangzi, if not Socrates, might have found most antipathetic. I have done so for two reasons. First, I believe this distinction can clarify the current debate about the presence, or absence, of skepticism in the Zhuangzi. That debate has been entirely concerned with the question of skeptical doctrines and recommendations, with the effect of obscuring the question of skeptical methods. The force of my distinction is to strengthen and emphasize the presence of skeptical methods in the Zhuangzi, and at least to suggest the presence of skeptical recommendations. Second, this method of analysis illustrates the importance of skeptical methods in both texts, a similarity that would simply not be apparent if the discussion focused on either skeptical doctrines or skeptical recommendations.

In conclusion, I would suggest that this examination of skepticism in the Zhuangzi and Theaetetus raises the broader problem of styles of reasoning in China and Greece. The prevailing tendency has been to talk about differences between Chinese and Greek philosophical arguments; I have chosen to look for similarities. I have argued that the Zhuangzi and Theaetetus are skeptical texts by virtue of their use of skeptical methods, and that skepticism may inhere in form, as well as content. If so, the arguments of Socrates and Zhuangzi may have more in common than we think, or than the rationalist tradition would admit.[64]

Notes

1. Unless otherwise specified, translations of Zhuangzi are taken from or based on Graham 1981.

2. Unless otherwise stated, all translations of Theaetetus are by M. J. Levett and M. F. Burnyeat in Burnyeat, The Theaetetus of Plato (Indianapolis: Hackett Publishing Company, 1990).

3. Other examples include Sextus Empiricus, Descartes (*Meditations* I), Hume, and Freud (*Interpretation of Dreams*, 83f).

4. For impermanence, see Li Bo's untitled poem on Zhuangzi. For questioning the content or source of knowledge, see Du Fu's 夢李白 *Meng Li Bo*, "Dreaming Li Bo." For translations of these poems see Obata Shigenyoshi, *Li Bo the Chinese Poet* (Tokyo, 1935) and David Hawkes, *A Little Primer of Tu Fu* (Oxford: Clarendon Press, 1967), 87–92.

5. See Paul Woodruff, "Plato's Early Theory of Knowledge" in *Companions to Ancient Thought: vol. 1 Epistemology*, Stephen Everson, ed. (Cambridge: Cambridge University Press, 1990), 61.

6. Skepticism flourished during some five hundred years between the fourth century B.C.E. and the third century C.E. The major academic skeptics were Arcesilaus (c. 315–c. 242 B.C.E.) and Carneades (c. 213–129 B.C.E.). The major Pyrrhonian skeptics were Pyrrho of Elis (c. 360–c. 270 B.C.E.), Aenesidemus (fl. first century B.C.E.), and Sextus Empiricus (fl. 200 C.E.). For general discussions of the history of Greek skepticism, see Edwyn Robert Bevan, *Stoics and Skeptics* (Oxford: Clarendon Press, 1913), Mary Mills Patrick, *The Greek Skeptics* (New York: Columbia University Press, 1929), and R. G. Bury, "Introduction" to *Sextus Empiricus*, vol. 1, Loeb Classical Library Edition (Cambridge, Mass.: Harvard University Press, 1933). Malcolm Schofield, Myles Burnyeat, and Jonathan Barnes, eds., *Doubt and Dogmatism: Studies in Hellenistic Epistemology* (Oxford: Clarendon Press, 1980), Myles Burnyeat, ed., *The Skeptical Tradition* (Berkeley, Calif.: University of California Press, 1983), Leo Groarke, *Greek Skepticism: Anti-Realist Trends in Ancient Thought* (Montreal: McGill-Oueens University Press, 1990), and Kjellberg 1994 discuss a range of more recent views. The major source for skeptical doctrines are the writings of Cicero, Sextus Empiricus, and Diogenes Laertius. All references to these texts are from the Loeb Classical Library Editions.

7. For discussion of the impact of skepticism on later philosophical traditions see Burnyeat 1983, 1–3, and Groarke 1990, 3.

8. Groarke opposes skepticism to such movements as Platonism, Aristotelianism, and Cartesianism (Groarke 1990, 4).

9. Phillip P. Hallie, "A Polemical Introduction" in *Selections from the Major Writings of Sextus Empiricus: Scepticism, Man and God*, Phillip Hallie, ed., Sanford G. Etheridge, tr. (Indianapolis: Hackett Publishing Company, 1985), 6.

10. Thus Sextus Empiricus describes skepticism as "ability, or mental attitude, which opposes appearances to judgments in any way whatsoever" ("Outlines of Pyrrhonism" (hereafter cited in the text as *OP*) 8). Sextus distinguishes his skepticism from the dogmatism of several important philo-

sophical predecessors: Heraclitus, despite his theory of flux; Protagoras, despite his relativism; Democritus, despite his distrust of sense perception; and Socrates and Plato, despite their didactic methods (*OP* 1.213–25).

11. Paul Woodruff describes this "definition-testing *elenchus*" in "The Skeptical Side of Plato's Method," *Revue internationale de philosophie* 156–7, 22–37.

12. Gregory Vlastos, "Socratic Irony," *Classical Quarterly* 37.1 (1987), 79–96.

13. For the distinction between doctrine and recommendation, and their mutual independence, see Gisela Striker, "Skeptical Strategies," in Schofield, Burnyeat, and Barnes 1980, 54–55.

14. This title has been variously interpreted and translated as: "essay on seeing things as equal" (Graham 1969–70), "sorting which evens things out" (Graham 1981, 48), and "discourse that equalizes things" (Hansen in Mair 1983, 26 and 50–52).

15. For purposes of this discussion, I restrict consideration of the *Zhuangzi* to the *Nei pian* or "Inner Chapters" of what is widely believed to be a composite work. By "Zhuangzi" I mean not the historical Zhuangzi, of which we know virtually nothing, but the coherent voice of the "Zhuangzi" of the *Qi wu lun*. For discussions of the textual history of the *Zhuangzi* see Graham 1986 and Roth 1991. For the importance of the *Qi wu lun* as a distillate of the arguments of the *Zhuangzi*, see Hansen in Mair 1983, 31.

16. Graham 1981, 9, Graham 1989, and Graham's responses to Hansen in Rosemont 1991.

17. Hansen in Mair 1983, 27 and 38. He also argues that the paradigm for skepticism was sense perception in Greece and language in China (Hansen in Mair 1983, 27, 30–34, 37–38, and 48–50). For further discussions of the problems of rationalism and skepticism, see Hansen's "Should the Ancient Masters Value Reason?" in Rosemont 1991, 196 and 203–5.

18. Allinson 1989. For a useful commentary on the arguments of this book see Bryan Van Norden, "Review of *Chuang-Tzu for Spiritual Transformation*" in *The Journal of Asian Studies* 49.2 (1990), 36–37.

19. Ivanhoe 1993 argues that Zhuangzi was a skeptic about language but not about certain kinds of knowledge.

20. Graham simply assumes skepticism (1989, 186 and 193–95). Hansen in Mair 1983 makes explicit arguments for a skeptical reading of the *Qi wu lun*, but does not distinguish kinds of skepticism. Ivanhoe 1993 discusses four kinds of skeptical argument, which he terms epistemological, sense,

ethical, and language skepticism. While he does not make the distinction, it is my impression that all four are variants of a skeptical thesis, rather than a skeptical method or recommendation.

21. Hansen in Mair 1983, 27 and Allinson 1989, 11. Hansen does separate the two in his argument that Zhuangzi is a relativist as opposed to an absolutist (in Mair 1983, 38–46).

22. In the case of relativism, the claim is that, if all knowing is a function of one's perspective, no one can advocate any one truth claim over another, including the claim that knowing is a function of one's perspective.

23. Wang 1961, 11 suggests that at the time he reclined on the cushion, he was already making use of the linguistic distinctions of the Confucians and Mohists. Up to that point, he had been in a state of disassociation, and had forgotten language.

24. 吹萬不同 *chui wan bu tong* (2/8), based on Graham 1981, 49. An alternative translation is "blow the ten thousand disputing voices," possibly the contradictory arguments of philosophers (Graham 1969–70, 149–50). Hansen further interprets the passage to raise implicitly the question of whether the distinctions of language are natural. In Hansen's view, this passage directly attacks the primitive Daoist position that language and its distinctions are unnatural, insofar as the users of these conflicting discourses are "natural" (Hansen in Mair 1983, 38–39 and in Hansen 1992).

25. For a discussion of the role of verse in the *Zhuangzi* , see my "Poetry in the *Zhuangzi*," *Journal of Chinese Religion* 22 (Fall, 1994): 103–116.

26. While the term *shi-fei* is often associated with the later Mohists, it does appear in Mencius at 2A6, 3B8, 4B31, 5A1, and 6A6 as a modality of moral sense.

27. For discussion of these skills, and of the problem of skill knowledge in general, see Ivanhoe 1993 and Raphals, *Knowing Words: Wisdom and Cunning in the Classical Traditions of China and Greece* (Ithaca: Cornell University Press, 1992). For a discussion of the importance of humor as an element in intellection, see Christoph Harbsmeier, "Humor in Ancient Chinese Philosophy," *Philosophy East & West* 39.3 (1989): 289–310.

28. Such a reading would provide an alternative to the general tendency to attribute "quietistic" attitudes to both mysticism and skepticism. For a vigorous attack on the latter see Hallie 1985, 6–9.

29. These three readings merit a separate study.

30. For further discussion of Zhuangzi's critique of Mencius, see Hansen in Mair 1983, 39–44.

31. By "Mencian" I mean either the position of Mencius himself or else one very much like it.

32. For support for this reading see Wang 1961, 16.

33. Hansen takes this claim one step further, to argue that *shi-fei* is not inherently natural (Hansen in Mair 1983, 41 and 1992).

34. From the perspective of Reading C, this passage seems to decribe a return from undifferentiated "mystical" experience to the perceptual and linguistic distinctions of the phenomenal world.

35. For a discussion of *you* "something" and *wu* "nothing" in Classical Chinese, see Angus Graham's "'Being' in Western Philosophy compared with *shi/fei* and *yu/wu* in Chinese Philosophy," *Asia Major* NS 7, Nos. 1–2 (1959), 79–112, reprinted in *Studies in Chinese Philosophy and Philosophical Literature* (Singapore: Institute of East Asian Philosophies, 1986).

36. Part of the humor of this passages lies in the parody of such cosmogonic accounts as *Laozi* 42. I am grateful to Harold Roth for calling this aspect of the passage to my attention.*

37. According to Shen Dao, the Great Way was capable of "embracing all things, but not of discriminating among them" (33/43–44, Watson 1968, 369). The Neo-Mohists responded: "To claim that all saying contradicts itself is self-contradictory" (Graham, *Later Mohist Logic, Ethics and Science* (Hong Kong: Chinese University Press, and London: School of Oriental and African Studies, 1978), 445.) For discussion of this passage see Hansen in Mair 1983, 38. Plato makes virtually the same case against Heraclitus when he rejects the Extended Flux theory of Heraclitus on the grounds that it leads to the impossibility of meaning in language (*Theaetetus* 179c–183c).

38. For discussion of Laozi-type monism in this passage, see Hansen in Mair 1983, 49 and 1992.

39. 因是 *yinshi*, "the 'adaptive' *shi*" that works by circumstance, is contrasted to 爲是 *weishi*, "the 'contrived' *shi*" that deems, which is the means by which boundaries are established (2/55). The "contrived" *shi*, which distinguishes a stalk from a pillar and Xi Shi from a leper, is contrasted with the dao, which interchanges these things and treats them as one (2/35–36). For translations of these passages see Graham 1969–70, 153 and 155.

40. For a concise summary of that debate see Woodruff 1986, 23–24.

41. Cicero, *Academica* 1.44–46.

---

*Loy makes a different suggestion about the relationship between Laozi and Zhuangzi (p. 55). See also Graham 1981, 126–128 for an argument that Laozi's creation as the mythic author of the *Daodejing* postdates the composition of the Inner Chapters.—Eds.

42. Cicero argues that Arcesilaus was a true follower of Plato (*Academica* 1.46.), that Socrates and Plato were skeptics (*Academica* 2.74.), and that Arcesilaus used their methods (*Academica* 2.77, *Finibus* 2.2, and *Natura Deorum* i.5.11).

43. Cicero, *Academica* 1.4.15–18. According to Socrates, others claim to know when they are ignorant; he himself knows only that he is ignorant, which is why Apollo judged him wisest of all, since wisdom is not to think you know what you do not (*Academica* 1.4.15–16). The reference to Apollo also occurs in Plato at *Apology* 21a.

44. Cicero, *Academica* 1.4.17. Cicero defends the original claim of Arcesilaus against both the dogmatic eclectics (represented by Varro in Cicero, *Academica* 1.16) and the New Academy of Arcesilaus (represented by Lucullus in Cicero, *Academica* 2.15). Diogenes Laertius (4.33) and Plutarch (*Adv.Col.* 1122a) attack the claims of Arcesilaus. For attacks by modern scholars see Sedley 1983.

45. Sextus, *OP* 1.213–25.

46. Sextus, *OP* 1.220–25 and 234; M.7.141–44, 9.64, 9.92, 9.105, and 10.70. A few concessions appear at *OP* 2.22 and M. 7.2 and 8.91–92.

47. Woodruff divides what he calls the definition-testing *elenchus* into two parts. First Socrates refutes a dogmatic interlocutor by showing that the questioner does not understand the conditions for successful definition (Woodruff 1986, 33). Next, Socrates (or his stand-in) takes the interlocutor's place and refutes views of his own, not because they are false, but because they are not definitions and thus not knowledge. I take it that Woodruff's emphasis is on the purpose, as distinct from the logical methods, of the *elenchus*. For a description of some of the latter see Gregory Vlastos, "Socratic Elenchus," *Journal of Philosophy* (1982), 711–714. The main difference between this Socratic method and skeptical argument forms is that Socrates claims knowledge of his own ignorance (Plato, *Apology* 23a–b) and Arcesilaus insists that he himself does not even know *that* (Cicero, *Academica* 1.45). The latter are strategies for inducing *epoche*, not proofs of ignorance (Woodruff 1986, 22–23, and 33).

48. Burnyeat 1990, 1.

49. For various versions of the positive reading, see Francis Macdonald Cornford, *Plato's Theory of Knowledge: the Theaetetus and Sophist of Plato Translated With a Running Commentary* (London: Routledge, 1935), 7, 28, 83 and *passim*, and H.J. Cherniss, "The Philosophical Economy of the Theory of Ideas" in Gregory Vlastos, ed., *Plato: A Collection of Critical Essays: vol. 1 Metaphysics and Epistemology* (New York: Doubleday and Company, Inc., 1971), 20–22. J. M. Cooper, "Plato on Sense-Perception and Knowledge

(Theaetetus 184–186)," *Phronesis* 15 (1970), 123–146, and Burnyeat 1990, 8 and *passim*, all present versions of the negative reading. The positive reading seems to be the prevalent view within Plato scholarship.

50. For purposes of discussion, I divide *Theaetetus* (151d–186e) into four components, based on Burnyeat 1990, 251–55. I have, however, combined the refutations of Protagoras into one section. They are: 1. Exposition of the three initial theses (151d–160e); 2. Refutations of Protagoras (161–179c); 3. Refutation of Heraclitus (179c–183c); and 4. Refutation by direct proof (183c–186e).

51. That is, a false pregnancy.

52. Edward Lee argues that Plato's representation of Protagoras is deeply ironic, and that Plato repeatedly represents Protagoras as holding views at odds with his actual views. Examples include speaking scornfully against persuasive speech and advocating fixed standards of validity that Protagoras' own philosophy precluded. See Edward N. Lee,"Hoist With His Own Petard: Ironic and Comic Elements in Plato's Critique of Protagoras (*Theaetetus*, 161–171)," in E. N. Lee, A. P. D. Mourelatos, and R. M. Rorty, eds., *Exegesis and Argument: Studies in Greek Philosophy Presented to Gregory Vlastos* (New York: Humanities Press,1973).

53. See Nicholas P. White, *Plato on Knowledge and Reality* (Indianapolis: Hackett Publishing Company, 1976), 157–62.

54. For discussions of Warring States thought as a response to the decline of the Zhou, see Graham 1989, 2–4.

55. For example, Liu Xie's (465–522 C.E.) description of Zhuangzi in the *Wen xin diao long*: "Zhuang Zhou attained freedom and spontaneity in his elucidation of the dao." See 王利器 Wang Liqi, 文心調龍校正 *Wen Xin Diao Long Jiao Zheng*, by 劉勰 Liu Xie. Shanghai: Guji chupan shu, 1980, 119 and Vincent Yu-chung Shih's translation, *The Literary Mind and the Carving of Dragons by Liu Hsieh: A Study of Thought and Pattern in Chinese Literature* (New York: Columbia University Press, 1959), 96. For a later example see Wang 1961.

56. For discussion of the *apraxia* argument, that skepticism is incompatible with daily life, see Striker 1980, 63–68.

57. *Theaetetus* 17a–171d.

58. For the details of this very interesting argument see Lee 1973, 255–59.

59. Graham 1969–70, 138.

60. Compare 2/24. Similar examples occur at 2/66, 2/86, and 2/30.

61. I am grateful to an anonymous reader for this observation.

62. See Lucien Levy-Bruhl, *La Mentalite Primitive* (Paris, 1922, *Primitive Mentality*, trans. L. A. Clare, London, 1923) and *Les Carnets de Lucien Levy-Bruhl* (Paris, 1949, *The Notebooks on Primitive Mentality*, trans. Pierre Riviere, Oxford: Blackwell Press, 1975), and also as described in G. E. R. Lloyd, *Demystifying Mentalities*, (New York: Cambridge University Press, 1980).

63. Following G. E. R. Lloyd's argument that the notion of a style of reasoning has more explanatory force than the mentalities (Lloyd 1980).

64. Earlier versions of this paper have been presented to the New England Seminar on Chinese Thought, the Religion Colloquium of Bard College, and the Philosophy Department of the University of Vermont. A released time grant from Bard College contributed to the preparation of this article, which is slightly revised from an earlier version of the same title published in *Philosophy East & West*. This paper has benefitted from the critical comments of Daniel Berthold-Bond, Susan Cherniak, Chad Hansen, P. J. Ivanhoe, Li Wai-Yee, Henry Rosemont, Harold Roth, Nathan Sivin, Bryan Van Norden, and an anonymous reader for *Philosophy East & West*.

THREE

Zhuangzi and Nāgārjuna on the Truth of No Truth

David Loy

To know how to stay within the sphere of our ignorance is to attain the highest. Who knows an unspoken discrimination, an untold Way? It is this, if any is able to know it, which is called the Treasury of Heaven.

—Graham 1981, 57

Ultimate serenity is the coming to rest of all ways of taking things, the repose of named things; no truth has been taught by a Buddha for anyone, anywhere.

—Nāgārjuna, *Mūlamadhyamikakārikā* 25:24, p. 262[1]

A Chinese legend has it that when old Laozi disappeared into the western frontier he journeyed to India and became Śākyamuni Buddha. I am not in a position to confirm or refute that story, but I enjoy speculating about another: Zhuangzi, the greatest Daoist philosopher, followed in the footsteps of his predecessor (whom he never mentions) by also traveling to India, where he . . . became Nāgārjuna, the greatest of the Buddhist philosophers.

Unfortunately for me, this second possibility is even less likely. One problem is the deathbed story in chapter thirty-two, where Zhuangzi declines the lavish funeral his disciples want to give him. There is also a worrisome historical discrepancy: Zhuangzi lived in the fourth century B.C.E., while most scholars place Nāgārjuna in the second century C.E.. No less troublesome, perhaps, is the radical difference in their philosophical styles. Zhuangzi is unparalleled in Chinese literature for his mocking and satirical tone, which directs its most acid humor at the pretensions of logic; Nāgārjuna is unparalleled in Indian thought for his laconic, knife-edged logic, which wields distinctions that no one had noticed before and many since have been unable to see the point of.

Despite these formidable objections, however, Zhuangzi and Nāgārjuna share something even more important: the targets and conclusions of their philosophies are remarkably similar, as I will try to show. For a start, both are antirationalists who present us with strong arguments for not believing in reason. According to A. C. Graham, "For Zhuangzi the fundamental error is to suppose that life presents itself with issues which must be formulated in words so that we can envision alternatives and find reasons for preferring one to the other" (Graham 1981, 6).[2] This error is quite a good characterization of what Nāgārjuna does, except for the fact that Nāgārjuna uses his dry distinctions to perform a self-deconstruction refuting the hope of logic to represent the world conceptually. His *magnum opus* the *Mūlamadhyamikākarikā* addresses the major philosophical problems of his day, not to determine the definitive position but to demonstrate that no conceptual solution is tenable. Like Zhuangzi, who "temporarily 'lodges' at the other man's standpoint" the better to show what is wrong with that standpoint (Graham 1981, 24), Nāgārjuna adopts his contemporaries' terminology in order to show what is wrong with that terminology.

On the surface, though, the *Zhuangzi* could hardly be more dissimilar. It offers a bewildering succession of anecdotes and arguments whose shifting tone makes it difficult and sometimes impossible to determine which voice represents the author. "Where then is the real Zhuangzi? . . . the text turns into a hall of mirrors where a frightening succession of images recedes into infinity and illusion becomes indistinguishable from reality" (Watson in Mair 1983, x). This postmodernist playfulness, which prefers posing questions to drawing conclusions, functions quite differently from Nāgārjuna's univocal dissection of this and that alternative. It subverts our need for a Master discourse, for that text which subsumes and unifies others into the truth—that Truth our philosophical labors try to stake out and lay claim to, the perfectly reason-able position that Zhuangzi loves to mock.[3]

What if there is no such Truth? Or is this insight itself the Truth? Is that a contradiction (and therefore impossible) or a paradox (which encourages a "leap" to a different level of understanding)? These questions will be ad-

dressed by considering what Zhuangzi and Nāgārjuna have to say about them.
Zhuangzi has been labeled a relativist and/or a skeptic, Nāgārjuna a skeptic
and/or a nihilist, but in their cases such bald designations put the cart before
the horse. We cannot understand whether Zhuangzi is a relativist without
first considering what the rest of us expect from the truth. We cannot appreciate their skepticism without considering what motivates the common sense
belief in objective knowledge. Instead of inquiring into what kind of a skeptic or relativist Zhuangzi is—that is, which of our boxes he would fit into
(and what fun he would have with that!)—it will be more fruitful to inquire
into the relationship between knowledge and other important themes for
him(no-self, mind-fasting, and dreaming.)The interesting issue, then, is not
whether the skepticism of Zhuangzi and Nāgārjuna is consistent with other
claims such as no-self, but to turn this around: What context do no-self,
meditation, dreaming and waking up, etc., provide for their understanding
of our understanding of knowledge?

The Illusion of Self and Things

Daoism and Buddhism are unique among the great religions in denying the
ontological self. *Anātma*, "non-self", is one of the three basic "facts" taught
by Śākyamuni Buddha, along with *anitya*, "impermanence", and *duḥkha*, "dis-
satisfaction". Two of his basic teachings deconstruct the self synchronically
into *skandha*, "heaps", and diachronically into *pratītya-samutpāda*, "dependent origination". These doctrines explain how the illusion of self is constituted and maintained. All experiences associated with the illusory sense-of-
self can be analyzed into one of five impersonal *skandhas* (form, sensation,
perception, volitional tendencies, and conditioned consciousness), with no
remainder: there is no transcendental soul or persisting self to be found over
and above their functioning.

This *skandha* analysis has, however, been overshadowed and even sub-
sumed into *pratītya-samutpāda*, the most important Buddhist doctrine. De-
pendent-origination explains "our" experience by locating all phenomena
within an interacting set of twelve factors (ignorance, volitional tendencies,
conditioned consciousness, the fetus, sense organs, contact, sensation, crav-
ing, grasping, becoming, new birth, suffering and death), each conditioning
and conditioned by all the others. In response to the question of how rebirth
can occur without a self that is reborn, rebirth is explained as one in a series
of impersonal processes that occur without there being any self that is doing
them or experiencing them. When asked to whom belong, and for whom
occur, the phenomena described in *pratītya-samutpāda*, the Buddha explained
that each factor arises from the preconditions created by the other factors;
that's all. The karmic results of action are experienced without there being

anyone who created the *karma* or who receives its fruit, although there is a causal connection between the act and its result.

As one would expect from its very different literary style, the *Zhuangzi* is less systematic in its critique of the self, yet the rejection is no less clear. Chapter one declares that "the utmost man is selfless" and chapter seventeen that "the great man has no self" (Graham 1981, 150). Chapter two, the most philosophical, begins with Ziqi in a trance, to reveal afterwards that "this time I had lost myself, didn't you know?" Like other anecdotes about mind-fasting, which explain how to lose one's self, these passages are not concerned with philosophically deconstructing the self into its elements, but they emphasize or presuppose the need to get beyond self.

Why is that so important? One problem with the self is its supposed identity: it provides the continuity that persists through change. Insofar as we value the self-identical, the world as the locus of transformation—which threatens the self—tends to be devalued. Yet Daoism and Buddhism agree that there is no such personal identity or continuity, which means that we are, in effect, depreciating everything that exists in order to cherish something illusory. Daoist emphasis on the ceaseless transformation of things does not reserve a corner for the self to watch from or hide away in, for it is the transformation of that "self" the *Zhuangzi* celebrates the most. On his deathbed Master Lai looks upon heaven and earth as a vast foundry and looks forward to being refashioned by the Master Smith. Will he be made into a rat's liver, or a fly's egg? (Graham 1981, 88–89). To resist this is to be preoccupied with the welfare of the self: with satisfying its desires and defending what are believed to be its interests.

Since self does not provide the desired identity, perhaps the most important of those interests is finding or constructing some such identity. That is, insofar as we have a sense-of-self we also feel a need to fixate it or stabilize it—a need, however, that can never be fulfilled if the self is indeed illusory. To have a sense of self without being able to know what this self is, to be preoccupied with something that cannot be secured because it does not exist—these are formulas for dis-ease (the Buddhist *duḥkha*). The implications of this for our understanding of truth will become important later when we consider the intellectual ways our minds seek a stable dwelling-place.

The other way to express the problem with self is that it is separate from other things. The subject that observes and manipulates objects becomes alienated from its world. And to experience oneself as separate from the world—as one of many things in it—is to experience the world as a collection of separate things, which according to both Daoism and Buddhism is a serious error.

Nāgārjuna emphasized that the Buddhist deconstruction of self is just as much a critique of thingness, of the self-existence of things. The first verse of the MMK asserts its thorough-going deconstruction of the *being of* all things: "No things whatsoever exist, at anytime or place, having risen by themselves, from another, from both or without cause." Paralleling the contemporary poststructural radicalization of structuralist claims about language, Nāgārjuna's argument merely brings out more fully the implications of *pratītya-samutpāda*. Dependent origination is not a doctrine about causal relations among things, because the mutual interdependence of phenomena means they are not really things.

The importance of this move becomes clearer when we realize that, although Nāgārjuna addresses the philosophical controversies of his time, his main target is that unconscious "metaphysics" that is disguised as the world we live in. If philosophy were merely the preoccupation of some intellectuals we could ignore it, but we are all philosophers. The fundamental categories of our everyday, common sense metaphysics are the self-existing things we interact with all the time—chairs, doors, cars, trees, etc.—which originate, change, and eventually cease; and in order to explain the relations among these objects the categories of space, time, and causality must also be employed. So we experience the world as a collection of discrete things, each of which has its own being (self) yet interacts causally with others in objective space and time. The problem with this understanding of the world is not only that it is erroneous but that it causes us to suffer, for we understand ourselves in the same way, as special instances of self-existing things that are nonetheless subject to the ravages of time and change, that are born only to grow old, become ill, and die.

But if I self-exist, how can I change? How could I die? For that matter, how could I have been born? This is the simple contradiction that Nāgārjuna uses to deconstruct self-being. That all phenomena appear and disappear according to conditions means that our usual way of perceiving the world as a collection of separately-existing things is a delusion. Nāgārjuna does not follow this critique by presenting the "correct" Buddhist metaphysics, however, for merely by subverting such ontological claims the Buddhist deconstruction of self-existence (especially our own) can allow something else to become apparent: something that has always been there yet has usually been overlooked in our preoccupation with satisfying desires and trying to make ourselves self-existent. For Nāgārjuna this is our everyday world experienced as *nirvāṇa*, since there is no specifiable difference whatever between them (MMK 25:19) except for our deluded way of "taking" the world. For Zhuangzi too the reason we experience this world as a collection of discrete things rather than as the Dao is that we misperceive it.

I have ignored chronology to discuss Nāgārjuna first because his analysis is more focused and easier to explicate, which means it can help us with some of the obscure yet important passages in the *Zhuangzi*, such as the following: "The men of old, their knowledge had arrived at something: at what had it arrived? There were some who thought there had not yet begun to be things—the utmost, the exhaustive, there is no more to add. The next thought there were things but there had not yet begun to be borders. The next thought there were borders to them but there had not yet begun to be 'That's it, that's not'. The lighting up of 'That's it, that's not' is the reason why the Way is flawed" (Graham 1981, 54). Instead of offering an account of social development or evolution, Daoist history is the story of a progressive decline in our understanding of the Way. Some of the old sages knew the ultimate, which is that there are no self-existing things; everything is a manifestation of the Dao. Later, people perceived the world as made up of things, but these things were not seen as separate from each other; their interrelationships and transformations meant the world was still experienced as a whole. After that, people came to see things as truly discrete, the world became a collection of objects, yet even they did not use discriminative thinking to understand the world. Once people employed and became trapped in their own dualistic concepts, the Dao was lost.

Zhuangzi often refers to the problem of "That's it, that's not"; when that way of thinking lights up, the Dao is obscured. What is he criticizing? One target is the logical analysis that philosophers go in for, in particular that of the Chinese sophists and Mohists of Zhuangzi's own time. Yet this by itself is too narrow, for (like Mādhyamika scholars who think Nāgārjuna's analyses are aimed only at certain Indian philosophical positions) it overlooks the discriminations that we have all learned to make in the process of coming to experience the world in the "ordinary" way other people do. Chapter two of the *Daodejing* (a text the *Zhuangzi* Inner Chapters never refer to)* discusses and by implication criticizes the conceptual dualisms that bifurcate into opposed categories: "When beauty is universally known as beauty, therein is ugliness. When goodness is universally known as goodness, therein is badness. Therefore being and nonbeing are mutually posited in their emergence," and the same is true for difficult and easy, long and short, etc. Nāgārjuna is less poetical and more explicit about the problem with such bifurcations: "Without relation to 'good' there is no 'bad', in dependence on which we form the idea of 'good'. Therefore 'good' [by itself] is unintelligible" (MMK 23:10). In the same way the concept "bad" is also unintelligible by itself (MMK 23:11). We distinguish between good and bad because we want to affirm one and reject the other, but their interdependence means we have both or neither: since the meaning of each is the negation of the other, one can consciously be "good" only by consciously avoiding "bad". In the same way my love of life is haunted by my hatred of death, hope for success is equaled by fear of failure, and so forth.

Insofar as all thinking tends to alternate between "That's it" and "That's

---

* For a different suggestion as to the relationship between Laozi and Zhuangzi, see p. 46, n. 36.—Eds.

not", between assertion and negation, this type of critique tends to end up incorporating all conceptual thinking, including all that we usually identify as knowledge. This most general understanding is consistent with Buddhist emphasis on letting go of all concepts and the *Zhuangzi* passages on mind-fasting, which negates such thinking. Yan Hui "expels knowledge" by learning to "just sit and forget" (Graham 1981, 92), and Old Dan teaches Confucius to practice fasting and austerities to "smash to pieces your knowledge" (Graham 1981, 132). Perhaps we can see how such a radical mental cleansing might also wash away the self, but what would that leave behind? Later we shall need to consider whether there is an alternative type of thinking which does not fixate on a "That's it" and a "That's not".

Other important passages in the *Zhuangzi* relate "That's it" thinking with dividing up the world into things, for example:

> [When a "That's it" which deems picks out things,] the Way interchanges them and deems them one. Their dividing is formation, their formation is dissolution; all things whether forming or dissolving in reverting interchange and are deemed to be one. Only the man who sees right through knows how to interchange and deem them one; the "That's it" which deems he does not use, but finds for them lodging-places in the usual. "The usual" is the usable, the "usable" is the interchangeable, to see as "interchangeable" is to grasp; and once you grasp them you are almost there. The "That's it" which goes by circumstance comes to an end; and when it is at an end, that of which you do not know what is so of it you call the "Way." (Graham 1981, 53–54)

Although our dualistic ways of thinking cause us to discriminate between things in the world and to see them as separate from each other, the Dao does not discriminate between things but treats them as a whole, for it transforms them into each other. The next sentence is more obscure: Burton Watson translates it as "Their dividedness is their completeness; their completeness is their impairment" (Watson 1968, 41). This seems to be making a point consistent with the alternation of *yin* and *yang* in the *Yijing*: things take form (*yang* movement) by individuating, yet with the completion of that movement (for example, maturity) the *yang* principle is fulfilled and begins to yield to *yin* dissolution; however, the Dao transforms them into each other, at whatever stage, because they are not separate from each other. Likewise, those who understand this clearly do not treat things as separate from each other. Such people are not trapped by discriminative concepts that fixate things into this or that, for their more fluid thinking is aware that such designations are always tentative, appropriate only for particular situations and purposes. Such tentative judgments are made because they are useful; realizing that judgments are to be made according to their usefulness frees one from rigid discriminations and enables us to perceive how things change into each other—and to realize *that* is close to realizing the Dao. The discriminations that are made according to particular circumstances cease when those circumstances change; what remains then is the world experienced as it is before our conceptual thinking divides it up: what is called the Dao.[4]*

According to this, the best judgments ("truths") are tentative because they are appropriate only for particular situations and different judgments are needed when those situations change. This perspective is expressed more clearly in the Liezi: "Nowhere is there a principle which is right in all circumstances or an action that is wrong in all circumstances. The method we use yesterday we may discard today and use again in the future; there are no fixed right and wrong to decide whether we use it or not. The capacity to pick times and snatch opportunities, and be never at a loss to answer events belongs to the wise."[5] If ethical relativism means denying a fixed moral standard by which to evaluate situations, one could hardly find a better formulation; yet the last sentence seems to confuse the issue again, by emphasizing a distinction that most contemporary versions do not reserve a place for. There is an important difference between the sage and the rest of us. Evidently it is not enough to defend such a relativistic position, or to be a relativist in practice, for those philosophers who accept relativism do not thereby become wise, and those who live relativistically do not thereby live wisely. Mahāyāna Buddhism makes a similar point with its doctrine of *upāya*, the "skillful means" with which the bodhisattva works for the liberation of all sentient beings, adopting and adapting whatever devices are suitable to the immediate task at hand, disregarding conventional moral codes and even the Buddhist precepts when necessary. This type of relativism too is reserved for beings who have attained a high level of spiritual development—the Buddhist equivalent of a Daoist sage.

The difference between them and us is that they are liberated by relativism, or into relativism, while the rest of us are more likely to become its victims, since the freedom it encourages panders to our preoccupation with satisfying insatiable desires. In other words, the difference is self. Those deluded by a sense-of-self are trapped in their own self-preoccupation; ethical relativism clears the way for such people to do whatever is necessary to get what they want. Since sages and bodhisattvas are liberated from self-preoccupation, because they do not experience others as objects whose well-being is distinct from their own, relativism frees them from the formal con-

---

*Compare Loy's account of the dao as the essential but incomprehensible unity of things with Kjellberg's decription of nature as involving differentia too subtle and wide-ranging to be captured in language (p. 13). See Schwitzgebel (p. 74) and Berkson (p. 112) for alternative ideas on the nature of the dao and the reasons for its ineffability.—Eds.

straints that the rest of us seem to need and allows them to get on with the task of apparently saving all sentient beings while actually doing nothing at all (a paradox embraced by both traditions). If the issue of ethical relativism in the *Zhuangzi* cannot be understood without also considering the role of self, is that also the case for other types of relativism—such as knowledge?

Being No-Thing

Much of our problem with understanding the Daoist and Buddhist critiques of self comes down to envisioning an alternative. What can it mean, not to have or not to be a self? In both traditions the answer is: to become nothing. The way to transcend this world is to forget oneself and become completely one with it, in which case one is so "empty" of any fixed form that one is able to become anything. That the Buddha (and our own Buddha-nature) has no fixed form by which he can be recognized is emphasized in Mahāyāna Buddhism, especially in the *prajñāpāramitā sutras* whose teachings are very similar to Nāgārjuna's. For example, in the *Diamond Sutra* the Buddha says that those who attempt to see him by form or sound cannot see him, and that he is not to be recognized by any material characteristic.[6] The other best-known Mahāyāna scripture, the laconic *Heart Sutra*, asserts that all form is *śūnyatā*, "emptiness", and that realizing our emptiness liberates us from the delusion of self.

For Zhuangzi too no-thingness characterizes the Dao itself, and becoming no-thing is a return to the source from which things including us arise: "There is somewhere from which we are born, into which we die, from which we come forth, through which we go in; it is this that is called the Gate of Heaven. The Gate of Heaven is that which is without anything; the myriad things go on coming forth from that which is without anything. Something cannot become something by means of something, it necessarily goes on coming forth from that which is without anything; but that which is without anything is forever without anything. The sage stores away in *it*" (Graham 1981, 103; emphasis Graham's). Having achieved this, the sage can "let the 心 *xin*, 'mind', roam with other things as its chariot" (Graham 1981, 71). A later chapter quotes the sage Guanyin:

> Within yourself, no fixed positions:
> Things as they take shape disclose themselves.
> Moving, be like water,
> Still, be like a mirror,
> Respond like an echo.
> Blank! as though absent:
> Quiescent! as though transparent.

Be assimilated to them and you harmonize,
Take hold of any of them and you lose. (Graham 1981, 281)

The mind as a mirror is perhaps the most important metaphor in the *Zhuangzi* and provides one of its most quoted passages, from the very end of the Inner Chapters: "Hold on to all that you have received from Heaven but do not think you have gotten anything. Be empty, that is all. The Perfect Man uses his mind as a mirror—going after nothing, welcoming nothing, responding but not storing" (Watson 1968, 97). In terms of the image, 忘心 *wang xin*, "self-forgetting" or "mind-losing", is the practice of polishing one's mind-mirror and keeping it clean of impurities. To say the least, such meditative techniques are also important in Buddhism, which is probably the richest of the world's contemplative traditions. Although Nāgārjuna mentions little about such practices, as a monastic he was doubtless familiar with them and they provide the context within which his work must be situated, especially its emphasis on *prapañcopaśama*, the cessation of conceptual ways of understanding, which is necessary if one is to experience things as they are. Burton Watson suspects that the *Zhuangzi* must originally have been accompanied by similar practices to help students realize what it is talking about, yet all that survives in the text are some references to controlled breathing (Watson in Mair 1983, xiii).[7]

By such practices the *xin* of the sage becomes "the reflector of heaven and earth, the mirror of the myriad things" (Graham 1981, 259). Nonetheless, the mirror metaphor, like all metaphors, has its limitations. To be a perfectly-polished mirror is not quite the same as being no-thing at all: there is still a dualism between the reflector and the reflected. This may encourage the tendency of contemplative types to stand back from the world, but Zhuangzi will have none of that: "To be transformed day by day with other things is to be untransformed once and for all. Why not try to let them go? For the sage, there has never yet begun to be Heaven, never yet begun to be man, never yet begun to be a Beginning, never yet begun to be things" (Graham 1981, 110–111). To forget oneself completely, truly to become nothing, means more than to reflect the transformations of things: it is to be wholly identified with them, to be them—in which case there are no things and no transformations, since "that which is without anything is *forever* without anything" (quoted above). Such a world is not a collection of things but is composed of events. Evidently someone who realizes she is no-thing remains no-thing even as she playfully assumes this or that form. When there is no thing or self that exerts itself to do things, there is the 自然 *ziran*, "spontaneity", of actions that are experienced as 無爲 *wuwei*, "no actions", of transformations that are just as much nontransformations.

When I forget my self I fall into the world, I become its manifold of interdependent phenomena transforming into each other. What does this mean for language and truth? Do they too become such a manifold?

The Ignorance of Truth and the Truth of Ignorance

To realize that there are no things is not to float in a porridge where each spoonful is indistinguishable from the next; it is to store away in the Gate of Heaven that remains no-thing even as all things arise from it and transform into each other. If we replace "things" in the previous sentence with "words," what would that imply about language?

According to Graham, grasping the Dao is a matter not of "knowing that" but of "knowing how," as shown by the many craftsmen Zhuangzi is fond of citing (Graham in Mair 1983, 8). This distinction is not as useful as one would hope,[8] but it is useful to consider: what would "knowing how" with *words* be like? It is no coincidence that Zhuangzi himself provides one of the greatest examples, and not only for Chinese literature.[9] Clearly there is a special art to this as well, which is not completely indifferent to logic and reasoning as we have come to understand them in the West, yet which is not to be completely identified with them. One of the delights of the *Zhuangzi* for Western readers is the way its polyvocal text disrupts our distinction between form and content, rhetoric and logic—a bifurcation that may be not "natural" but an unfortunate legacy of the Western intellectual tradition.

What is the knowing-how with words that Zhuangzi shows? "The Way has never had borders, saying has never had norms. It is by a 'That's it' which deems that a boundary is marked" (Graham 1981, 57). A "That's it" that *deems* is speech that fixates things and becomes fixated itself, which Zhuangzi repeatedly contrasts with the more fluid "That's it" that *goes by circumstances*, that which changes when circumstances change. The parallel here between things and words is so close that it is more than a parallel, for they reflect each other: Our language fixates the world into things, and once they are fixated the words that fixate them are also fixated—into "the truth." In contrast to the everyday world of rigidly differentiated objects, the Dao is not an otherworldly denial or transcendence of things, but their no-thingness that enables their interpenetration and incessant transformation into each other; in contrast to the everyday use of words that fixates things by fixating categories, the Dao does not involve an ineffable rejection of language as inevitably dualistic and delusive, but celebrates language such as we find in the *Zhuangzi*, a playfulness possible when we are no longer trapped by and in our own words. "Words exist because of meaning; once you've got the meaning you can forget the words. Where can I find a man who has forgotten words so I can have a word with him?" (Watson 1968, 302). Here we are delighted by the tension between needing to escape words that "deem," and the conclusion that delights in words that do not deem.

Why do we cling to words that deem? As one would expect, here too the problem is self. "Saying is not blowing breath, saying says something; the only trouble is that what it says is never fixed" (Graham 1981, 52). That's no trouble at all if we don't need to fixate on our words, but the problem is we do: The transformation of words, like the transformation of things, is terrifying to a necessarily insecure (because illusory) self that is always seeking to secure itself. How uncomfortable it is to realize that our opinion of something is wrong and needs to be changed; how much more anxious do I become when I start letting go of all my opinions about the world and, most of all, my opinions about myself—to let go of the self-image whereby my-self is fixated. If the self is that which needs to settle on "That's it" or "That's not", without such a self there is no need to dwell on one perch only: "What is It is also Other, what is Other is also It. There they say 'That's it, that's not' from one point of view, here we say 'That's it, that's not' from another point of view. Are there really It and Other? Or really no It and Other? Where neither It nor Other finds its opposite is called the axis of the Way. When once the axis is found at the centre of the circle there *is no limit to responding with either*, on the one hand no limit to what is it, on the other no limit to what is not" (Graham 1981, 53; emphasis mine). "It is easy to keep from walking; the hard thing is to walk without touching the ground" (Watson 1968, 58). And it is easy to keep from talking; the hard thing is to talk without needing to touch a ground. According to Graham's gloss, it is easy to withdraw from the world and live as a hermit, it is harder to remain above the world while living in it. Yet without a self we float quite easily, if its need to ground itself is what weighs us down.

In place of our usual distinction between knowledge and ignorance, this yields a knowing that becomes indistinguishable from a kind of ignorance. "How do I know that what I call knowing is not ignorance? How do I know that what I call ignorance is not knowing?" (Graham 1981, 58). What we usually consider knowing—deeming that something "is *this*"—can reveal our ignorance about the transforming nature of language and things. What is usually understood as ignorance—not settling finally on "It's *this*" or "It's *that*"—can reflect our insight into that nature. If "we have the axis on which things turn, and to start from have that which is other than ourselves, then our unravelling will resemble failing to unravel, our knowing will resemble ignorance" (Graham 1981, 63). This "ignorance" of the sage allows her to play with truths freely insofar as she feels no need to fixate herself by fixating on any particular one.

The exception will be when we want to accomplish things in the world, yet that is no problem for the sage, whose free roaming harbors no such schemes. "Since the sage does not plan, what use has he for knowledge?" For him our usual "knowledge is a curse," whereas "utmost knowledge doesn't plan" (Graham 1981, 82).

As this last quotation suggests, Zhuangzi's understanding of knowledge and ignorance can be formulated into two levels of truth. Such a two-truths doctrine is also essential to Buddhism, especially Mahāyāna, and its paradigmatic formulation is by Nāgārjuna: "The teaching of the Buddhas is wholly based on there being two truths: that of a personal everyday world and a higher truth which surpasses it. Those who do not clearly know the true distinction between the two truths cannot clearly know the hidden depths of the Buddha's teaching. Unless the transactional realm is accepted as a base, the surpassing sense cannot be pointed out; if the surpassing sense is not comprehended nirvāṇa cannot be attained" (MMK 24:8–10). Śākyamuni himself made an implicit distinction between words that deem and words that change with circumstances when he compared his own teachings to a raft that may be used to ferry across the river of saṁsāra to the other shore of nirvāṇa and then abandoned, not carried around on one's back. Nor did Nāgārjuna understand his own writings as committing him to a particular view: "If I had a position, no doubt fault could be found with it. Since I have no position, that problem does not arise."[10] How could he avoid taking a position? There is no position to be taught because there is no truth that needs to be attained; all we need to do is let go of delusion: "Ultimate serenity [or beatitude: śiva] is the coming to rest of all ways of taking things, the repose of named things; no Truth has been taught by a Buddha for anyone, anywhere" (MMK 25:24). The Aṣṭasāhasrikā, probably the oldest and most important of the prajñāpāramitā sutras, begins by emphasizing the same point:

> No wisdom can we get hold of, no highest perfection,
> No Bodhisattva, no thought of enlightenment either.
> When told of this, if not bewildered and in no way anxious,
> A Bodhisattva courses in the Tathagata's wisdom.[11]

In the Diamond Sutra, Sūbhuti asks the Buddha if his realization of supreme enlightenment means that he has not acquired anything. "Just so, Subhuti. I have not acquired even the least thing from supreme enlightenment, and that is called supreme enlightenment."[12] Then it could just as well be called supreme ignorance—as long as that is not confused with ordinary ignorance.

How does this reconcile with the two-truths doctrine enunciated by Nāgārjuna above, which emphasizes the importance of the higher truth in attaining nirvāṇa? No truth is the higher truth: not a more abstract or profound set of concepts, but an insight into the circumstance-changing nature of all truth. That makes it sound easy, yet the rub is that such a realization requires letting go of oneself, which is seldom if ever easy. The bewildered anxiety that the Aṣṭasāhasrikā mentions are the rule rather than the exception. The basic problem, again, is that discriminating between ignorance and truth—rejecting the one, grasping the other—is an intellectual way (is especially the intellectual's way) the self tries to find some secure ground for itself. With such discriminations we tame the mystery and terror of the world into the truths that are necessary for us to live because they teach us what the world is, who we are, and why we are here. Untold millions have killed and died defending such truths: in religion, it is faith in the doctrine that can save us and that therefore needs to be defended at all costs against heretics; less dramatically yet more intimately for many of us, it can also be the "liberating insights" of psychoanalysis and deconstruction, etc., or the "enlightening" Asian wisdom of Buddhism and Daoism. This is not to deny that they can be liberating and enlightening; but only when we do not need to secure our selves can we become comfortable with and able to *live* the lack of such a higher truth to identify with.

Then the truth of no-truth must always self-deconstruct. On the one hand, it needs to be expressed somehow, for without that there is no Daoist or Buddhist teaching and no help for the benighted. As Nāgārjuna puts it, the transactional realm—our everyday use of language and understanding of truth—is necessary to point out the surpassing sense of truth, that there is no higher truth whose understanding liberates us. Yet what one hand offers the other must take away. No statement of this paradox can be final, pretending to offer a definitive understanding, for to do so makes us like the would-be sage who realized that no one should have disciples and promptly organized a group of disciples to disseminate this teaching. And our intellectual understanding of these issues is liable to make us into converts who, in effect, join his band of disciples.*

Dreaming of Waking Up

Last night Zhuang Zhou dreamed he was a butterfly, spirits soaring he was a butterfly (is it that in showing what he was he suited his own fancy?), and did not know about Zhou. When all of a sudden he awoke, he was Zhou with all his wits about him. He does not know whether he is Zhou who dreams he is a butterfly or a butterfly who dreams he is Zhou. Between Zhou and the butterfly there was necessarily a dividing; just this is what is meant by the transformation of things. (Graham 1981, 61)

Everything in this world can be taken as real or not real; or ✓ both real and not real; or neither real nor not real. This is the Buddha's teaching. (MMK 18:8)

The meaning of Zhuangzi's celebrated dream has been much debated and always will be, since the ambivalence of its meaning is clearly as much Zhuangzi's intention as the ambivalence of the dream. The central tension of the story is between Zhuang Zhou waking up and Zhuang Zhou wondering

---

* See Berkson (p. 115) for a related analysis of Zhuangzi's dao as "self-deconstructing."
—Eds.

whether he has indeed awakened. What is the difference? The story does not want to persuade us that this world is a dream, but to raise doubts about whether this world is a dream. Evidently ignorance on this matter is more valuable than knowing the answer. Is that because ignorance is preferable, if we want to truly wake up and experience things as they really are? Or is ignorance itself waking up?

Insofar as we try to understand Zhuang Zhou's dream, it is helpful to place it in context by considering the two other important passages on dreaming in the Inner Chapters. "How do I know that the dead do not regret that they ever had an urge to life? . . . While we dream we do not know we are dreaming, and in the middle of a dream interpret a dream within it; not until we wake do we know that we were dreaming. Only at the ultimate awakening shall we know that this is the ultimate dream. Yet fools think they are awake, so confident that they know what they are, princes, herdsmen, incorrigible! You and Confucius are both dreams, and I who call you a dream am also a dream" (Graham 1981, 59–60). This dreaming is less ambiguous than Zhuang Zhou's. We are all dreaming, which we will realize when we finally awaken. This assertion must be understood in its wider context, which wonders whether we are wrong to love life and hate death. Perhaps those who do so are exiles who have forgotten the way home. If so, life itself is the ultimate dream and death the ultimate awakening.

Despite Nāgārjuna's unwillingness in the epigraph above to commit himself to one view at the cost of the other, there are prominent passages in the Mahāyāna scriptures that also unambiguously assert that this world is unreal and dreamlike. In chapter two of the *Aṣṭasāhasrikā*, for example, Subhuti declares that beings, all objective facts, and even the Buddha and *nirvāṇa* itself are like an illusion and a dream.[13] The *Diamond Sutra* concludes with the remark that we should view things as like a bubble, a lightning flash, a dream.[14]

There is one more important dream in the Inner Chapters of the *Zhuangzi*: "You dream that you are a bird and fly away into the sky, dream that you are a fish and plunge into the deep. There's no telling whether the man who speaks now is the waker or the dreamer. Rather than go toward what suits you, laugh: rather than acknowledge it with your laughter, shove it from you. Shove it from you and leave the transformations behind; then you will enter the oneness of the featureless sky" (Graham 1981, 91). This dream is more like the butterfly dream; the speaker does not know whether he is awake or dreaming. But why is it so important for us to know that? What in us needs to know which is which? Instead of dreaming about waking up, perhaps we should consider why we are so afraid of dreams. What makes a dream a dream? Things in a dream are unreal in the sense that they do not have any objective stability or self-existence. They are constantly appearing, disappearing, and transforming into something else. Yet that is also true for

this world, according to Zhuangzi and Nāgārjuna! In which case the distinction between them becomes less important. To wake up, then, is to realize
there is only the dream. To dream of waking up from that dream is to fantasize
about attaining a Reality that will save me from my empty, unfixed, transforming nature, which makes me uneasy because I want to be self-identical.
If so, to "wake up" from my constantly-changing nature (in which I become,
say, a butterfly) is actually to fall asleep into the ignorance that thinks "I"
am this body, this particular self within a collection of other discrete things.
To dream I am a butterfly, etc., is to wake up to my selfless, endlessly transforming nature.

Like other dualistic categories, however, the concept of dreaming has
meaning only in relation to a concept of waking up and leaving the dream
transformations behind. Yet the Zhuangzi says that the alternative to dreaming
is not another world or higher dimension but "the oneness of the featureless
sky." Such a featureless oneness is indistinguishable from no-thing-ness. It is
important to forget oneself and experience this no-thing-ness—to become
no-thing—because that extinguishes the self; and it is just as important not
to remain in that featureless oneness because, in Buddhist terms, that is
"clinging to emptiness." As the *Heart Sutra* puts it, form is not other than
emptiness, but emptiness is not other than form. Their nonduality is the
great dream which we awaken not from but to.

Notes

1. All *Mūlamadhyamikākarikā* (hereafter cited in the text as "MMK")
references are to Mervyn Sprung's translation in his edition of Candrakīrti's
Lucid Exposition of the Middle Way (Boulder, Colo.: Prajna Press, 1979).

2. For a more detailed discussion of rationalism and antirationalism, see
A. C. Graham, *Reason and Spontaneity* (London: Curzon Press, 1985) and
Unreason Within Reason: Essays on the Outskirts of Rationality (La Salle, Ill.:
Open Court Press, 1992).

3. "It is well worth remarking that most philosophical work, down to
the humblest journal article, has been presented with the air of 'Here is the
truth; the inquiry into this topic may now cease, because all alternative
views are incorrect.' . . . if a philosopher understands that a final, definitive
account is impossible, and chooses to mirror this in his or her manner of
presentation, this could change everything. The philosophy must then be
tentative and exploratory. It cannot be serious in the way in which most
philosophy is serious" (Joel J. Kupperman, "Not in So Many Words: Chuang-
tzu's Strategies of Communication," *Philosophy East & West* 39:3 (July 1989),
311–318).

4. In accordance with the linguistic turn in contemporary philosophy, some commentators understand this and similar passages to be about language: for example, the nominalistic realization that "names have only a conventional relation to objects," or that no language-game is absolute, for each is only internally self-justifying. (See, for example, Graham 1981, 10 and Hansen in Mair 1983, 45–47 and passing.) Such interpretations overlook or de-emphasize the integral relationship between the words we employ and the world we experience: When our concepts change, the world they organize also changes. John Searle makes this point well: "When we experience the world we experience it through linguistic categories that help to shape the experiences themselves. The world doesn't come to us already sliced up into objects and experiences: What counts as an object is already a function of our system of representation, and how we experience the world in our experience is influenced by that system of representation. . . . Our concept of reality is a matter of our linguistic categories" (in Bryan Magee, ed., *Men of Ideas* (New York: Viking Press, 1978), 184). When our conceptual categories change, then, so does the world *for us*.

5. A. C. Graham, trans., *Lieh-tzu* (London: John Murray, 1960), 163–164.

6. In *The Diamond Sutra and the Sutra of Hui Neng*, A. F. Price, trans. (Boston: Shambhala, 1990), 47, 21.

7. In the Inner Chapters, Huzi "levels out the impulses of the breath" (Graham 1981, 97), and the True Men of old "breath from their heels" (Graham 1981, 84).

8. As P. J. Ivanhoe points out, Zhuangzi's examples are all benign, for we do not encounter any assassins or pickpockets (Ivanhoe 1993, 651). If grasping the Dao is a matter of knowing-how, however, then (contra-Graham) it is not clear why their skills should not also qualify them. We cannot cross-examine wheelwright Pian about his personal life, but our century provides some counter-examples. Consider the case of Picasso, arguably the greatest painter of our times, yet, if we believe half the stories told by friends and acquaintances, he was often a moral monster due to his egoism, a *self*-centeredness usually insensitive to those around him. We cannot deny his genius—that the Dao often flowed through his painting—but that was not enough to make him a sage. Although romanticism has familiarized us with such inconsistencies, it remains difficult to reconcile Picasso as a master artist who knew-how with a view of the Dao as simply knowing-how. In order to understand what makes someone a sage, we seem to need something more: what the "knowing how" of *living* is.

9. P. J. Ivanhoe describes Zhuangzi as a "connoisseur of words" (Ivanhoe 1993, 640).

10. *Vigraha-vyavartani,* verse 29.

11. Edward Conze, trans., *The Perfection of Wisdom in Eight Thousand Lines and its Verse Summary* (Bolinas, Calif.: Four Seasons Foundation, 1973), 9 (ch. 1, v. 5).

12. Price 1990, 43. I have substituted "supreme enlightenment" for Price's "consummation of incomparable enlightenment."

13. Conze 1973, 98–99 (ch. 2, v. 5).

14. Price 1990, 53.

FOUR

Zhuangzi's Attitude Toward Language and His Skepticism[1]

Eric Schwitzgebel

A tension stands at the heart of the *Zhuangzi*. Sometimes, Zhuangzi seems to advocate radical skepticism and relativism. This occurs especially in his second chapter, the "Discussion on Making All Things Equal."[2] At other times, however, Zhuangzi seems to make a variety of factual claims and to endorse and condemn various ways of living, in apparent disregard of any skeptical or relativist considerations. His advocacy of uselessness in the fourth chapter, for example, would seem to be an instance of this (Watson 1968, 63–66). Naturally, then, the question arises: how can we reconcile Zhuangzi's apparently skeptical and relativist passages with his apparently nonskeptical, nonrelativist ones? Surely this is one of the most fundamental questions an interpreter of Zhuangzi must face. The answer given will color the rest of what one says about the text.

In recent years, a variety of answers to this question have been proposed. Some authors, like Chad Hansen, have argued that Zhuangzi is sincere in defending radical skepticism and relativism, at least regarding evaluative judgments. If Zhuangzi nonetheless expresses evaluative opinions, it is only because it is as natural for him to do so as it is for birds to sing in trees (Hansen in Mair 1983, 38–40).[3] Others have tried to limit Zhuangzi's skepticism and relativism in various ways so there will be no conflict in his position. A. C. Graham believes that even if Zhuangzi sweeps away all moral and prudential standards, still the imperative "respond with awareness" will remain in force (Graham in Mair 1983, 12 ff. and Graham 1989, 193). Presumably, then, Graham would say it is only this lesson and its natural adjuncts that Zhuangzi means to convey in the non-skeptical parts of his work. Robert Eno argues that Zhuangzi is relativistic only regarding what set of skills one ought to master to connect oneself to the Dao, but he is not relativistic at all regarding the value of connecting with the Dao by means of mastering *some* set of skills or other (Eno in Smith 1991, 24).* Robert Allinson argues that Zhuangzi's relativistic and nonrelativistic statements fit into a coherent picture because they are meant to apply to people in "unawakened" and "awakened" states of consciousness, respectively (Allinson 1989, 122). And this is only a sample of the proposals that have been put forward to resolve the tension between the skeptical and nonskeptical, relativist and nonrelativist elements in Zhuangzi's work.

In this paper, I shall offer a solution to the interpretative puzzle at hand. My focus will be on Zhuangzi's skepticism, although I believe that many of the same arguments can be applied to his relativism. My position can be summed up rather simply: Although Zhuangzi *argues for* radical skepticism, he does not *sincerely subscribe* to it. In other words, Zhuangzi's skepticism is "therapeutic"—he endorses it more with the desire to evoke particular reactions in the reader than as an expression of his heartfelt beliefs.

I am aware that this position may strike the reader as something of a cop-out. It seems too easy. Faced with *any* passage that conflicts with one's interpretation, couldn't one just toss up one's hands and declare the author not to be speaking sincerely? I agree that there are excellent reasons to avoid this as a general interpretative method. But I hope in the course of this paper to convince the reader that Zhuangzi is an exceptional case.

It is difficult to tell to what extent this view has been anticipated by previous English-language interpreters of Zhuangzi. Certainly I disagree with those, like Hansen, who take Zhuangzi to be a sincere and radical skeptic, and also with those, like Graham, Eno, and Allinson, who take the skeptical passages in the *Zhuangzi* to be sincere arguments for a more limited sort of skepticism. One possible earlier proponent of the therapeutic view of Zhuangzi's skepticism is Arthur Waley. Waley does not seem to hold that Zhuangzi is very skeptical at all, attributing to him, among other things, such nonskeptical positions as opposition to war and the ideals of invulnerability and technological primitivism (Waley 1939, 94–95, 76–77, and 98–99, respectively). Although Waley translates two of the major skeptical passages from the *Zhuangzi* (the butterfly dream and the irresolvability of arguments), he puts the first at the end of a passage in a section called "death" and makes no comment on it (Waley 1939, 54 and 25–26). Regarding the second, he says only that it is a parody of the logicians (Waley 1939, 24). That Waley calls the passage a "parody" suggests that he thinks it is not to be

---

* On the issue of skill, see also the contributions to this volume by Eno and Yearly.—Eds.

taken as a sincere endorsement of skepticism; but without further comment, this suggestion remains only a hint. H. G. Creel also finds it "doubtful that they [the Daoists] actually expected to be taken altogether seriously," but like Waley he does not follow through on the remark.[4] A more recent author who discusses the therapeutic view of Zhuangzi's skepticism in some detail is Victor Mair, but his paper to this effect is infrequently cited (Mair 1983). Other recent authors discuss the therapeutic view, but with different ideas of its scope. Lee Yearley brings it up mainly to warn against it (Yearley in Mair 1983, 137–138). Paul Kjellberg applies it to Zhuangzi's relativism but not to his skepticism (Kjellberg 1993, 96–98, 126–146, 170–171). P. J. Ivanhoe applies it to Zhuangzi's *ethical* skepticism and relativism, but not elsewhere (Ivanhoe 1993).[5]

Since I believe that the key to a therapeutic interpretation of Zhuangzi's skepticism lies in a better understanding of his attitudes toward language, much of my paper shall be devoted to examining these attitudes. In particular, I shall defend two theses: first, that Zhuangzi hopes to elicit in the reader an inclination to take words less seriously than most of us tend to, and second, that Zhuangzi is willing to use assertions to provoke changes in the reader's attitudes, without much regard for the truth of these assertions or their consistency with the rest of the text. In the second half of the paper I shall argue that Zhuangzi is not a skeptic—at least not a radical skeptic. I shall draw a distinction between radical, or "philosophical," skepticism and "everyday" skepticism, and I shall argue that although Zhuangzi asserts philosophical skepticism, he does so only therapeutically, intending the reader to draw from his assertions a rather more sensible form of everyday skepticism.

The latter part of this paper depends upon the former in two ways. First, unless one accepts the general claim that Zhuangzi is willing to argue for things he does not believe, the claim that he does so in the particular case of skepticism will not seem plausible. Second, some sense must be made of what Zhuangzi is doing when he asserts philosophical skepticism, if he does not intend to be convincing the reader of its truth. I shall argue that Zhuangzi means to assist the reader in taking her beliefs less seriously. This view fits quite neatly with the view expressed in the first part, that Zhuangzi wishes to see the reader take words, and what people can express with words, less seriously.

Taking Words Less Seriously

As I have just suggested, I believe Zhuangzi would like to see us take what people have to say—the claims and evaluations they make, the distinctions they draw—less seriously.[6] I shall often say simply that Zhuangzi wishes to see us take *words* less seriously. To take something "less seriously," for the purposes of this paper, is to reduce one's esteem for it, put less stock and credence in it, and be willing to play around with it in a disrespectful way for humorous or other ends. I think it is rather clear that Zhuangzi takes this attitude toward those claims, evaluations, and distinctions that we may put into words. From beginning to end, the Inner Chapters are stuffed with passages seemingly designed to reduce our seriousness in the face of assertion, whether that assertion is Zhuangzi's own or someone else's.

The *Zhuangzi* begins[7] with the story of Kun, a huge fish roe that turns into a bird thousands of miles across and journeys to the southern darkness (Watson 1968, 29–31). Zhuangzi claims that this story is recorded in a book called the *Universal Harmony*. Neither the claim about the fish nor the claim about the book seem sincerely intended to convince. Instead—as Watson suggests in a footnote[8]—Zhuangzi seems to be mocking the texts, histories, and tales of antiquity, as well as the philosophers of other schools who cite them to support their assertions. If so, then this passage is designed to incline us to take such stories and such philosophers less seriously.

But the story of the Kun has more to it than this. Zhuangzi also uses it to make a point about perspective.[9] The cicada and the little dove laugh at the Kun (now called Peng) and say that when they make an effort to fly, they may get as far as the elm or sapanwood tree but sometimes they don't make it and just fall down on the ground. They are full of self-pride, and judging the Peng by comparison with themselves, they conclude that he cannot in fact make the full journey that the *Universal Harmony* records. I believe that there is meant to be an implicit comparison here between the reader and these small birds. Like them, we judge the tale by comparison with our own capacities and find it implausible. Being small creatures, we cannot understand great things like the Peng (and the rest of the *Zhuangzi*?). On this interpretation of the passage, Zhuangzi clearly hopes that we do not take our own views too seriously, realizing that we are small creatures with limited perspectives.

Finally, Zhuangzi is setting himself up to have what *he* says taken less seriously. He undermines his own credibility by telling such a tale and frustrates the reader's natural inclination to interpret the book as expressing the true opinions of its author. This passage, then, sets the stage beautifully for a book full of fantastical tales and wild assertions, and it casts doubt on the credibility of all the three players in any work of philosophy: the reader, the author, and the author's opponents. Except in the case of the reader and the little birds, Zhuangzi's focus is not so much on the merit of the positions as it is on the use of words. What is called into question in this passage is not Zhuangzi's or the other philosophers' *beliefs* so much as their honesty and the quality of their argumentative technique. In Zhuangzi's case, it is a lack of a reliable connection between what he says and what he believes that undermines his credibility. In the case of the other philosophers, it is a failure to restrain themselves to only legitimate forms of support. For diverse reasons, then, what Zhuangzi, the philosophers, and the reader have to *say* has failed to earn respect.

A few pages later, Zhuangzi speaks more explicitly about language. A person named Jian Wu describes the speech of one Jie Yu as "big and nothing to back it up . . . wild and wide of the mark, never coming near human affairs." However, Lian Shu, who seems to speak for Zhuangzi, responds that "from his dust and leavings alone you could mold a Yao or a Shun" (Watson 1968, 33–34).[10] The description of Jie Yu's speech sounds a bit like a description of Zhuangzi's own, or at least some of it. The Kun/Peng story could certainly be described as wild and never coming near human affairs. As if to bolster an implicit comparison here, Zhuangzi's friend Huizi a little later on describes Zhuangzi's words as "big and useless," and Zhuangzi does not object (Watson 1968, 35). I doubt, then, that Zhuangzi would be too bothered if the reader did not place much credence in his words.

In fact, Zhuangzi uses several devices throughout the Inner Chapters that seem deliberately intended to prevent the reader from taking too seriously anything he has to say. One such device is his straight-faced telling of fantastical tales. Another is putting his own words in other people's mouths.[11] More than half of the Inner Chapters is in quotation.[12] Zhuangzi's words are spoken by madmen, cripples, beggars, and dukes alike—and many of them by Confucius. Sometimes, especially with Confucius, it is hard to know whether the words being spoken are meant to have Zhuangzi's approval or disapproval.[13] At other times, Zhuangzi will make a claim, apparently in his own voice, then turn around and bring it into question.[14] One such example is the following: "Because right and wrong appeared, the Way was injured, and because the Way was injured, love became complete. But do such things as completion and injury really exist, or do they not?" (Watson 1968, 41). Zhuangzi goes on to discuss completion and injury further, but without any clear consequence for his claims about love and the Way. This first claim is left hanging, its presuppositions brought into doubt but never satisfactorily clarified.

If Zhuangzi seeks to prevent his own words from being taken too seriously, so also does he seek to prevent the words of others from being taken too seriously. Two techniques he uses toward this effect are mockery and reversal. Mocking someone's speech, if effective, is a direct way of dispelling seriousness about it. The mocker's usual aim in mockery is to discredit the subject of the mockery and get the hearers (or readers) to laugh at him. By reversal, I mean Zhuangzi's tendency to make statements that are the reverse of seeming truisms or ordinary judgments. To the extent that Zhuangzi may succeed in casting a truism in doubt, he succeeds to some extent in undermining the credibility of any statement that seems less certain than the truism initially did.

The *Zhuangzi* is full of mockery, but one of the most successful mockeries is the mockery of logic that occupies a large part of the second chapter. A. C. Graham tries valiantly to make logical sense of all the arguments in this chapter, but the attempt seems strained (Graham 1981, 52–56). The following passage, for example, is most naturally read as a deliberate jest at the expense of the logicians:

> Now I am going to make a statement here. I don't know whether it fits into the category of other people's statements or not. But whether it fits into their category or whether it doesn't, it obviously fits into some category. So in that respect it is no different from their statements. However, let me try making my statement.
>
> There is a beginning. There is a not yet beginning to be a beginning. There is a not yet beginning to be a not yet beginning to be a beginning. There is being. There is nonbeing. There is a not yet beginning to be nonbeing. Suddenly there is nonbeing. But I do not know, when it comes to nonbeing, which is really being and which is nonbeing. Now I have just said something. But I don't know whether what I have said has really said something or whether it hasn't said something. (Watson 1968, 42–43)[15]

In other parts of the Inner Chapters, Zhuangzi's mockery takes on a variety of other targets, including the sages, burial customs, and—a particular favorite of his—Confucius.

Another technique Zhuangzi employs to encourage his reader to take less seriously what people say is reversal, defined briefly above. Some of the ordinary truisms that Zhuangzi reverses include: that we should strive to be useful (see, for example, Watson 1968, 35, 63–66), that death is worse than life (see, for example, Watson 1968, 47, 80, 83–87), and that one should seek benevolence and righteousness (see, for example, Watson 1968, 90).[16] One might read these reversals as evidence that Zhuangzi actually thought that we ought to be useless, disregard the difference between life and death, and forget benevolence and righteousness. But another possibility—one that I think coheres better with the body and the tone of the *Zhuangzi*—is to look at these reversals not as full-blown attempts to convince, but merely as attempts to undermine our faith in these truisms, to shake our convictions to a certain extent, and thereby reduce our likelihood of putting too much stock in such claims. Raising such doubts may be necessary for fruitful inquiry or action.

But I am anticipating myself somewhat, since my interpretation of what Zhuangzi is doing with his reversals depends on my view that Zhuangzi does not always subscribe to the positions he argues for, and my defense of this latter view does not come until later. The main point of the present section is only this: to make plausible the view that Zhuangzi wishes to see his readers take what people have to say less seriously. Exactly which devices assist Zhuangzi toward this end may be a matter of some debate, although I think they include much of what we find in the *Zhuangzi*: improbable tales, statements made and then questioned, dubious and incomprehensible claims, Daoist utterances from unlikely or disreputable sources, mockery, inconsistencies, and reversals of ordinary judgments.

Reasons to Take Words Less Seriously

I have argued *that* Zhuangzi wishes us to take less seriously what people have to say, but I have not yet provided any reasons *why* Zhuangzi might wish such a thing. What follows are three reasons I think Zhuangzi may have had for wishing us to take words less seriously. In discussing these three reasons, I shall be laying out the basic components of what I take to be Zhuangzi's philosophy of language.*

First Reason To Take Words Less Seriously: the Ineffability of Skill[17]

Zhuangzi wishes to provoke in the reader a certain amount of disrespect for human assertion in part, I believe, because he sees people as tending to overestimate the capacity of words, and rules expressible in words, to capture what is important in the world and to provide a successful basis for action.[18] The clearest statement of Zhuangzi's views on this point, ironically, is found in the Outer Chapters and so may not have come from Zhuangzi himself.[19] The passage is worth quoting in its entirety.

> Duke Huan was in his hall reading a book. The Wheelwright Pian, who was in the yard below chiseling a wheel, laid down his mallet and chisel, stepped up into the hall, and said to Duke Huan, "This book Your Grace is reading—may I venture to ask whose words are in it?"
> "The words of sages," said the duke.
> "Are the sages still alive?"
> "Dead long ago," said the duke.
> "In that case, what you are reading there is nothing but the chaff and dregs of the men of old!"
> "Since when does a wheelwright have permission to comment on the books I read?" said Duke Huan. "If you have some explanation, well and good. If not, it's your life!"
> Wheelwright Pian said, "I look at it from the point of view of my own work. When I chisel a wheel, if the blows of the mallet are

---

* Compare Schwitzgebel's account of the problem with language to Kjellberg (page 13), Loy (page 57) and Berkson (page 112).—Eds.

too gentle, the chisel slides and won't take hold. But if they're too hard, it bites in and won't budge. Not too gentle, not too hard— you can get it in your hand and feel it in your mind. You can't put it into words, and yet there's a knack to it somehow. I can't teach it to my son, and he can't learn it from me. So I've gone along for seventy years and at my age I'm still chiseling wheels. When the men of old died, they took with them the things that couldn't be handed down. So what you are reading there must be nothing but the chaff and dregs of the men of old." (Watson 1968, 152–153)

For Wheelwright Pian, rules expressible in words are inadequate to convey the special knack required for the successful carving of wheels. Likewise, he believes that explicit rules and statements cannot convey whatever it is the duke seeks in the book he is reading.[20] Since the duke's book contains the words of sages, we might suppose that he hopes to get from it the keys to virtue, power, happiness, successful living, or some such. If Wheelwright Pian is speaking for Zhuangzi, we may guess that Zhuangzi holds these things also to elude adequate formulation in words.

In the Inner Chapters, the clearest example of a special knack like the wheelwright's which cannot be conveyed in words is in the story of Cook Ding.[21] As Cook Ding describes himself, when he first began cutting oxen he could see only the whole ox, but as time passed he saw less and less of it. Now, he says, "I go at it by spirit and don't look with my eyes. Perception and understanding have come to a stop and the spirit moves where it wants" (Watson 1968, 50–51). Cook Ding, in setting aside perception and understanding, seems to be doing what "Confucius" later describes as "fasting of the mind" (Watson 1968, 57–58). It is important to note that Cook Ding is described as having latched on to "the secret of caring for life," since this suggests, as does the story of Wheelwright Pian, that what Zhuangzi sees as ineffable are not just the skills of particular crafts, but the skills required for successful living in general.

Perhaps there are others in the Inner Chapters who are meant as negative examples, performing actions artlessly and clumsily, in the rigid fashion that would presumably be characteristic of those who use explicit doctrines and linguistically expressible rules to guide their behavior. The logician Huizi would be an obvious candidate (at least when he is not exercising his skill at logic-chopping), and indeed in the first chapter we find him smashing a huge gourd because he cannot find a use for it that fits with his simple rules for the use of gourds—the gourd was too heavy for a water container and too large and unwieldy for dippers (Watson 1968, 34). Zhuangzi is disgusted with him and suggests that he might have used the gourd as a great tub for floating around on rivers and lakes. On the same page, we find reference to a man of Song who is successful in selling ceremonial hats in Song, but fails to sell them in Yue where the people have different customs and no use for such hats. The error common to both Huizi and the man of Song is that they find a practice successful in their usual context and so attempt to apply it in a new and different situation, where it fails. Perhaps it is not that Huizi and the man of Song follow rules in their behavior that leads them astray *per se*—more sophisticated rules would have sufficed to save them from their errors—but the errors they make are characteristic of the types of errors that anyone who is rule- and doctrine-bound will tend to make. They are errors of excessive rigidity.

Think of the difference between a beginning and an expert cook. The beginning cook will follow the directions in the cookbook exactly, and so doing may be successful in a limited range of circumstances. She guides her behavior by explicit, linguistically formulated rules, the rules in the cookbook.[22] If there is any kind of change in circumstances—if the ingredients available are just a little different from what is called for, or if there is a shortage of oven space, or if the diners have tastes that require some accommodation—the beginning cook runs a substantial risk of failure. Like Huizi or the man of Song, she will be at a loss if the rules she knows do not lead to the result she desires. As her cooking improves, however, she will begin, like Wheelwright Pian, to develop a skill that eludes precise formulation in words. She will be able to improvise on recipes and adapt to a wide variety of changes in circumstance; she will know how and how much to knead a loaf of bread to get the rise she desires; she will know how the soup would taste if she added another bay leaf. This kind of knowledge is acquired only by practice, and could not be expressed in a thousand cookbooks.*

Zhuangzi would like his readers to appreciate that most things of human importance are like cooking in this respect. Consider as further examples: walking, talking, teaching, making a good impression, being a good husband or wife, maintaining one's health. To all these things, there is a knack that cannot be summed up in words. This is part of why Zhuangzi would like to see us take words less seriously.

Second Reason To Take Words Less Seriously: the Limitations of Human Judgment

It would be a mistake, I think, to hold that the ineffability of skill is the only, or even the primary, reason for Zhuangzi's stand against taking what people have to say too seriously. Another very important set of considerations are

---

* Note that Schwitzgebel here values skill for the efficiency and adaptability with which it accomplishes its goals. This is different from Yearley's focus on the psychological or "spiritual" fulfillment that accompanies skillful performance (p. 158). It is also different from Kjellberg's emphasis on the ability of the skillful individual to select goals well in a changing and unpredictable world (p. 12), the absence of which ability keeps Huizi from being a paradigm of skill even though he is an effective arguer. —Eds.

Zhuangzi's opinions about the limitations of human judgment. If what we believe about a subject is suspect, then clearly, so also is what we have to say about the subject.

I shall not at this point, however, discuss Zhuangzi's views regarding the limitations of human judgment. I do not mean to slight the importance of these considerations as justification for Zhuangzi's view that we should take less seriously the things people say and the claims they make. On the contrary, I believe that such considerations may be the strongest among those that Zhuangzi can adduce in favor of such a conclusion. Nonetheless, a discussion of Zhuangzi's views about the limitations of human judgment could only be properly conducted hand-in-hand with a discussion of Zhuangzi's skepticism, since obviously the two are intimately related, perhaps even indistinguishable; and the discussion of skepticism awaits the elaboration of some further points. I pause here only to highlight one thing: To the extent Zhuangzi manages to bring into question the warrant for our beliefs, he grants us license to take with a grain of salt any claims we may make on the basis of those beliefs.

Third Reason To Take Words Less Seriously:
What Words Have To Say Is Not Fixed[23]

Finally, I shall consider what probably comes to mind most readily when Zhuangzi's "view of language" is discussed: what he explicitly says about language in the "Discussion on Making All Things Equal." Like most of Zhuangzi's other claims in this chapter, I think his claims here about language are exaggerated. But even under the weakest possible interpretation, what Zhuangzi says about words in this chapter suggests that he thinks they ought to be taken less seriously.

Zhuangzi's claims about language in this chapter are rather mysterious at a first reading. One thing that seems to be important are boundaries. Zhuangzi says, "The Way has never known boundaries; speech has no constancy. But because of [the recognition of a] 'this', there came to be boundaries" (Watson 1968, 43). Boundaries and categories are also associated with the injury of the Way (Watson 1968, 41), and presented as foreign to it (Watson 1968, 40–41). Apparently on the basis of such claims, Zhuangzi says that the sage does not discriminate, and that "those who discriminate fail to see" (Watson 1968, 44). What can Zhuangzi mean by all this?

It is crucial to notice that the use of words requires drawing boundaries between things. Thus, the remarks about boundaries and speech are related. Suppose the two of us are together at an aquarium and I remark, "How beautiful that green and yellow striped fish is!" To make such a remark meaningfully, I must presume that distinctions of some sort can be drawn between a fish and what is not a fish, what is green and what is not green, what is beautiful and what is not beautiful, and so on. I need not presume that these distinctions can be made absolutely precise, nor do I need to be able to outline plausible criteria for distinguishing between the things in question—but I do need to be able to pick out to my own satisfaction at least a few clear cases on either side of these distinctions. If I would be at a loss to think of any design that I would not call a stripe, or if I could not to my own satisfaction come up with plausible examples of things that were not fishes, my remark at the aquarium would be meaningless. Or, if meaningful, its meaning would at least be inscrutable to those around me.[24] I might just as easily have said it while pointing at a water fountain.*

Thus, boundaries are crucial to language. Seeming to acknowledge this, Zhuangzi says that the Way has never known boundaries and that the sage does not discriminate between things. Of particular importance in understanding this claim, I think, is a passage a few pages farther along in which talk of "discriminations" surfaces again. A man named Wang Ni three times says he doesn't know (actually he *asks* how he could know), and then says,

> If a man sleeps in a damp place, his back aches and he ends up half paralyzed, but is this true of a loach? If he lives in a tree, he is terrified and shakes with fright, but is this true of a monkey? Of these creatures, which one knows the proper place to live? Men eat the flesh of grass-fed and grain-fed animals, dear eat grass, centipedes find snakes tasty, and hawks and falcons relish mice. Of these four, which knows how food ought to taste? Monkeys pair with monkeys, deer go out with deer, and fish play around with fish. Men claim that Maoqiang and Lady Li were beautiful, but if fish saw them they would dive to the bottom of the stream, if birds saw them they would fly away, and if deer saw them they would break into a run. Of these four, which knows how to fix the standard of beauty for the world? The way I see it, the rules of benevolence and righteousness and the paths of right and wrong are all hopelessly snarled and jumbled. How could I know anything about such discriminations? (Watson 1968, 45–46)

In this passage, Wang Ni adopts a type of relativism toward aesthetic and moral judgments, and uses it as a basis for rejecting aesthetic and moral discriminations.[25] Since this is one of the clearest examples of a passage in the Inner Chapters of the *Zhuangzi* in which a reason is given for the rejection of discriminations, we might look at it as a clue. We wish to know what basis there might be for the general rejection of discriminations that Zhuangzi says characterizes the sage. Perhaps it is some more general form of relativism?

If we continue to look at the Watson translation, as we have been doing, it is hard to find any passage that unambiguously suggests such a generalized

---

*Compare Berkson's account of "relational relativism" (p. 104).—Eds.

form of relativism. There is a passage, however, that although ambiguous on Watson's translation, comes out strongly relativistic on Chad Hansen's translation (Hansen in Mair 1983). In Hansen's translation, 是 *shi*, when contrasted with 非 *fei*, is intended to mean affirmation, and *fei* denial. Where a slash divides two words the first is Chinese, the second an English translation. Colons separate alternate English translations.

> There is nothing that is not bi/that, there is nothing that is not shi/this. From bi/that you do not see it; from zhi/know:mastery you zhi/know it. Thus it is said: "bi/that comes from shi/this and shi/this is based on bi/that." This is the theory of the simultaneous birth of *shi-bi*. . . . Shi/this is also bi/that. Bi/that is also shi/this. There is one *shi-fei*, here is one *shi-fei*. Is there really shi/this and bi/that? Or is there no shi/this and bi/that? Where neither shi/this nor bi/that is in opposition, we call "axis of daos." When the axis begins to generate a circle you can respond without limit. There is no limit to what you can *shi* and no limit to what you can *fei*.[26]

Having already noted the importance for language of categories—boundaries between "that" and "this"—we can see that this passage suggests a radical view of words and distinctions. For any distinction we might wish to make, Zhuangzi argues, and for any object that might be classified on one side or the other of the distinction, there is a perspective from which the object will be classified on one side (this) and a perspective from which the object will be classified on the other (that). Thus, from one perspective the green and yellow striped thing I am pointing at will fit into the category "fish"; from another perspective, it will not fit into that category. From one perspective the "fish" is green and yellow, from another perspective it is not. There is no limit to what one can affirm and deny.[27] As if to illustrate, Zhuangzi says (a few pages later), "There is nothing in the world bigger than the tip of an autumn hair, and Mount Tai is tiny. No one has lived longer than a dead child, and Pengzu died young. Heaven and earth were born at the same time I was, and the ten thousand things are one with me" (Watson 1968, 43).[28] If however, as Zhuangzi seems to suggest in these passages, words cannot reliably be attached to things, any word potentially picking out any object, then there can be no verbal communication or transfer of meaning between people, unless merely by accident. Zhuangzi raises this possibility at the beginning of his discussion of words, suggesting that they may really be no different from the peeps of baby birds (Watson 1968, 39).

This is a very radical position to ascribe to Zhuangzi, and it runs against objections and difficulties similar to those surrounding his skeptical arguments. If Zhuangzi thinks words have no meaning, what are we to make of his text? Should we just give up on the task of interpreting him at all? Although it is a tired observation, I think it is a compelling one: if Zhuangzi thought words had no meaning, it would be strange of him to say so. It is worth observing that at one point Zhuangzi even *corrects* Huizi's interpretation of a phrase, saying "that's not what I mean" (Watson 1968, 75).

My response to what Zhuangzi has to say about words is very much like what I shall say about his skeptical arguments. Zhuangzi need not mean all that he says and need not believe all that he argues for. In fact, I shall argue, it is appropriate for him not to, given his philosophical stance. Still, we should not grant that Zhuangzi speaks purposelessly or presents arguments completely at odds with what he believes. It would seem that Zhuangzi's point in bringing up the perspective relativity of words and statements is to attack other philosophers—Confucians, Mohists, and other "ordinary men" who make fine discriminations "and parade their discriminations before others" (Watson 1968, 44). To the extent that Zhuangzi raises doubts in our minds about the fixity of words and the universality of judgments, he prevents our taking too seriously such doctrines and discriminations. Regardless of whether one takes Zhuangzi at his word in these passages on language or whether one takes a more moderate view like my own, the passages indicate that Zhuangzi believes some reduction of our faith in the credibility of categories and distinctions is in order.

The three arguments just presented are intended to be arguments Zhuangzi might have given for taking what people have to say less seriously. As stated, however, they do not prove exactly what I wish them to prove. Even if in each of the three cases the arguments were to be taken literally and found wholly persuasive, it seems that their end is only this: to show that we ought not put too much stock and credence in what people have to say. The two conclusions are not quite equivalent. One might imagine, for example, a deadly earnest skeptic who did not put much faith in people's words, but nonetheless took those words quite seriously and in a grave and diligent manner sought in every case to prove their claims groundless. The difference between reducing one's stock and credence in a claim and refusing to take it seriously is one of attitude. One who does not take a claim seriously will be willing, for example, to play around with it with disrespectful humor. One who merely finds a claim not entirely credible may or may not be so willing.

Zhuangzi does not provide any *argument* that one should, in reducing one's stock and credence in what people have to say, also go the extra step and take what they have to say less seriously. Still, I think it is clear that he wishes the reader to go this extra step. In the first section of this paper, I outlined some of Zhuangzi's rhetorical devices toward this end. In the present section I have outlined some arguments he may have given to encourage the reader to cast aside at least the most substantial obstacle to her taking words less seriously: an undue faith in the reliability and usefulness of what people have to say.

Must Zhuangzi Mean What He Says?

So far I have only explored the first of the two attitudes toward language I attribute to Zhuangzi. I have gone into the issue in some depth not only because it has relevance to the remainder of this paper but also because I feel it warrants elaboration in its own right. In what follows, however, I shall be more brief.

Recall that the central aim of this paper is to defend the position that Zhuangzi is not a skeptic in any strong sense of the word. Since I believe that there are passages in the Inner Chapters of a radically skeptical sort, I am faced with a tension that requires resolution. We might formulate this tension as a question: If Zhuangzi is not a skeptic, why does he appear to make skeptical arguments? I seek to resolve this tension by arguing that Zhuangzi does not sincerely endorse the radical skepticism he defends. In other words, when speaking as a skeptic, Zhuangzi does not mean what he says.[29] If there is an important point to be drawn from Zhuangzi's skeptical passages (and I think there is), it is not what one would gather from a literal reading of them. However, because there is a strong presumption that an author, when speaking as a philosopher (and not as a writer of fiction), believes what he asserts, I hope to show two things to counteract this presumption: (a) that Zhuangzi both has a general disposition to assert things he does not believe and has a good reason for doing so, and (b) that strong evidence exists elsewhere in the text to suggest that Zhuangzi is not a skeptic. The argument toward (b) shall not appear until the next section of this paper. The present section is devoted to the defense of (a), which may be seen as a restatement of what I described in the opening section as Zhuangzi's second attitude toward language.

It should be clear that Zhuangzi's first attitude toward language feeds into his second. To the extent Zhuangzi is disinclined to take words seriously he will be predisposed to utter things without careful regard for their truth. Like Zhang Wuzi (Watson 1968, 47), Zhuangzi speaks reckless words and hopes to be listened to recklessly. He tells absurd tales such as that of the Kun/Peng and that of the shaman who could predict the fortune of a man and the day of his death "as though he were a god himself" (Watson 1968, 94–95). He weaves fanciful dialogues in which it is sometimes hard to judge what voice, if any, is meant to be his own. He mocks, teases, and mouths absurdities. In short, Zhuangzi exhibits a *playfulness* with language that pays little heed to truth. Some examples of such playfulness have already come out in this paper. Many more can be found in the text. Just to cite one further example:

> Tian Gen was wandering on the sunny side of Yin Mountain. When he reached the banks of the Liao River, he happened to

meet a Nameless Man. He questioned the man, saying, "Please may I ask how to rule the world?"

The Nameless Man said, "Get away from me you peasant! What kind of dreary question is that! I'm just about to set off with Creator. And if I get bored with that, then I'll ride on the Light-and-Lissome Bird out beyond the six directions, wandering in the village of Not-Even-Anything and living in the Broad-and-Borderless field. What business do you have coming with this talk of governing the world and disturbing my mind?" (Watson 1968, 93–94)

Often, as here, it is clear that Zhuangzi intends to be taken with a grain of salt.

But even when Zhuangzi seems to be speaking in earnest, we cannot be sure that the conclusions most obviously to be drawn from his tales are exactly the conclusions he endorses. Consider this story from the Outer Chapters:[30] "Zhuangzi was walking in the mountains when he saw a huge tree, its branches and leaves thick and lush. A woodcutter paused by its side but made no move to cut it down. When Zhuangzi asked the reason, he replied, 'There's nothing it could be used for!' Zhuangzi said, 'Because of its worthlessness, this tree is able to live out the years Heaven gave it'" (Watson 1968, 209). So far the story looks quite familiar: it is similar to two parables in the Inner Chapters about trees whose uselessness enables them to live out their natural term (Watson 1968, 63–65). The moral of all three stories seems obvious, if a little perverse: strive to be useless, so that you may live undisturbed and uninjured by the demands of others (cf. the story of Crippled Shu, Watson 1968, 66). But the story in the Outer Chapters continues,

> Down from the mountain, the Master stopped for a night at the house of an old friend. The friend, delighted, ordered his son to kill a goose and prepare it. "One of these geese can cackle and the other can't," said the son. "May I ask, please, which I should kill?"
>
> "Kill the one that can't cackle," said the host.
>
> The next day Zhuangzi's disciples questioned him. "Yesterday there was a tree on the mountain that gets to live out the years Heaven gave it because of its worthlessness. Now there's our host's goose that gets killed because of its worthlessness. What position would you take in such a case, Master?"
>
> Zhuangzi laughed and said, "I'd probably take a position half-way between worth and worthlessness. But halfway between worth and worthlessness, though it may seem to be a good place, really isn't—you'll never get away from trouble there. It would be very different, though, if you were to climb up on the Way and its Virtue and go drifting and wandering, neither praised nor damned, now a dragon, now a snake, shifting with the times, never willing to hold one course only." (Watson 1968, 209)

In this last part of the story, Zhuangzi goes halfway back on his original position, settling between worth and worthlessness; then he suggests that even this position is not the ideal, and offers an alternative that is rather difficult to comprehend, probably half in jest and half as a pointer toward something he cannot or does not wish to state explicitly.[31] Quite possibly his point is one about the rejection of rigid rules on the matter (which might be seen by the unenlightened as a kind of "halfway" position). But if we take this dialogue to be authentic, it casts into question the function of the parables on uselessness in the Inner Chapters. Why should Zhuangzi tell a parable with a moral to which he himself does not subscribe?

Perhaps Zhuangzi knows that his readers could not be convinced to abandon completely their desire to be useful. What he hopes for instead, and what he aims at in telling these parables, is to persuade the reader to rethink her commitment to usefulness, reduce it, and bring it into line with an appreciation of uselessness. In Lee Yearley's words, Zhuangzi may be employing a "rhetoric of exaggeration" intended to shake our normal perception of the world (Yearley in Mair 1983, 137).[32]

Yearley offers an example of how the rhetoric of exaggeration might work in another situation. We are supposed to imagine ourselves having a gangrenous leg and Zhuangzi's advising us not to go to the hospital to have it treated. Zhuangzi points out that the leg has a variety of new colors and really is much more interesting than the usual sort of leg. If we object that the complications may be fatal? Zhuangzi's response, in this imaginary dialogue, would be to ask why it is we think life better than death. The function of such a stance on Zhuangzi's part would be merely to provoke reflection and generate new ideas. He himself, we imagine, would go to the hospital in a similar situation. If the parables on uselessness in the Inner Chapters are indeed meant to function like this imaginary dialogue, as is suggested by the story from the Outer Chapters cited above, then they provide an example of a gap between what Zhuangzi says and what he believes—and not just when Zhuangzi is mouthing obvious nonsense or speaking *qua* fiction writer, but when he is making a substantial philosophical point.

Even if the story from the Outer Chapters is not authentic, it should strike us as plausible. Given the wildness of some of Zhuangzi's claims, it is natural for the reader to suspect that at least sometimes Zhuangzi employs, in the Inner Chapters, a rhetoric of exaggeration. And if we admit this possibility, why not concede the chance that Zhuangzi, in his skeptical arguments specifically, does not subscribe to the position for which he seems to be arguing?

Before concluding this section, I have two more remarks to make in defense of the view that Zhuangzi does not always mean what he says. The first remark is this: If Zhuangzi sincerely believes something like what I have presented as his "first reason to take words less seriously"—that is, that most of what is important in the world is not expressible in words—then he probably does not think that his ideas, no matter how earnestly he attempts to express them, can be given full justice by the words he uses. Thus, to some extent he cannot quite believe what he says. Furthermore, if Zhuangzi sincerely adopts anything like the perspectivism about categories that I offered as his "third reason to take words less seriously," then for this reason also we have license to wonder about the connection between what he appears to be saying and what he believes. I think these points are worth noting, although by themselves they cannot quite explain the appearance of skeptical passages in a nonskeptical text. The first cannot do so because it cannot account for *radical* deviations between what Zhuangzi says and what he believes, but only for small deviations and for confusing approximations. I believe that the second cannot do so because I believe that Zhuangzi does not in fact subscribe to a perspectivism about categories sufficiently radical to justify our attributing such a large divergence between what he appears to say and what he means to be saying by it.

As noted in earlier sections, Zhuangzi sees limitations and problems with the use of words that lead him to advocate their being taken less seriously. However, if Zhuangzi were simply to *say* that he thinks words ought to be taken less seriously, he would risk undermining his own project, for he would tempt the reader to take him as speaking in a serious vein. The reader, then, might reject Zhuangzi as a man who does not practice what he preaches; or, if the reader found Zhuangzi's arguments convincing, she might be inclined to replace a serious Mohism, for example, with a serious adherence to what Zhuangzi says. The latter, I suspect, Zhuangzi would judge to be a scant improvement. Thus, Zhuangzi is better off not quite saying what he thinks about any particular issue, or at least making it unclear which among the things he says are the things he means sincerely. Zhuangzi does best to work by example and parable, weaving ridiculous tales, confounding and mocking his opponents, squawking absurdities. And if in the end the reader takes no doctrine, no earnestly expressed judgment, no concoction of words too seriously, Zhuangzi's or otherwise, Zhuangzi will have succeeded in his project. We ought to be quite wary, then, of what Zhuangzi says, since he has good reason to connect it only tenuously with what he believes.

Zhuangzi's Skepticism

Finally, I am ready to present my position on the apparently skeptical passages in the *Zhuangzi*. First I shall draw a distinction between skepticism in the philosopher's sense, or radical skepticism, and skepticism in an everyday sense. Then I shall defend the following position: Although Zhuangzi argues for radical skepticism, in the end he is only a skeptic in the everyday sense. This claim may be broken into three component claims: (1) Zhuangzi argues for (at least one version of) radical skepticism; (2) Zhuangzi is not a radical skeptic; and (3) Zhuangzi is a skeptic in the everyday sense. Each of these component claims shall be supported in turn.

Two Kinds of Skepticism

When nonphilosophers speak of a skeptic, they usually mean either some-one who does not subscribe to a particular claim or body of claims (for example, a "skeptic about parapsychological phenomena" or a "religious skep-tic"), or they mean someone who holds higher standards of evidence than most, usually in a particular domain (for example, "she tends to be skeptical about what she reads in the newspapers," or "he is skeptical about the claims of modern science," although one might also hear "so-and-so is a skeptical person in general, and hard to convince"). The philosophical position "skep-ticism," in any of its various forms, is something quite different. Roughly, a skeptic is someone who thinks that none of her beliefs constitute knowl-edge, or at least none of her beliefs in some quite broad and general domain, such as beliefs about the "external world," or beliefs arrived at inductively. Although your Uncle Randolf may be a skeptic about paranormal phenom-ena and quite a skeptical fellow in general, it is unlikely that he is a skeptic in the philosopher's sense, unless he is either a madman or (perhaps) a philosopher.

Up to this point, when I have claimed that Zhuangzi is not a skeptic, I have meant that he is not a skeptic in the radical, philosopher's sense. From this point on, however, I shall not refer to "skepticism" *simpliciter*, but to either "radical skepticism" or "everyday skepticism."*

Zhuangzi Argues for Radical Skepticism

I shall now defend the first component of my position on Zhuangzi's skepti-cism: that he argues for radical skepticism. My strategy shall consist prima-rily in just presenting what I see to be the more radically skeptical passages from the Inner Chapters, since I think they more or less speak for them-selves.

In saying that Zhuangzi argues for radical or philosophical skepticism, I do not mean to presume that there is a single unified position, "philosophical skepticism," for which Zhuangzi argues. Rather there are a number of posi-tions that fall into a class the members of which might be described as "philo-sophical skepticisms."[33] As noted above, these positions have in common radical, unusual doubt regarding some broad range of propositions. Descartes' skepticism about knowledge obtained via the senses is a famous example of such skepticism. Because we cannot be sure we are not dreaming, Descartes

---

* See editors' note on page 29.—Eds.

argues in his first *Meditation*, we cannot have knowledge through our senses; so long as it is possible that we are dreaming, sensory knowledge is an impossibility.[34] Zhuangzi makes a point that may be construed in a similar way. "Once Zhuang Zhou dreamt he was a butterfly, a butterfly flitting and fluttering around, happy with himself and doing as he pleased. He didn't know he was Zhuang Zhou. Suddenly he woke up and there he was, solid and unmistakable Zhuang Zhou. But he didn't know if he was Zhuang Zhou who had dreamt he was a butterfly, or a butterfly dreaming he was Zhuang Zhou. Between Zhuang Zhou and a butterfly there must be *some* distinction! This is called the Transformation of Things" (Watson 1968, 49). Heavy weather has been made over this passage, and I do not wish to provide a detailed analysis of it.[35] However, it is easy to construe as an example of radical, philosophical skepticism. Zhuangzi does not know whether he is a butterfly or a human being. Presumably, then, he cannot arrive at any knowledge through his senses: he does not know whether there is really a writing desk and ink in front of him or whether there are flowers in front of him instead. If he did, he would know whether he was a butterfly or not.[36] Furthermore, no indication is given in this passage to suggest that any of us are better off than Zhuangzi in this respect.

Another passage, which perhaps warrants comparison with Sextus Empiricus' skepticism regarding the resolvability of arguments,[37] is the following: "Suppose you and I have had an argument. If you have beaten me instead of my beating you, then are you necessarily right and am I necessarily wrong? If I have beaten you instead of your beating me, then am I necessarily right and are you necessarily wrong? Is one of us right and the other wrong? Are both of us right or are both of us wrong? If you and I don't know the answer, then other people are bound to be even more in the dark" (Watson 1968, 48). Still another skeptical passage is the discussion between Nie Que and Wang Ni:

> Nie Que asked Wang Ni, "Do you know what all things agree in calling right?"
> "How would I know that?" said Wang Ni.
> "Do you know that you don't know it?"
> "How would I know that?"
> "Then do things know nothing?"
> "How would I know that? However, suppose I try saying something. What way do I have of knowing that if I say I know something I don't really not know it? Or what way do I have of knowing that if I say I don't know something I don't really in fact know it?"
> (Watson 1968, 45)

Other passages in the *Zhuangzi* seem to presuppose some form or other of radical skepticism:

Now I have just said something. But I don't know whether what I
have said has really said something or whether it hasn't said something. (Watson 1968, 43)

If the process continues, perhaps in time [the Creator will] transform my left arm into a rooster. In that case I'll keep watch on the
night. Or perhaps in time he'll transform my right arm into a cross-
bow pellet and I'll shoot down an owl for roasting. Or perhaps in
time he'll transform my buttocks into cartwheels. Then, with my
spirit for a horse, I'll climb up and go for a ride. What need will I
ever have for a carriage again? (Watson 1968, 84)

Moreover, when he is changing, how does he know that he is really
changing? And when he is not changing, how does he know that
he hasn't already changed? (Watson 1968, 88)

There are a number of other examples. Given the brevity of the Inner Chapters, such radically skeptical passages warrant a fair bit of attention.

I do not think that one who chooses to read these passages as sincere
attempts by Zhuangzi to express some form of philosophical skepticism can
avoid the conclusion that Zhuangzi's skepticism is enormously broad and
unconstrained. Those who would limit Zhuangzi's skepticism must contend
with these passages in one way or another. It has been proposed by Kjellberg
and Ivanhoe, for example, that Zhuangzi is merely a skeptic about the capacity of language accurately to describe things in the world.[38] Such a form
of skepticism might, with only a little strain, account for the Nie Que and
the irresolvability of arguments passages, but Zhuangzi's butterfly dream passage does not seem to depend on language in any way, nor, arguably, does
the passage cited from page 84 or the animal relativism passage on p. 44–45
(since animals have no language).[39] Even Hansen, who seems to be willing
to allow that Zhuangzi's skepticism and relativism are quite extreme, says
that they are confined to "evaluative distinctions made in prescriptive discourse" (Hansen in Mair 1983, 33).[40] Thus Hansen's account runs against
the same passages that Kjellberg's and Ivanhoe's do.[41]

Graham's account has difficulty with different passages. Graham claims
that Zhuangzi's relativism does not extend to the imperative "respond with
awareness," which, he says, "we all take for granted" (Graham 1983, 11–
12). But to support this position, Graham must set aside the Wang Ni passage, for Wang Ni (at least in the part of the passage quoted above[42]) seems
unlikely to endorse *any* imperative, no matter how universally agreed upon.
Graham says of his imperative that it amounts only to preferring intelligence
to stupidity and reality to illusion (Graham in Mair 1983, 12). But couldn't
one dispute these preferences? Then, following the irresolvability of arguments passage (Watson 1968, 48), Zhuangzi would be forced into skepticism
on this matter also.

It may sound as though I am objecting to these authors' attempts to limit Zhuangzi's skepticism. I am not. I sympathize completely with their wish to read Zhuangzi as less than utterly skeptical. In fact, I believe the text demands such a reading. The point here is rather that no interpretation of the *Zhuangzi* along such lines could possibly cohere with a literal interpretation of everything in the Inner Chapters. At some point, the alert interpreter of the *Zhuangzi* will have to admit that Zhuangzi does not always mean what he says. Once this is admitted, if the interpreter wishes to go on and defend a view of exactly what it is Zhuangzi is skeptical about, mere appeal to passages in the *Zhuangzi* that support the proposed form of skepticism is not enough. Some general account of when and when not to take Zhuangzi at his word is required. I would like to see interpreters of the *Zhuangzi*, in general, pay more attention to this issue.

After reading the whole of the Inner Chapters, there is a natural temptation to try to read passages such as those cited above as not broadly and radically skeptical, since the overall tone of the Inner Chapters does not suggest such utter skepticism. The result of succumbing to this temptation is likely to be an unfortunate compromise: on the one hand, to do justice to the rest of the Inner Chapters these passages may be interpreted as less skeptical than they actually are, while on the other hand, to do justice to these passages, Zhuangzi's overall view may be seen as more skeptical than it really is. So long, however, as we are willing to grant a distinction between what Zhuangzi *argues for* and what he *believes*, there is no need either to twist these passages into something other than they immediately appear to be, or to see Zhuangzi as actually subscribing to skeptical views that stand starkly in tension with the rest of his work.

Zhuangzi Is Not a Radical Skeptic

Despite the fact that Zhuangzi argues for radical philosophical skepticism, I do not think he is a skeptic in this sense. Although this is the central thesis of this paper, it is a thesis for which it is difficult to provide a single coherent argument, since much of what I think makes it believable is an overall impression of the Inner Chapters that cannot be conveyed in any particular short collection of passages.

Still, I think the view admits of some defenses that may be put down on paper. One defense is to point to certain ideas in the Inner Chapters that seem to shine through the fog created by Zhuangzi's playful and frustrating use of language. Zhuangzi would like to see a greater appreciation of uselessness, less fear of death and poverty, less dogmatism, less ambition, less devotion to the state. Only a person reading with her eyes half-open could miss these themes in the book. Zhuangzi seems to have definite convictions, then, about how people ought to live. But if he were a philosophical skeptic of the radical sort suggested by the passages above, such convictions would be totally out of place.

Another defense of the view that Zhuangzi is not a philosophical skeptic is to issue a challenge to the reader: If Zhuangzi were a philosophical skeptic, then there would have to be some particular set of propositions or issues about which he was skeptical. What could this set be? The set would have to be broad enough to warrant the sweeping skepticism that inhabits the passages cited above, yet consistent with the various positive stands he seems to take through the rest of his work. Could it be that Zhuangzi rejects the possibility of sensory knowledge? Then he would have to deny that Cook Ding or Wheelwright Pian knew what they were doing. Could Zhuangzi be a skeptic regarding the issue of how one ought to live? Then his advocacy of equanimity in the face of death and the appreciation of uselessness, et cetera, would hardly make sense. Zhuangzi might be a skeptic about the power of words to convey unchangeable truths, but as I noted earlier such a skepticism would hardly be sufficient to account for the passages cited above. The butterfly dream passage, for instance, makes no reference to words.

On page seventy, Zhuangzi has a character say that you ought to "know what you can't do anything about" and be content with it. On page ninety-three, he has another character say that the sage, when he governs, "makes absolutely certain that things can do what they are supposed to do, that is all." Zhuangzi also says that "he who knows what it is that Heaven does, and knows what it is that man does, has reached the peak" (Watson 1968, 77). On the same page it is suggested that the True Man, whoever he is, has true knowledge. A little earlier on, Zhuangzi describes a man who "governs Heaven and earth, stores up the ten thousand things, . . . unifies the knowledge of what he knows, and in his mind never tastes death" (Watson 1968, 69). In all these passages, Zhuangzi seems explicitly to presuppose the possibility of various sorts of knowledge. These passages do not command as much attention as his philosophically skeptical passages and they primarily concern people in their (possibly unattainable) ideal state, but these passages may nonetheless be of some value in the argument that Zhuangzi is not a philosophical skeptic.

The idea that it would be odd or inappropriate for Zhuangzi to advocate changes in our ways of life if he were a philosophical skeptic requires a little more clarification. Although I hope that it seems plausible enough on its surface, this claim rests on a presumption that may be challenged, that is, that a philosophical skeptic regarding propositions or issues of a certain type would not advocate any position that falls within the scope of his skepticism. But this is not obviously the case. For example, one might be a philosophical skeptic not because one has any greater doubt about things than an ordinary person, but rather because one sets impossibly high standards on what is to count as knowledge. Then, one may be a philosophical skeptic and advocate as much as one pleases, so long as one avoids the word "know" (知 zhi) and its cognates.[43] I suppose one could resolve the tension between Zhuangzi's skeptical claims and his substantive positions by taking such a line, but one might think that if Zhuangzi had a definitional focus of this sort, he would be careful not to use "know" in the passages cited above. Likewise, such an explanation of Zhuangzi's "skepticism" could hardly explain such things as his positive appraisal, without any reference to the word "know," of Clansman Tai who sometimes thought he was a horse and sometimes thought he was a cow (Watson 1968, 92).

Another way to excuse Zhuangzi for making positive claims despite global philosophical skepticism is suggested by Chad Hansen (Hansen in Mair 1983, 39). According to Hansen, Zhuangzi, though a philosophical skeptic, naturally has opinions and a desire to express them, by virtue of being human. It would make no more sense for him to attempt to prevent himself from opining and disputing than it would for him to try to stop the wind in the hollows or the peeps of baby birds. Although I believe this view of Zhuangzi has merit, it would attribute to him a degree of inconsistency I find difficult to accept. On Hansen's view, presumably, Zhuangzi is both of the opinion that a driving success for political ambition is misguided (the opinion he naturally has and expresses) and of the opinion that moderate ambition is no more warranted than driving ambition (his skeptical/relativist position).[44] I would prefer, if at all possible, to see Zhuangzi's views as more coherent and ordinary than this.

The best argument that Zhuangzi is a radical skeptic is that he sometimes seems to advocate radical skepticism. Although initially this looks like quite a compelling argument, I hope I have been able to take some of the sting out of it with my defense of the view that Zhuangzi does not always believe what he seems to endorse. Thus, the door is opened for arguments of the sort given in this section to convince us that Zhuangzi is indeed not a radical skeptic.

The reader may raise another objection at this point, for it might appear that I have worked myself into something of an interpretive predicament. On the one hand I argue that Zhuangzi does not wish for his words to be taken too seriously and that he does not always mean what he says. On the other hand, I ascribe to Zhuangzi particular views on the basis of what he does say. But if I think that there is no firm and reliable connection between what Zhuangzi says and what he believes, what is to prevent me from thinking, for instance, that he was an orthodox Mohist who simply scribbled down a lot of things he did not believe?

My answer to this objection depends on considering Zhuangzi as having been reasonably capable of predicting what effects his writings might have had upon the sympathetic reader.* I think it is fair for us to assume that

---

*Compare Schwitzgebel's attention to the expected effect of Zhuangzi's arguments on the reader to Kupperman's accounts of them as "educating" the emotions (p. 193) and to the descriptions of Zhuangzi's project as "therapeutic" by Kjellberg (p. 7) and Ivanhoe (p. 200).—Eds.

Zhuangzi thought these effects would be salutary, and to infer from facts of this sort something about his real philosophical positions. (I would, in fact, advocate this as a general technique for interpreting the Inner Chapters.) I have discussed at length one such effect that Zhuangzi might have hoped to induce in the reader: an inclination to take words less seriously. If we suppose that Zhuangzi did in fact aim at this effect, then it seems reasonable to infer that he thought people in general (or perhaps his audience in particular—scholarly, philosophical types) ought to take less seriously what people have to say. Another effect at which I think Zhuangzi aimed was the reduction of the reader's confidence in her own beliefs. I believe that he hoped to achieve this effect in part by means of the skeptical passages. But this is the topic of the next, and final, subsection.

Zhuangzi Is a Skeptic in the Everyday Sense

If Zhuangzi is not a philosophical skeptic and does not subscribe to the positions he endorses in his more philosophically skeptical passages, the question naturally arises, why did he write these passages in the first place? I believe he wrote these passages with a therapeutic intent—that is, to jolt the reader into a certain kind of everyday skepticism, a kind of open-mindedness that consists in putting somewhat less faith than is standard in one's own and others' beliefs.[45] Such open-mindedness may be both an epistemic and a moral boon, leading not only to a receptiveness to new evidence but also to a tolerance of people with different beliefs.*

Such a project would clearly be akin to Zhuangzi's project of making us take less seriously what we have to say. In fact, it may be described as the project of making us take less seriously what we believe. As I noted in an earlier section, the second project supports the first: if we refuse to take our beliefs too seriously, we cannot take too seriously the claims we use to express these beliefs. One might attempt to separate the two projects, arguing that although Zhuangzi wishes to have us take our words less seriously, he hopes that we hold our beliefs in earnest. To me this sounds like an improbable scenario. Not only do the skeptical passages, even if read as insincere, suggest against this, but so also do Zhuangzi's frequent attacks on conventionally accepted beliefs (such as that one ought to be useful) and his humorous endorsement of those who have quite peculiar beliefs. It is likely, then, that Zhuangzi does in fact aim to reduce the seriousness with which we take our beliefs. If so, then the skeptical passages seem a useful tool toward that effect.

It is possible of course that the skeptical passages will be too effective, and produce in the reader a full-blown philosophical skepticism, rather than a more modest kind of everyday skepticism. Possible, but unlikely. Few philosophical skeptics are made by the reading of philosophical skepticism. By far

---

* See Ivanhoe's discussion of David Wong's views (pp. 207–209). —Eds.

the more common effect is a momentary twinge of doubt, a brief amusement, and eventually a willingness to concede that we probably do put more stock in our beliefs than they truly deserve. My position is that Zhuangzi appreciated all this. His skeptical arguments are not meant to be taken literally and are not intended to convert the reader to any sort of radical skepticism. Rather, what Zhuangzi sought to do with his skeptical arguments was to generate the more modest type of doubt that is the province of the everyday skeptic.

Notes

1. I would like to thank Kirk Gable, Kim Kempton, P. J. Ivanhoe, and Bryan van Norden for their kind and useful comments on earlier drafts of this paper.

2. See Watson 1968, 38–49. "Discussion on Making All Things Equal" is Watson's translation of the Chinese *Qi Wu Lun*, the title of the second chapter of the Zhuangzi. There has been some debate over how exactly to translate the title of this chapter (see, for example, Allinson 1989, 133–137, and Graham 1981, 48), but for my purposes nothing in particular hinges on it.

In the paper, I will be focusing almost entirely on the Inner Chapters (chapters one through seven) of the *Zhuangzi*, which I take to be the authentic core of the book. It may be that the writer of the Inner Chapters was not named "Zhuangzi." These chapters may not have even been written by a single person. I do not think that it matters much for my arguments one way or another. The Inner Chapters have a stylistic and thematic unity that suggest the work of a single person or multiple people of similar mind and intent. It is to that person or those people that I mean to refer when I use the name "Zhuangzi."

3. Hansen alters his position somewhat in *A Daoist Theory of Chinese Thought* (New York: Oxford University Press, 1992).

4. Herrlee Creel, *Chinese Thought from Confucius to Mao Tse-Tung* (Chicago: University of Chicago Press, 1953), p. 114.

5. In Allinson 1989 there are also occasional suggestions that a therapeutic approach to Zhuangzi's relativism might be appropriate (see, for example, p. 23), but these suggestions evaporate in Allinson's more detailed analysis of relativism and in his discussions of particular skeptical passages (Watson 1968, 14–22, 78–96, 122–126). Allinson does, however, seem to want to attribute therapeutic intent to some other types of passages, such as those that consist of double-headed questions and the passages about use-

lessness (see, for example, 23–27, 167). Wong 1984 also briefly discusses a therapeutic view of Zhuangzi, but without particular attention to his skepticism, as does Wu 1982, 33–36.

6. See Mair 1983 for a rather different defense of this view.

7. Whether this is due to Zhuangzi himself or later compilers is uncertain, and for my purposes it does not really matter.

8. Watson 1968, 29. See also Wu 1990, 59.

9. What exactly this point is has been the subject of much debate. See, for example, Allinson 1989, 41–44, Hansen in Mair 1983, 51, and Wu 1990, 69–75.

10. Yao and Shun were legendary sage kings of the past, cultural heroes held up as exemplars by the Confucians.

11. Allinson 1989, 38 makes a similar point.

12. Although there are no quotation marks in Classical Chinese, the form "X *yue*" clearly indicates direct quotations.

13. See Allinson 1989, 157–166, for an interesting discussion of Zhuangzi's use of Confucius as a mouthpiece.

14. Graham may be right in interpreting some of these claims as doctrines of opponents, merely brought up for dispute and so not really asserted—but even Graham does not venture to interpret in such a way all the claims Zhuangzi makes and then questions. The example I give is not so interpreted by Graham. See Graham 1981, 51–56 for some examples of this interpretive technique.

15. I use the Watson translation here, as usual. Graham's translation is quite different, and he attempts to reconstruct something of a coherent argument from it in a long note that follows. As one might guess, however, even Graham's reconstruction only makes dubious sense.

16. Actually, these truisms seem less obviously truisms once one realizes that they are key assumptions of Mohism, Yangism, and Confucianism, respectively. On seeking and forgetting, especially, see Cua 1977.

17. Many of the ideas expressed in this section are extensions of ideas suggested to me my P. J. Ivanhoe, and can be found in his 1993. See also Eno 1991, Kjellberg 1993, 99–112, and Graham 1989, 199–202.

18. In the contemporary West, the most ardent spokesman for this position has been Michael Polanyi. See, for example, chapters 9–12 of his *Knowing and Being: Essays*, Marjorie Greene, ed. (London: Routledge, Kegan, and Paul, 1969).

19. Graham considers this passage to be from the "School of Zhuangzi." See Graham 1981, 139–140.

20. It is interesting to note that even if the sages were alive, Wheelwright Pian would have to hold that their writings could not convey what it is the duke seeks. The issue of their death is a red herring.

21. Following Watson's translation, I shall refer to the cook as "Cook Ding," but see Kjellberg 1993, 34, and Wu 1990, 285, for different interpretations of the cook's name.

22. Actually, even understanding and carrying out linguistically formulated rules requires certain ineffable skills. But this only means that the same kind of analysis can be applied at different levels of behavior: the clumsy cook may be very skillful at walking across the room to pull ingredients off the shelf.

23. This section owes a substantial debt to Hansen in Mair 1983 and Graham 1989. They are surely right in casting the kinds of arguments that appear here as part of a dialogue with the Mohists and the School of Names. I shall not explore issues of historical context here, however.

24. I do not intend to be taking any controversial stands here on the use of the word "meaning." My central point is the one about inscrutability, which I take to be fairly obvious. Notice, however, that not every noun and adjective in English works in the way I describe. For example, one can use the word "thing," even if one cannot imagine anything that is not a thing.

25. It is interesting to note, however, that Wang Ni's argument for moral relativism here hinges entirely on aesthetic examples.

26. Hansen in Mair 1983, 45-46. The passage translated here is the same as the one translated in Watson 1968, 39–40. Italics are Hansen's. Hansen's Wade-Giles romanization has been converted to Pinyin.

27. Graham and Hansen also take this to be the natural conclusion of Zhuangzi's arguments. See Graham 1981, 53 and Hansen in Mair 1983, 45–46.

28. Mount Tai is a paradigm example of a large mountain. Pengzu lived from the twenty-sixth to the seventh centuries B.C.E. by traditional dating.

29. I suppose one could quibble at this point about what Zhuangzi is really "saying" in the skeptical passages. If we allow that in some sense he is "saying" something rather different with the passages than what is conveyed by their literal meaning (such as that we should be more modest in our epistemic self-evaluations), then in the same sense we can allow that Zhuangzi does "mean what he says."

30. Graham considers this passage to be from the "School of Zhuangzi." See Graham 1981, 121.

31. The passage contains an ambiguity I shall leave unresolved: Is the final position meant to express a change of mind (or phrasing) and a revision of his "halfway" position, or is Zhuangzi drawing a distinction between the position he would take and the ideal course, which perhaps he is incapable of taking? For my discussion, nothing of import hangs on the resolution of this ambiguity.

32. Yearley does not counsel that we unreservedly see Zhuangzi as employing a rhetoric of exaggeration. He would like us to see also a radical side of Zhuangzi—a side of Zhuangzi that I am doing my best to render mundane, or as Yearley would say, "conventional."

33. Ivanhoe 1993 discusses several such skepticisms in relation to Zhuangzi.

34. See Descartes, and for a useful discussion of it, Barry Stroud, *The Significance of Philosophical Skepticism* (Oxford: Clarendon Press, 1984). Of course, Descartes' skepticism is not confined to dream-doubt in the early *Meditations*, and Descartes argues against philosophical skepticism in his later *Meditations*.

35. Some of the heaviest weather is drummed up in Allinson 1989, 71–110, and Wu 1990.

36. This assumes what is sometimes called "the closure of knowledge under known consequence"—that is, that if one knows that p and one knows that p implies q, then one knows that q. Although this principle of closure seems plausible, at least when one is consciously considering both p and p implies q, some have argued against it. See for example Fred Dretske, "Epistemic Operators," *Journal of Philosophy* 67 (1970).

37. For a comparison of Zhuangzi and Sextus, see Kjellberg 1994.

38. See Kjellberg 1993 and Ivanhoe 1993. Eno 1991 and Yearley in Mair 1983 seem to endorse similar views.

39. The latter passage is cited on pp. 110–111 of this paper . Ivanhoe 1993, 642-643 interprets the butterfly dream as a general allegory on spiritual awakening (which presumably involves, among other things, skepticism about linguistic categories; Ivanhoe 1993, 648-651), and so, apparently, does not take the passage as revealing sincere doubt about the possibility of knowledge through the senses. Kjellberg describes the passage as marked by Zhuangzi's "usual hyperbole" (1993, 134).

40. Compare his *Language and Logic in Ancient China* (Ann Arbor: University of Michigan Press, 1983), 92, and *A Daoist Theory of Chinese Thought* (New York: Oxford University Press, 1992), 292–296.

41. Hansen strives admirably, but not quite satisfactorily I think, to show how such passages can be worked into a linguistic view of Zhuangzi's skepticism in Hansen 1992, 292–296.

42. That is, the first part of the passage in question. As the passage continues, Wang Ni seems to grow less and less skeptical, until, at the end of the passage, he is sketching a portrait of the "Perfect Man" (Watson 1968, 46). I do not think this change in Wang Ni undermines my point at all. Indeed, I take it as support for my position that Zhuangzi does not sincerely subscribe to Wang Ni's skepticism (though he may not support Wang Ni's conception of the Perfect Man, either).

43. Or, in the Chinese, 知 *zhi*. I take Peter Unger to be advancing a skepticism of this sort in his *Ignorance: a Case for Skepticism* (Oxford: Clarendon Press, 1975).

44. Actually, Hansen argues in his 1992, 290 that the relativist cannot compare perspectives along an evaluative dimension at all, even to say they are equal. But this only moves my objection up a level: on the one hand Zhuangzi seems to be comparatively evaluating approaches to life while on the other hand, as a relativist, according to Hansen, he must deny that such approaches are evaluatively comparable.

45. I take the ideal of open-mindedness I am arguing for here to be compatible with that laid out by Kjellberg in his 1993, 139–146.

FIVE

Language: The Guest of Reality—
Zhuangzi and Derrida
on Language, Reality, and Skillfulness

Mark Berkson

Philosophers and writers striving for truth have continuously searched for a vehicle that would deliver the world unmolested to the human mind. For some, this has been the pure light of reason, for others direct perceptual experience. Yet what all philosophy and literature share in common is that they are in a *language*. Ultimately, then, philosophers have had to confront the problem of language, not only in regard to how thought is conveyed in text, but also to how the world is experienced by those searching for truth or meaning, for the inquiry must be conducted from within the edifice of language. While some have looked at language as a transparent window, others have seen it as a prison house. In the end, all of those concerned with the possibility of gaining access to truth must think seriously about the relationship between the individual, language and reality.

Two thinkers who deal extensively with this problem are the fourth-century B.C.E. Daoist thinker Zhuangzi and the contemporary French philosopher and literary critic Jacques Derrida. While both have been labeled iconoclasts, and their ideas seen as subversive, they have both had a profound influence on their traditions. Some modern thinkers have found the comparative study of their views on language to be a fruitful source of insight,[1] and many of them have emphasized what have been labeled Derrida's and Zhuangzi's "essential similarities" (Xie and Chen 1992, 373). One has gone so far as to write, "With the exception of the difference in emphasis, Zhuangzi and Derrida make essentially the same statement" (Yeh 1983, 115). Indeed, there are significant similarities: both thinkers frequently take aim at the same targets and often employ similar rhetorical weapons. Yet their purposes in doing so, their ultimate goals, are vastly different. This crucial, but often overlooked, point should militate against seeing Zhuangzi as a fourth-century B.C.E. deconstructionist or Derrida as a twentieth-century Daoist. In this paper, I will discuss the treatment of language in Zhuangzi and Derrida and its relationship to their overall projects. I will show that while they both had similar negative projects, Zhuangzi differed from Derrida in presenting a positive picture as well. Exploring this distinction will, I hope, help to shed light on the projects of both.

Response to Tradition

Zhuangzi and Derrida are language skeptics for they both doubt the ability of language to present reality objectively; language, they argue, cannot be seen as a vehicle that can deliver a picture of the world as it actually is. There can be no "true accounts" of the world in the form of propositional claims. From this insight, they both launch attacks on traditional philosophy based on the fact that it tries to use language in this way. Before delving more deeply into their philosophies of language, I will look briefly at the traditions to which they are responding.

Both are challenging traditions that put *meaning* into language in an authoritative way. They see all efforts to describe the world accurately in language as illusory, for language itself inevitably foils the attempts. They view the traditional philosophy that precedes them as misguided, arguing that it cannot be a conveyer of pure reason or truth because of the disruptive and self-undermining effects of the language it must, by necessity, use. Philosophers cannot dispense with language and arrive at truth; philosophy will always remain trapped in language.

Derrida was a product of late-1960s France, a period infused with a revolutionary zeal aimed at overthrowing traditional structures. Derrida and others in the poststructuralist movement directed their spirited protest in two directions, institutional and theoretical. The institutional target was the French academic establishment, seen as an ossified preserver of traditions. The academic scene is described by John Ellis: "An unusual degree of rigidity and conservatism prevailed in French universities in the midsixties when deconstruction emerged. A version of literary history and biography that had gone unchanged since the nineteenth century held complete sway in the field. . . . nowhere was there more conformism in what was taught to university students. There was one truth, and it was contained in Gustave Lanson's literary history of France, which students were required to commit to memory."[2] The second target was represented most immediately by the structuralist movement, which looked for meaning behind the structures found in literature, media, social institutions, and elsewhere. Structuralists believed that one can decode these structures to find the center, the deeper meanings underneath the primary level of the form (the signifier). This is not to say that structuralists were conservative; Roland Barthes, who held many structuralist assumptions, wrote subversive essays. Derrida himself was greatly influenced by the structuralist movement.

Traditionally, forms were looked at simply as windows to see through; by turning his gaze at the forms themselves, Barthes forces the reader to acquire a new stance of attention toward the different levels of meaning presented. Barthes argues that most readers who encounter myth see the simple first-order meaning. He works to decode the structures and expose the deeper levels. For Barthes, myth is a form of speech that is *ideologically charged*, but the charge is hidden. In unpacking the political signification, the subtext is exposed and the myth is decoded.[3]

What Derrida refutes is that there is any ultimate meaning that one can get to, there is no decoding to be done, for there is no center to reach. Derrida is responding to those conservative elements in structuralism that claim that texts have meanings hidden in them, and that the critic's job is to seek them out, to decode them, and expose the meanings underneath the signs. Christopher Norris describes conservative structuralism as a view that "lends support to traditional ideas of the text as a bearer of stable (if complicated) meanings and the critic as a faithful seeker after truth in the text. . . . Deconstruction is avowedly 'poststructuralist' in its refusal to accept the idea of structure as in any sense given or objectively 'there' in the text."[4]

While structuralism is Derrida's most immediate precursor, his ultimate target is "logocentrism," seen by him as the ruling illusion of Western metaphysical thought since Plato, which can be defined as the belief that one can get at "the truth" (the origin, objective reality) through "the word." Ellis defines logocentrism as "a belief that there is an order of meaning existing independently of the structure of any given language that is the foundation for all else" (Ellis 1989, 35). Derrida believes that this is a kind of ethnocentrism of the West derived largely from phonocentrism, the belief that speech is close to a Platonic realm of pure ideas and that writing must strive to represent speech as accurately as possible in order to be closer to this realm. He writes, "logocentrism is an ethnocentric metaphysics. It is related to the history of the West."[5]

Derrida, in one of his most important works, *Of Grammatology*, states that his project is to negate logocentrism, the "metaphysics of presence." He wants to get away from notions that have permeated Western philosophy and literary theory—that there is "presence" beyond the words, that words can get to something "real" beyond the text, that there is an ultimate "transcendental signified" that can form the foundation of a language system. Derrida identifies "logocentrism and the metaphysics of presence as the exigent, powerful, systematic, and irrepressible desire for such a (transcendental) signified" (Derrida 1976, 49). A signifier cannot simply, transparently yield a view to a transcendental signified, truth, or meaning. For Derrida, any such signified is "always already" a sign, inscribed and mediated, eluding any attempts at finding it in pure form. He sees himself as dismantling centuries of thinking, of turning the philosophical world upside down.[6]

Zhuangzi has a number of opponents, that include both the Confucians and two schools that focus largely on language and employ it analytically, the Neo-Mohists and dialecticians. Zhuangzi, whose closest friend was a member of the latter group, shows great familiarity with their techniques.

Confucius provides a conservative response to societal dissolution, a return to the *li* of the Zhou dynasty, a carefully organized set of rituals, ceremony, and etiquette that govern human behavior and interhuman relations. While there is some debate among Confucian thinkers as to how rigidly the rituals are to be applied, all Confucians to some degree put emphasis on them, believing them to be in harmony with the cosmos. One of the two most important Confucian interpreters of the classical period, Mencius, finds the source of these *li* in human nature itself, within the human *xin* "heart/mind". Mencius describes the structure of the human *xin*, exactly what components it is composed of, and how this structure is properly developed and reflected in Confucian ritual. This idea has its literary parallel in what Jonathan Culler calls the structuralist belief that "structures of meaning correspond to some deep-laid mental 'set' or pattern of mind" (Norris 1991, 3). (Mencius' and the structuralists' notions of innate structures of morality and meaning, respectively, might be seen as akin to Chomsky's innate linguistic structures.)

Language, itself a form of ritual, occupies an important place in the Confucian scheme. Names, titles, and roles must be used properly. The Confucians called for the "rectification of names," whereby the proper matching up of name and reality would bring order to society. The Neo-Mohists took the philosophical position of consequentialism, using sophisticated styles of analytic argumentation in debate that most closely resemble those of the West. Chad Hansen demonstrates that Zhuangzi was very familiar with the styles and methods of argumentation of this school and concludes that "Zhuangzi is a skeptical, relativistic reaction to the philosophy of language of the Neo-Mohists" (Hansen in Mair 1983, 27).

Zhuangzi objects to these other schools on many grounds. They all put a great deal of faith in the power of rational, discursive language and the power of the human *xin* to find solutions through learning, thinking, or disputation. For Zhuangzi, it is the Mencian belief that the *xin* should be the governor of the body that has people in trouble in the first place. Furthermore, both the Confucians and the Mohists have a strong notion of the sage or the political order as a moving force behind societal change. Zhuangzi challenges the idea that politics should be a vehicle for change. Benjamin Schwartz writes, "The historic Zhuangzi moves further than any ancient Chinese thinker in the direction of denying any function to the political order in 'correcting things'."[7] Zhuangzi maintains that the more effort is put into fixing things, the more problems will be created.

What he objects to most is what he sees as the absolutism of Confucians and Mohists, both of whom appeal to Heaven as the source of their normative visions; they both argue that they have determined *shi* "right" and *fei* "wrong", and that their way is objective, immutable, and applies to all individuals. Zhuangzi responds with a relativism based largely on perspectivism and language skepticism. This is the angle Zhuangzi uses to challenge the views of his opponents, arguing that both Confucians and Mohists suffer from the same problem—they are trapped in their limited perspectives. Zhuangzi writes, "You can't discuss the ocean with a well frog—he's limited by the space he lives in. . . . You can't discuss the Way with a cramped scholar—he's shackled by his doctrines" (Watson 1968, 97).

The Challenge to Language

Language Skepticism and Relativism

Zhuangzi and Derrida challenge these traditions with a skepticism of language borne largely from a recognition of language's perspectival and relational relativism. The first describes the relativity of language based on the position of the one using it, who is "always already" operating from within a system of meanings and concepts (what is "here" for one person is "there" for another), while the second describes the recognition that all words or claims within a given language system have meaning only relative to other words or claims that they are set against ("small" is only "small" relative to "large"). There can be no objective representation of reality, for language divides reality up in an arbitrary way that provides meaning only in a relational sense.

This recognition leads to an awareness that any claim must be made from a certain position and that the world is always seen under some description. This means that a writer, before she puts pen to paper, is already bound in a system from which she cannot extricate herself. The tools she is able to use, the concepts with which she can define and describe the world, are already given to her and are, from the beginning, contaminated with centuries of sediment. Derrida writes, "the writer writes *in* a language and *in* a logic whose proper system, laws and life his discourse by definition cannot dominate absolutely. He uses them only by letting himself . . . be governed by the system. . . .The person writing is inscribed in a determined textual system" (Derrida 1976, 158, 160). In a way, then, the text writes the writer as much as the writer writes the text; as the writer can never completely dominate the language she is using, the language can do things the writer did not know or intend.

In an important sense, then, the individual subject, standing apart and making meaning, disappears. There is neither a transcendental subject nor a world outside and independent of the text; rather it is language itself that creates, uses, and speaks them. Language has its own life and its own momentum. Each word contains "traces" of other words in the language system (echoes of words that define it, words that it is not, words that provide difference, words that precede and follow it, previous uses of the word and uses in other texts). In fact, words are only traces, what Derrida calls the "absence of origin," for one cannot get back to the "original" or "true" meaning of any word. Thus, the writer is not a point of origin, for she can never be in complete control of her writing. Writing is, after all, moving counters around within the system of language, and these counters are already laden with traces. There is no point outside the language and logic system that the writer can stand on in order to get a full grasp of the system in which she is working.

Daoism has always shown a deep skepticism of the efficacy of language, so much so that the *Daodejing*, the most famous early Daoist text, advocates abandoning language altogether and returning to the ancient practice of knotting rope to communicate. The very first line of that text reads, "The Dao that can be spoken is not the eternal Dao." Another line reads, "Those who speak do not know; those who know do not speak."

Zhuangzi also shows some of the skepticism of language seen in the *Daodejing*, but he has a much more sophisticated understanding of it and spends far more time addressing the problems and paradoxes of language. (Ironically, he uses it more beautifully than any other classical Chinese thinker.) In one of Zhuangzi's most famous passages on language, he states:

> Saying is not blowing breath, saying says something; the only trouble is that what it says is never fixed. Do we really say something? Or have we never said anything? If you think it different from the twitter of fledgelings, is there proof of the distinction? Or isn't there any proof? By what is the Way hidden that there should be a genuine and a false? By what is saying darkened that sometimes "That's it" and sometimes "That's not"? Wherever we walk how can the Way be absent? Whatever the standpoint how can saying be unallowable? The Way is hidden by formation of the lesser, saying is darkened by its foliage and flowers. And so we have the "That's

it, that's not" of Confucians and Mohists, by which what is *it* for one of them for the other is not, what is *not* for one of them for the other is. If you wish to affirm what they deny and deny what they affirm, the best means is Illumination. (Graham 1981, 52)

Many of Zhuangzi's most important ideas on language are contained within this passage. The problem with language for Zhuangzi is that it depends on the perspective of those speaking, the context and the relation to other words. Thus, while words *do* say something, what they say changes all of the time and cannot be fixed with certainty. The problem with philosophical discourse, such as that between Confucians and Mohists, is that it puts faith in the power of language to take a firm stand and convey ultimate reality.

What this passage also shows is that for Zhuangzi, there *is* an ultimate reality, a true Way.[8] He states, "Wherever we walk, how can the Way be absent?" Thus, the Way is everywhere, but it is hidden when distinctions are made and relied upon. Where does this leave language? Zhuangzi never says that words have no meaning, or that language should not be allowed. In fact, the problem is that *all* statements, not none, are allowable, for they are all, from some standpoint, true. This is what he means by "Whatever the standpoint, how can saying be unallowable?" Zhuangzi asks playfully if language is really different from the twittering of birds, mere sounds. He seems to suggest that, in an important way, it is not. (Yet he goes on to show that some chirps are more *effective* than others.) Graham concludes that Zhuangzi "sees it as the lesson of disputation that one is entitled to affirm or deny anything of anything" (Graham 1981, 53). It is by means of *illumination*, lighting up all sides to expose the relativity and equality of different positions, that one is taught this lesson.

The idea of perspectival relativism leads both Zhuangzi and Derrida to recognize that there is no absolute, correct interpretation of texts or events. Derrida, as will be shown, sees the text as the site of an infinite play of signs that produces numerous (perhaps infinitely) possible meanings.[9] This puts the reader in the role of *producer* rather than consumer; the reader uses the text to create meaning, for there is no stable meaning present in the text.

As no one individual can provide the objectively correct interpretation, there is no way to ultimately adjudicate disputes. Both Zhuangzi and Derrida see the difficulty in deciding between different positions, for each individual's interpretation is dictated from his or her perspective. Stanley Fish, commenting on Derrida's version of this idea, states, "What we have here then are two critics with opposing interpretations, each of whom claims the same word as internal and confirming evidence. Clearly they cannot both be right, but just as clearly there is no basis for deciding between them. One cannot appeal to the text, because the text has become an extension of the interpretive disagreement that divides them."[10]

Zhuangzi also discusses this difficulty in adjudicating disputes:

Suppose you and I have had an argument. . . . Is one of us right and the other wrong? Are both of us right or are both of us wrong? . . . Whom shall we get to decide what is right? Shall we get someone who agrees with you to decide? But if he already agrees with you, how can he decide fairly? Shall we get someone who agrees with me? But if he already agrees with me, how can he decide? Shall we get someone who disagrees with both of us? . . . Shall we get someone who agrees with both of us? . . . Shall we wait for still another person? But waiting for one shifting voice [to pass judgment on] another is the same as waiting for none of them. . . . Forget distinctions. (Graham 1981, 43–44)

Saussure and Relational Relativism

The idea of relational relativism can be understood more clearly by looking closely at the thought of Ferdinand de Saussure. Saussure sees that meaning in language comes not from any absolute mapping of words onto the world, but through the *difference* that exists between words in a given language system. For Saussure, language cannot be understood in individual terms, but synchronically; any individual speech act (*parole*) draws on a language system (*langue*) that must be viewed as a whole.

He provides insight into the arbitrary nature of signifiers, for they gain their meaning only in relation to other words.[11] Signifiers are defined not by signifieds but by other signifiers.[12] (A word is what it is by virtue of what it is not.)* This difference comes in two ways. The first is that of *phonic* difference, for example that "cat" is "cat" because it is not "bat" or "rat" (or "cot" or "cab," etc.). These tiny differences in sound create the profound difference in meaning. His more revealing insight is in the second form of difference, that of *conceptual* difference.

The world is not divided up in any natural way; divisions arise only when human beings impose them on the world *via* language. There are not things that are naturally "large" until compared with those things we decide to call "small." Not just the word, but the concept itself is an "arbitrary creation of a language and does not necessarily exist outside of that language" (Ellis 1989, 45).

One example that illustrates conceptual difference is provided by John Ellis and uses water temperature. The temperature of water rises in a smooth continuum without any divisions inherent in its nature (until it changes form). In applying concepts, human beings make decisions as to what constitutes "cold," "cool," "warm," and "hot." Other cultures make different

---

* Compare Berkson's account of "relational relativism" to Schwitzgebel's analysis of the role of boundaries in language (p. 78).—Eds.

divisions using different words. Ellis shows, using German and English, that words commonly thought to have the same meaning (for example, "hot" and "heiss") actually correspond to different temperature ranges.[13] Neither is "correct," for water itself can never be "hot." It is only hot to an individual interacting with it and applying the concept from within a system of terms. Thus, *how* we see the world depends on the language we inherit. The differences and categories are not "out there" in the world, but in the finite language developed to classify and organize the chaotic and infinite world for us. The relationship between signifier and concept is arbitrary in that it is *chosen* (agreed upon by the linguistic community), but not totally random: A given sign occupies a distinct and important position within the system.[14]

This arbitrariness and dependence on difference is, for Derrida, a source of great instability. Not only must words be located within the language system to derive their meaning, but the meaning of words continuously changes with context. Derrida would argue that, as a sign is "iterable" or citable, the possibility of alteration is built into the sign itself; it can never mean the same thing twice, for it always appears in a different context. He writes, "Every sign . . . can be cited. . . . In so doing it can break with every given context, engendering an infinity of new contexts in a manner which is absolutely illimitable."[15] What is reproduced is inevitably altered, a possibility that is inscribed within even the first use of the mark. Even in the phrase "Blah blah," the second word does not have the same "meaning" as the first by virtue of the fact that it follows a "blah."

Zhuangzi has many affinities with Saussure in this regard. Zhuangzi recognizes that there are facts about the world, but the way these are labeled and divided are arbitrary. This is why Zhuangzi states, "Things are so because they are called so. What makes them so? Making them so makes them so" (Graham 1981, 35). Zhuangzi states that the "name is only the guest of reality" (Graham 1981, 26). Names have no permanent status as definitive description. They are only temporary invitees, serving a job that is useful, but provisional and limited. Thus, there can be no correct account, as all accounts are relational and relative. They both recognize that when an infinite world is divided up into finite categories, arbitrary human choice will play the defining role. Zhuangzi warns, "If you use what is limited to pursue what has no limit, you will be in danger" (Graham 1981, 46).

Elsewhere, Zhuangzi states, "The Way has never known boundaries; speech has no constancy. But because of [the recognition of a] 'this', there came to be boundaries. . . . The sage embraces things. Ordinary men discriminate among them and parade their discriminations before others. So I say, those who discriminate fail to see" (Graham 1981, 39). In embracing all things, the sage sees the relativity of all things, while others are trapped in taking arbitrary distinctions for "truth."

Zhuangzi speaks often of the relational aspects of words. He writes, "From the point of view of differences, if we regard a thing as big because there is a certain bigness to it, then among all the ten thousand things there are none that are not big. If we regard a thing as small because there is a certain smallness to it, then among the ten thousand things there are none that are not small. If we know that heaven and earth are tiny grains and the tip of a hair is a range of mountains, then we have perceived the laws of difference" (Graham 1981, 101). Zhuangzi's and Derrida's awareness of the relativistic quality of language leads them to attack systems of thought founded on theories of opposition.

The Problem of Binary Opposites

Their insight into language as a relational system of arbitrary signifiers leads Zhuangzi and Derrida to focus a great deal of attention on overturning "binary" logic, the idea that binary opposites naturally divide the world. Much of philosophy and literary criticism is based on the analysis of categories of binary opposites: right/wrong, light/dark, good/bad, true/false, etc. Both thinkers try to overturn the assumption that the world can be carved up in such natural dichotomies, for each term derives its meaning from the existence of the other, and ultimately blends in smoothly with the other.

Deconstruction, as will be shown below, denies origins, ultimate meaning, and first principles. These can always be shown simply to be *part* of a system, rather than the foundation for it. Such principles are always defined by what they *exclude*, by their opposite. This creates the system of binary pairs that has driven the traditions to which Derrida and Zhuangzi respond. The structuralist tradition, for example, uses opposites (light/dark, nature/culture) as methods of analysis to unlock the meaning in texts. Derrida tries to deconstruct these pairs, to show how they ultimately collapse into each other. Terry Eagleton sees this as a principal concern of deconstruction in general, writing, "'Deconstruction' is the name given to the critical operation by which such oppositions can be partly undermined, or by which they can be shown to partly undermine each other in the process of textual meaning."[16]

Eagleton points out that what is "outside" is also "inside"; in other words, while what is light is defined as what is *not* dark (thus, dark is kept outside of light), the very idea of darkness is deeply embedded in light as what gives it its very meaning. Deconstruction shows how the frontier between the two members of a pair dissolves, how each inheres within the other. Derrida states in an interview, "the movement of *differance*, as that which produces different things, that which differentiates, is the common root of all the oppositional concepts that mark our language, such as, to take only a few examples, sensible/intelligible, intuition/signification, nature/culture, etc. As a common root, *differance* is also the element of the *same* . . . in which these oppositions are announced."[17] Derrida attempts to create a nonbinary logic, a system that uses paradox and subverts the law of noncontradiction. Barbara

Johnson states, "In its deconstruction of the either/or logic of noncontradiction that underlies Western tradition, Derrida's writing attempts to elaborate an 'other' logic."[18]

There is a political agenda underlying much of the opposition to binary opposites, for such pairs are often typical of ideologies that want to elevate one side at the expense of another: central/marginal, white/black, male/female, etc. Derrida writes, "an opposition of metaphysical concepts (for example, speech/writing, presence/absence, etc.) is never the confrontation of two terms, but a hierarchy and the order of subordination" (Derrida 1988, 21). By showing how such pairs collapse into themselves, deconstruction subverts the attempt of the dominant side to keep the other excluded.[19]

This gives rise to the deconstructive technique of seizing a marginal element of the text to subvert the "dominant" theme. The dominant must do a great deal of work to keep the "Other" at a distance, for if the Other is brought too close and shown to be inherent in the dominant, the pair collapses and the original "meaning" of the text is destroyed by the emergence of its opposite. This is the technique employed in "That Dangerous Supplement," where Rousseau's dichotomies of nature/culture and speech/writing are unraveled by using the recurring word "supplement" to break down the artificial barrier erected between them (Derrida 1976, 141–164). Norris writes, "Wherever the primacy of 'nature' (or speech) is opposed to the debasements of 'culture' (or writing), there comes into play an aberrant logic which inverts the opposition and cuts away the ground of its very meaning" (Norris 1991, 35).

Daoism has always been concerned with the role of binary opposites, and the *Daodejing* has a number of passages that deal with these pairs. In one chapter, there is a section that shows how opposites are mutual causations of each other, and that only when one is recognized does the other come into play:

> When the people of the world all know beauty as beauty,
> There arises the recognition of ugliness.
> When they all know the good as good,
> There arises the recognition of evil.
> And so: Being and non-being produce each other;
> Difficult and easy complete each other;
> Long and short contrast each other;
> High and low distinguish each other;
> Sound and voice harmonize each other;
> Front and behind accompany each other.[20]

Zhuangzi's clearest and most eloquent exposition on this theme occurs in the following passage, where he shows the relativity of binary opposites: "Everything has its 'that', everything has its 'this'. . . . So I say, 'that' comes out of 'this' and 'this' depends on 'that'—which is to say that 'this' and 'that' give birth to each other. But where there is birth there must be death; where there is death there must be birth. . . . Where there is recognition of right there must be recognition of wrong; where there is recognition of wrong there must be recognition of right. Therefore the sage does not proceed in such a way, but illuminates all in the light of Heaven. He too recognizes a 'this' but a 'this' which is also a 'that', a 'that' which is also a 'this'" (Graham 1981, 35). Thus, Zhuangzi's attack on binary opposites comes from his aware-ness of perspectival and relational relativism. But Zhuangzi, unlike Derrida, believes there is a way to escape this. In order to become a sage, one must "illuminate all in the light of Heaven." One escapes the perspectivism of human-centered points of view trapped within systems by escaping the sys-tems altogether in a Heaven's-eye view that illuminates all things to show their relativity and ultimate equality (but not identity). Using the image of light, most people can be seen shining flashlights on different spots, think-ing they have found the complete truth; from within their limited perspec-tives, they argue their positions. When the lights are turned on, all are seen to be arguing different aspects of the same thing. *Elephant fable*

Practically, what would holding such a position be like for the sage? It is doubtful that one could maintain the Heaven's-eye view consistently and truly see the equality of all things. But if the sage can achieve this insight for even a short time, he or she can reenter the world of human perspective with the knowledge of the relativity of all claims, and will no longer stand entrenched in a position of "absolute, objective truth." This is why the sage still "recognizes a 'this', but a 'this' which is also a 'that'." Zhuangzi can be understood as holding the view that competing thinkers do not really dis-agree. They simply divide up the world into It and Other from different standpoints. While all things *are* equal from Heaven's point of view, ulti-mately we are human beings who occupy a particular place in the world. The ability to *recognize* the existence of a Heavenly point of view will be enough to change how one lives, for it will give one a greater awareness that allows one to live a natural, *human* life without being trapped in the false confidence of one's limited perspective.

Zhuangzi discusses this using the metaphor of "the piping of Heaven." Zhuangzi describes the piping of Heaven as "blowing on the ten thousand things in a different way, so that each can be itself—all take what they want for themselves, but who does the sounding?" (Graham 1981, 32). In other words, each individual is unique and sounds different (will have a different viewpoint and nature), but underlying all is the sound of Heaven; behind all of the differences, there is an all-encompassing, underlying Dao. Those who do not see this are stuck in their limited perspective, thinking that they have the whole truth. Zhuangzi criticizes such individuals, stating, "They cling to their position as though they had sworn before the gods, sure that they are holding on to victory" (Graham 1981, 32).

The commentator Wang Fuzhi (1619–1692) emphasizes this aspect of Zhuangzi's thought.[21] His interpretation is that Zhuangzi's work is composed of dyads that have meaning only when they are put together (like the wind and the pipes that only sound when they come in contact with each other). The interaction between the two partners in a dyad produces sound and life; the key to understanding the Dao is not in either member of the dyad, but in their dynamic interaction. This is represented by *liang xing*, "walking with both things", which means one should not get trapped in either side of the dyad, but accept both halves. One should not apply conventional categories, but rather foster a receptivity to all things. Zhuangzi believes that the problem with Confucians and Mohists is that they get trapped on one side of the dyad, either *shi*, "right"/"that's it", or *fei*, "wrong"/"that's not" and argue against the other from that position. Much of Zhuangzi's therapy is designed to get the individual to escape this trap, to achieve the Heaven's-eye view (or simply an awareness of its existence), and to maintain that state of receptivity and awareness.

We can now have a richer appreciation of Zhuangzi's statement that "words have something to say," but what they say "is not fixed." By focusing on the relativity, ambiguity and relational nature of language, he takes down the barriers separating words considered opposite by traditional points of view. Graham writes that for Zhuangzi, "words have no fixed meanings except in the artificial conditions of intellectual debate" (Graham 1981, 26). The sage does not get caught up in these conditions, but sees language as the dynamic process it is. According to Wu Kuang-ming, Zhuangzi opposes opposition, he has a "position of no position." What this "affirmative nonposition" means is that "Zhuangzi affirms every view. . . without being stuck in it. Life is larger than logic. . . Zhuangzi is at home everywhere."[22]

Methods: Apophatic Language

As authors, both Zhuangzi and Derrida run into a problem: How can one who is a language skeptic trying to undermine the view of language as a conveyor of truth, meaning, or reality *use* language to perform the task? How can they work within language when they mistrust it, and how can language be dismantled from within language? They are both very conscious that any attempts to "prove" their positions via rational, discursive language will only undermine themselves. They resort to other methods that bring about the desired effect without falling prey to their own destructive power.

Zhuangzi and Derrida are both antirationalists and language skeptics, doubting the ability of reason and language to reach or communicate ulti-mate reality and truth.[23] As such, they face a problem if they want to com-municate—they must necessarily talk about what is uncommunicable. Yet they both recognize that the problem is not with language and reason per se, but only a certain use of them. With the correct understanding, language can serve an important purpose in bringing the reader closer to the right frame of mind, pointing him or her in the right direction (even if that direction leads to recognizing the failure of language itself). For antirationalists like Zhuangzi and Derrida, what language *does* is more important than what it says. To this end, both of them (like other antirationalists such as Plotinus and Nāgārjuna) use apophatic language.[24]

The word "apophasis" is Greek for "denial" and comes from the world *apophanai*, which means "to deny." In its common usage it means to mention something by not mentioning it (for example, "We won't talk about the fact that you lied to me first," or "I won't mention your criminal record"). In this paper I will take it to involve 1) a recognition that nothing about the topic can be said directly or referentially, and 2) the subsequent use of language in a negative or indirect way. In this sense, it is trying to say something without really saying it.[25]

Apophatic language has a number of characteristics, all of which are found in the writing of Zhuangzi and Derrida. The first of these is the apol-ogy and pact.[26] The writer often begins with an apology that says, in effect, although I have no choice but to use language here, I won't be using it in *that* way, and please don't take it as such. Michael Sells describes this as an "acknowledgment that the terms used in reference to the unlimited are in-correct and should not be taken referentially" (Sells 1985, 50). This involves a pact between the reader and writer that, although language is going to be used, it must not be taken as definitive and referential. The reader must initially accept an essentially incorrect or misleading use of language and names, and continuously keep in mind that language is being used in a "tem-porary," withdrawing and pragmatic way (like the Wittgensteinian ladder that can be kicked away once it has done its job). The other elements of apophatic language are the undermining of binary logic; the use of "antirational" or nondiscursive language (for example, analogical or symbolic language, puzzle, paradox, humor or play, stories and parables, and visual imagery); and self-undermining, regression and *reductio ad absurdum*. (We have already seen many examples of these, above.)

Derrida, like Zhuangzi, recognizes that words say something but have no fixed meaning, and he conveys this idea through words "under erasure."* While he leaves the word on the page, which is an acknowledgment that

---

* Compare Derrida's idea of writing "under erasure" to Sextus Empiricus' description of skeptical arguments as "crossing themselves out on their own" (p. 7).—Eds.

something is being said, he puts a line through it to call into question exactly *what* is being said. This is his apophatic marker. He recognizes that if he is to write, particularly about loaded concepts such as "experience," then he must do it "according to this sort of contortion and contention which the discourse is obliged to undergo" (Derrida 1976, 60). This is his apophatic apology. Having no way out, he uses words (particularly those that carry with them the kind of heavy philosophical baggage that can lead the reader astray) with "embarrassment," saying "we can only make use of (them) under erasure." Iris Murdoch says of this practice, "This 'embarrassing' device, of using a crossed-out word, is intended to alert us to an unusual, stripped, deconstructed sense of a concept which no better words can at present be found to exhibit."[27]

Another angle on this idea is Derrida's idea of "both/and" rather than "either/or." When a text is deconstructed, the original (traditional) meaning is not simply destroyed or replaced by another. It is called into question by showing how the opposite meaning can be supported by other elements of the text. The original idea is *both* subverted *and* retained, showing that no single reading is privileged, and that any one reading contains its opposite. (Similarly, the iterability of a mark "implies *both* identity *and* difference" (Derrida 1988, 53). The mark is neither completely the same nor completely different.) The entire text is left "under erasure," with both the original and opposing meanings left in tension.

Derrida emphasizes that deconstructive readings always leave themselves open to further dismantling. He writes, "the enterprise of deconstruction always in a certain way falls prey to its own work" (Derrida 1976, 24). Deconstruction, for Derrida, is not a theory or a position, but an activity, a dynamic project. It is not advocating any particular reading, but throwing all readings open to question. Derrida takes pains to point out the interrogative nature of the deconstructive project in *Positions*: "It has never been a question of opposing . . . any center to any other center. *Of Grammatology* is not a defense and illustration of grammatology. . . . *Of Grammatology* is the title of a *question*: a question about the necessity of a science of writing . . . (and) a question about the limits of this science" (Derrida 1978, 13). Derrida uses the idea of play and games to describe the deconstructive project, often exhibiting a rhetorical playfulness and flair (see, especially, *Limited Inc.*).[28] For him, the game is in the subverting of rules, creating new texts from old, tipping sacred cows, and showing how texts always unravel if pulled in the right place. He writes, "We think only in signs. . . . One could call *play* the absence of the transcendental signified as limitlessness of play. . . . Here, one must think of writing as a game within language" (Derrida 1976, 50). As anyone who has read Derrida knows, he is fond of making ambiguous, paradoxical, and contradictory statements in an effort to change our way of thinking and overturn traditional Western modes of thought. In *Dissemination*, he writes, "It is thus not simply false to say that Mallarmé is a Platonist or a Hegelian. But it is above all not true. And vice versa" (Derrida 1981, 207).

Zhuangzi continuously turns his own skepticism and wit on himself, deftly escaping the error of taking a position, showing confidence in propositions or labeling another "wrong." Zhuangzi prefaces one discussion by stating, "I'm going to try speaking some reckless words and I want you to listen to them recklessly" (Graham 1981, 42); this is a way of entering into an apophatic pact with the listener. Elsewhere, he begins a speech by saying, "Now I am going to make a statement here. I don't know whether it fits into the category of other people's statements or not. But whether it fits into their category or whether it doesn't, it obviously fits into some category. So in that respect it is no different from their statements. However, let me try making my statement." After making the statement, which is an argument against the possibility of being able to capture the unity of all things in distinctions, Zhuangzi says, "Now I have just said something. But I don't know whether what I have said has really said something or whether it hasn't said something" (Graham 1981, 38). He does not want the words themselves to carry too much weight; he wants the reader/listener to take them lightly, recklessly. Listen to them, he advises, but do not put too much trust in them to express something stable.*

Elsewhere, Zhuangzi illustrates the self-contradictory nature of making any statements at all about a Dao which encompasses all things. He states, "We have already become one, so how can I say anything? But I have just *said* that we are one, so how can I not be saying something? The one and what I said about it make two, and two and the original one make three. If we go on this way, then even the cleverest mathematician can't tell where we'll end. . . . Better not to move, but to let things be!" (Graham 1981, 39). Zhuangzi is making the point that as soon as one *says* that "everything is one," already there are two things, the unity and what one has said about it. Thus, saying can never capture true reality, the Dao. The best thing to do is not to make distinctions, but to "let things be."†

Zhuangzi is playful and poetic. The technique he uses more than any other is that of humor, for he recognizes that if he takes a position, if he attacks another as "wrong," he is committing the same mistake that he is trying to overcome. He laughs at himself and his positions and hopes that he can get others to laugh at themselves and their positions. Whereas Derrida still emphasizes a certain kind of reading and careful analysis that depends on the intellect, on seeing connections and making arguments (as in "That Dangerous Supplement"), Zhuangzi rejects the use of the mind and appeals directly to intuitive, nonrational experience (see below).

---

*Compare Schwitzgebel's contribution to this volume.—Eds.
†Compare p. 122–23, note 8. See also the editors' note on p. 57.—Eds.

Thus, both Zhuangzi and Derrida undermine traditional theories of meaning and opposition. But Derrida stops here, having dismantled those systems he opposes. His deconstructive technique emphasizes, in the words of John Ellis, "debunking the old." However, Zhuangzi, as I will argue, goes on. While undermining and dismantling are important techniques, and a destabilized foundation is a critical *intermediate* position for Zhuangzi, he ultimately uses the awareness fostered by such a position to move the listener or reader into a deep connection with the underlying reality of the Dao.

Derrida: Skillful Undermining

In the deconstructive method, Derrida teaches a kind of reading that undermines any attempt to establish a definitive, or "privileged," interpretation of the text (for any such attempt will only deconstruct itself). Thus, Derrida does not provide a *reading* of a text, but rather a *method* or *process* of reading that ensures that no single reading can ever emerge. The text cannot be a source of meaning and concepts, but a constantly changing, unstable nexus of signifiers, an *activity*. Those who claim that Derrida does not believe in "reality" are distorting his position. It is not that he claims that there is no reality, but rather that we can have no unmediated or noncontextualized access to reality. All we as human beings have is text, inscribed and mediated intermediaries between ourselves and anything that might be "out there." "Text" for Derrida does not simply mean books, magazines, and other paper products; anything inscribed with signs counts as text. This includes the human mind. It is Derrida's position that not even direct perception can give us the world, for the mind is "always already" inscribed, like a writing pad, with concepts, categories, and language (Norris 1987, chapter 6). We always see the world under some interpretation that is inherently unstable, and can only be "provisional and finite" (Derrida 1988, 150). One of his earliest works is an attack on Husserl, who claims that reality can be directly present through perception to human consciousness. For Derrida, then, neither the world "out there" nor the self within can ever be directly present to us. All we have access to are signifiers that, rather than corresponding in any direct way to the world, have meaning only in relation to other signifiers. This is why Derrida claims that there is "nothing outside the text," and that all we have is an infinite "play of signifiers" that can never get outside of text. Derrida writes: "In the absence of a center or origin, everything became discourse. . . . that is to say, a system in which the central signified, the original or transcendental signified, is never absolutely present outside a system of differences. The absence of the transcendental signified extends the domain and the play of signification infinitely."[29] Since, as pointed out by Saussure, signifiers are defined by difference, what any given signifier means is dependent on all of the things it does not mean. Thus, there is in every signifier a "trace" of all of the other signifiers that it is not, and it is defined largely by absence. While every signifier hints at a presence (of a signified), always there is an absence contained within it as well. Derrida sees texts as continuous plays of presence and absence in signifiers, and he uses the word *differance* to capture this idea. There are two meanings to the neologism *differance*, one being "differ" and the other being "defer." In the former we see the Saussurian idea of difference providing meaning. Derrida points out that signifiers also defer meaning, as it always depends on other signifiers (and these on still others), meaning will always be incomplete. Derrida argues that any signified in turn becomes a signifier for something else (for example, a dictionary defines words with other words, which in turn are defined by still others).

Derrida points out that people have always needed the idea of an ultimate, transcendental signified to provide meaning. The hope is that at the end of a chain of signifiers will be a pure meaning beyond which there is no other, something like a Platonic form or God that will provide an absolute foundation upon which the edifice of language can be constructed. This, for Derrida, is an illusion, for we are always left with only text. He writes, "There is not a single signified that escapes . . . the play of signifying references that constitute language" (Derrida 1976, 7). Elsewhere he writes: "That the signified is originally and essentially . . . trace, that it is *always already in the position of signifier*, is the apparently innocent proposition within which the metaphysics of the logos, of presence and consciousness, must reflect upon writing as its death" (Derrida 1976, 73). Another way to think about this is that the meaning of any word depends on its context within the sentence, on words yet to come; the meaning of the sentence depends on the paragraph, which depends on the text, which depends on the meaning of words in other texts and ultimately the *langue* as a whole. As the entire language system is brought in, we are always, in some sense, waiting for the completion of any given meaning.

Beginning with the notion that meaning depends on context, Derrida undermines the stability of meaning by trying to demonstrate "why a context is never absolutely determinable" (Derrida 1988, 3). He writes that it is not only that "nothing exists outside context, as I have often said, but also that the limit of the frame or the border of the context always entails a clause of nonclosure" (Derrida 1988, 152). Given the Derridean picture of textuality and language, what kind of reading does he advocate? Derrida, despite being elusive and paradoxical, does advocate a particular way of reading, a type of skillful interaction with the text, that applies the insights of deconstruction. For Derrida, there is a way that the critical reader *should* approach a text.

The reader must be the creative producer of the text, working to undermine the standard meaning advanced by the author.[30] Derrida writes that the relationship between what a writer does and does not command in the language he uses is a "signifying structure that critical reading should *produce*" (Derrida 1976, 158). Derrida argues that we must go beyond readings that merely repeat the text (what he calls "doubling commentaries"). While these are perhaps necessary as an initial approach, they are not sufficient. He states, "To produce this signifying structure obviously cannot consist of reproducing . . . the conscious, voluntary, intentional relationship that the writer institutes" (Derrida 1976, 158). The reader must use the text to produce new, contradictory readings.[31] In "That Dangerous Supplement," Derrida produces a reading that Rousseau could never have "intended," a reading that, using only the word "supplement," overturns one of Rousseau's main theses. Deconstructive readings must never use anything outside of the text; they are a form of infiltration, operating from within. They need bring in no weaponry of their own, for the language of the text being read already contains in it the seeds of its own overturning. Any reading "cannot legitimately transgress the text toward something other than it, toward a referent . . . or toward a signified outside the text. . . . *There is nothing outside the text*" (Derrida 1976, 158).

In order to maintain the illusion of meaning given by the traditional interpretation (the dominant element of the binary opposite), the text must relegate any ideas that might undermine its intent to the periphery. This is why deconstruction often uses words, phrases, or tropes found in the margins, the footnotes, or "unimportant" details as wedges to get into the text and overturn its central ideas. The barrier between the two elements of the binary pair is stripped away and each is shown to inhere within the other. Terry Eagleton writes, "Derrida's own typical habit of reading is to seize on some apparently peripheral fragment in the work—a footnote, a recurrent minor term or image, a casual allusion—and work it tenaciously through to the point where it threatens to dismantle the oppositions which govern the text as a whole" (Eagleton 1983, 133). Deconstruction is ultimately a technique to show how each text undermines itself, betrays itself, and defeats its own attempt at conveying meaning.*

Derrida's picture is ultimately *negative*. It subverts any attempt to get at reality, undermines all possible interpretations, and shows how any text unravels itself. Derrida points out a great many problems of meaning and interpretation but provides no solution, believing that there is no solution to provide. He has no positive picture, no way to get out of an infinite play of signifiers, a text filled with sediment and traces, in which meaning and reality always remain elusively out of reach. He states; "I try to write in the space in which is posed the question of speech and meaning. I try to write the question:

---

*Compare Loy's account of Daoism and Buddhism as "self-deconstructing" (p. 63).
—Eds.

(what is) meaning to say? Therefore it is necessary in such a space, and guided by such a question, that writing literally mean nothing" (Derrida 1978, 14). His project is that of calling into question. He writes, "To make enigmatic what one thinks one understands by the words 'proximity', 'immediacy', 'presence'. . . is my final intention in this book" (Derrida 1976, 70). Terry Eagleton concludes, "In deconstruction, the winner is the one who has managed to get rid of all his cards and sit with empty hands" (Eagleton 1983, 147).

Zhuangzi: From Undermining to Skill

There are a great number of similarities in Zhuangzi's and Derrida's negative pictures. Like Derrida, Zhuangzi sees the relational, arbitrary component of language; he tries to foster a deep distrust in the powers of reason, conceptual thinking, and discursive language. He believes that no propositions can adequately capture the world, and that the usual logic of binary opposites obscures and distorts rather than reveals. Both Zhuangzi and Derrida deny that ultimate categories of reality can be conveyed directly to the human mind without being altered by language.

Yet, unlike Derrida, Zhuangzi does not stop here. The reason that Zhuangzi dismantles the usual structure of language and reason is to allow a deeper intuition to emerge from within and come into play, an intuition that has been obscured by societal linguistic and conceptual schemes. This allows one to react naturally and spontaneously to the world, rather than through rational decision-making models or preconceived biases. One becomes aware of the true nature of reality, the patterns and movement of nature. One's intuitions allow one to tap into the deep, underlying pulse of the Dao, a pulse normally covered up by the static of human thinking and social constructs; in this way, one attains sagehood and learns to live skillfully (see below).

In this positive picture (and in *having* a positive picture), Zhuangzi departs radically from Derrida. Whereas both are skeptical of reason and perception, Derrida believes this leaves us with no avenue of access to reality; we are left only with text, and we are trapped within an intermediary that can never reach its final destination. Zhuangzi believes there *is* a way the world truly is and that we *do* have access to it if only we give up the usual methods of reason and language and rely on natural intuition. Thus, there is more than just text; there is *unmediated access* to reality. For Zhuangzi, certain kinds of language cover up not absences, but true presences.

Zhuangzi, as shown above, *uses* language in the form of humor, paradox, and parable to undermine our confidence in rational, discursive language. For Zhuangzi, language is not bad per se, it is only a certain type of language that keeps us from discovering the true nature of the world. Language, when creatively and therapeutically used, can bring one to the state needed to discover the deeper reality.

Once the words have done their job, conveyed their intention, and produced a certain state of mind, they should be forgotten. While words should not present theories or positions, they *can* move people; they can shock us out of a certain logic and can be slippery enough that we cannot grab onto them and get stuck with the word instead of the idea it conveys. P. J. Ivanhoe writes that words used in this way "appeal to the spirit and not the rational part of the self" (Ivanhoe 1993, 649). According to Zhuangzi; "The fish trap exists because of the fish; once you've gotten the fish, you can forget the trap. The rabbit snare exists because of the rabbit; once you've gotten the rabbit, you can forget the snare. Words exist because of meaning; once you've gotten the meaning, you can forget the words. Where can I find a man who has forgotten words so I can have a word with him?" (Graham 1981, 140). In the playful last line, Zhuangzi shows that he wants to talk; he does not advocate silence. But he only wants to talk with those who understand the proper role of language.

Zhuangzi proceeds to give illustrations of the place one finds oneself if one escapes these conventions (after he is done "tearing down"), and these are given with his examples of artisans and craftsmen who represent the sage who lives skillfully. These are people who, rather than "knowing that" (as those who debate with propositions do), "know how." They have a knack for living, for moving smoothly through the world. While this knack cannot be definitively described in words, it can be shown through exemplars. Some of the most famous examples are as follows:

> Cook Ding was cutting up an ox for Lord Wenhui. At every touch of his hand, every heave of his shoulder, every move of his feet, every thrust of his knee—zip! zoop! He slithered the knife along with a zing, and all was in perfect rhythm. . . . "Ah, this is marvelous!" said Lord Wenhui. "Imagine skill reaching such heights!" Cook Ding laid down his knife and replied, "What I care about is the Way, which goes beyond skill. When I first began cutting up oxen, all I could see was the ox itself. After three years I no longer saw the whole ox. And now—now I go at it by spirit and don't look with my eyes. Perception and understanding have come to a stop and spirit moves where it wants. I go along with the natural makeup, strike in the big hollows, guide the knife through the big openings, and follow things as they are." (Graham 1981, 47)

In another example, a man dives into a swirling waterfall so swift that "no fish or other water creature can swim in it," but emerges unscathed. When asked how he stays afloat, he replies: "I began with what I was used to, grew up with my nature, and let things come to completion with fate. I go under with the swirls and come out with the eddies, following along the way the water goes and never thinking about myself. That's how I stay afloat" (Graham 1981, 126). Elsewhere:

> Woodworker Qing carved a piece of wood and made a bell stand, and when it was finished, everyone who saw it marveled, for it seemed to be the work of the gods or spirits. When the marquis of Lu saw it, he asked, "What art is it you have?" Qing replied, "My skill is concentrated and all outside distractions fade away. After that, I go into the mountain forests and examine the Heavenly nature of the trees. If I find one of superlative form, and I can see a bell stand there, I put my hand to the job of carving; if not, I let it go. This way, I am simply matching up 'Heaven' with 'Heaven'." (Graham 1981, 127)

> Duke Huan was in his hall reading a book. The Wheelwright Pian . . . said to Duke Huan, "This book Your Grace is reading—may I venture to ask whose words are in it?" "The words of sages," said the duke. "Are the sages still alive?" "Dead long ago." said the duke. "In that case, what you are reading there is nothing but the chaff and dregs of the men of old!" "Since when does a wheelwright have permission to comment on the books I read?" said Duke Huan, "If you have some explanation, well and good. If not, it's your life!" Wheelwright Pian said, "I look at it from the point of view of my own work. When I chisel a wheel . . . the blows of the mallet [must be] . . . not too gentle, not too hard—you can get it in your hand and feel it in your mind. You can't put it into words, and yet there's a knack to it somehow. I can't teach it to my son and he can't learn it from me. So I've gone my seventy years and at my age I'm still chiseling wheels. When the men of old died, they took with them the things that couldn't be handed down. So what you are reading there must be nothing but the chaff and dregs of the men of old." (Watson 1968, 152–3)

There are other "skill stories," but the main lessons may be drawn from these four. First, there is a way the world really is, a true reality, an underlying Dao. While this cannot be accessed through words, it can be experienced by those who lose themselves in a skill, whose rational mind falls away to leave room for intuition. "Knowing that" may be important for acquiring the skill originally, but once one "has it," one must reach the point of "knowing how," a point where one loses the self, the rules and concepts, and enters a type of "pure experience." It is only when "perception and understanding stop and spirit moves where it wants" that one can achieve this state. It is in such states that, in a sense, the sage no longer acts; rather, the Dao acts through the sage.* These are states often reached by great musicians or athletes who are so absorbed in the moment that they simply perform effortlessly and spontaneously. Like Cook Ding moving his knife through the hollows and openings, and the diver moving through the swirls and eddies, one who lives in this mode will move effortlessly through the currents of the world.

Second, each individual has a spontaneous nature that will emerge and respond when one escapes the prison of rationality. The diver simply "grew up with (his) nature"; Woodworker Qing, who empties himself completely before going out into the woods, matches up the Heavenly nature within him with the Heaven without. This is the goal of the sage—acting from the true inner nature, the sage taps into the Dao, matching up "Heaven with Heaven."

Finally, what Wheelwright Pian points out is that skillful living cannot be described in words; it is a "knack" that must be acquired. The most important things cannot be handed down, even by sages.

What these skillful sages have in common is a mind that is open and responsive to the situation, a mind that does not bring preconceptions along with it.† This allows these sages to respond with intuition in complete awareness. Zhuangzi describes the perfect man as one who "uses his mind like a mirror . . . responding but not storing. Therefore he can win out over things and not hurt himself" (Graham 1981, 95). Zhuangzi advocates the technique of "fasting of the mind," which seems to suggest emptying the mind of its preconceptions, logic, and tendency to want to dominate the other organs of the body; this state, like the state achieved by the skillful artisans described above, will allow the intuition and innate tendencies to take over. The method is "don't listen with your mind, but listen with your spirit. . . . Spirit is empty and waits on all things. . . . Emptiness is the fasting of the mind" (Graham 1981, 54). The mind, emptied of preconceptions, will be continuously receptive and aware, tenuous, and clear like a mirror, reflecting all things. In this state, one can react spontaneously to the world.

Sages live in the world without getting caught up in it, just as Zhuangzi, the skillful user of language, uses language without getting caught up in it. For Zhuangzi, "the hard thing is to walk without touching the ground" (Graham 1981, 54). This is the ultimate goal of the sage, and shows that the sage is in the world, but not of it; within language, but not its prisoner. Zhuangzi's sages are not recluses or hermits; they remain in the world. He does not, like Laozi, advocate any return to a primitive, rural utopia. Such a view would be putting a value on one form of social organization over another, falsely believing one to be the cure for our illness. The freedom that

---

*See editors' note on page 154.—Eds.

†Compare the ideal of openmindedness in Kjellberg and Schwitzgebel.—Eds.

Zhuangzi advocates is an inner one. This is what he means by "roaming free inside the cage." Thus, for Zhuangzi, while language cannot give a complete picture of the Dao ("The Dao that can be spoken is not the eternal Dao"), it can play an important role in bringing one to a state where one *can* have access to the Dao. The skillful use of language, the kind that is dynamic, changes with the situation and responds freely to the situation, plays a critical role in Zhuangzi's therapy. It must be evocative rather than declarative, tentative rather than affirming. What language *does* to the reader of the *Zhuangzi* is more important than what is says. Its ultimate goal is to produce the awareness, spontaneity, and skill of a Cook Ding or a Wheelwright Pian.

Conclusion

There are important similarities in how Zhuangzi and Derrida approach language; both of them share a similar *negative* project. They both point out the relativistic, arbitrary elements in language. Both employ apophatic language in order to dismantle the rationalist project and undermine the reader's confidence in the ability of language to carry or convey stable meaning or absolute reality. They both use a variety of techniques to unravel others' positions, poke holes in arguments, and show the absurdity of certain claims. Both advocate approaches that will put the reader or listener in a certain state of mind—skeptical, receptive to paradox, open to the acceptance of both sides of binary opposites.

However, Derrida leaves us with only the negative picture. He proposes only a technique for dismantling, whereas Zhuangzi provides a therapy for better living. While language might be no different than the "twittering of birds," Zhuangzi wants to chirp a uniquely therapeutic song. He moves the reader in a certain way; while many of his stories defy analysis and rational understanding, it is that very fact that allows his therapy to work. Perhaps it is only when the reader throws up his hands and realizes the mind won't get him all the way, that the deeper intuitions are allowed to take over and the positive picture takes shape.

Derrida would critique the notions of the Dao, unmediated access to reality, true nature, and intuition as falling back into the metaphysics of presence, believing there is a way out of and beyond text.[32] Derrida would see any attempt at soteriology as wishful thinking. We must, he would argue, become reconciled to the absence of any such salvific presence. He would reject Zhuangzi's formulation of language as the guest of reality. For Derrida, reality is the guest of language.

Zhuangzi's reply would probably be in the form of an attempt to free the deconstructionist from getting stuck in the discourse of deconstruction so that he could *experience* the Dao. Ultimately, arguing back and forth is no way to get at the Dao. Language can only take one part of the way, and no amount of "convincing" can do what direct experience can do. Only skillful activity, and the practice of techniques such as "sitting in forgetfulness" and "fasting of the mind," can give one access to the Dao.[33]

While much would remain unsettled, Zhuangzi, I believe, would be immune from the kind of argument that Zhang Longxi levels against him—namely, that he suffers from the sort of logocentrism that has plagued thinkers like Plato in the West. Zhang writes, "Since intuition is what Daoism emphasizes . . . this contrast between intuition and expression already includes the East in the tradition of the metaphysics of presence. Logocentrism, therefore, does not inhabit just the Western way of thinking" (Zhang 1985, 394–395). While certain thinkers in the "East" may, indeed, fall into this kind of logocentric thinking, Zhuangzi is not one of them. Unlike Plato, he does not bring one to any solid ground, trying to get us instead to cultivate the tenuous, mirrorlike mind. One cannot construct the edifice of language on the "presence" of the Dao, in the way one could with transcendental signifieds like the Platonic forms or God, because the Dao is not a stable "thing" that can provide such a foundation. It is always elusive, always evading language; in no way, then, can it logocentrically support or be revealed by language. While there may be a "presence" in Zhuangzi that is absent in Derrida, it cannot be described as a logocentric one.

Thus, Derrida teaches a *skillful* form of reading in order to *undermine*, call into question, and subvert. Zhuangzi works to *undermine* rational modes of thought in order to allow one to reach a state of *skillful* living. Zhuangzi has a *soteriology* that Derrida lacks. For Zhuangzi, language itself is not the problem. The fact that we are "spiritually sick," contaminated with the viruses of reason, social constructs, conceptual schemes, and entrenched positions and traditions, is what keeps us separated from the Dao and from a life of moving effortlessly through the world. Zhuangzi's apophasis has a soteriological aim; it points to the Dao. Zhuangzi gives us medicine to take; his text is the therapy. Derrida would see this as, at best, the illusory comfort of a placebo, and, at worst, a way to slip us the poison of presence.

There is no soteriology in Derrida's system; nor is there any "ultimate reality" to see. His message is that we cannot be "saved" (in fact, our only sickness comes from the false belief that we can be saved) and if there is an ultimate reality, we can never know it and never get there. All we can do is recognize this fact and destroy our old, quaint illusions about meaning, reference, and presence. Knowing that any attempt to get out of the text is futile, the deconstructionist simply plays within it. The apophasis of Derrida, then, points nowhere except back at the text itself; apophasis can only point at itself.[34] Zhuangzi would see Derrida as still fettered by text, unable to be freed until skill or fasting of the mind carries him out of the new prison in which he has found himself after deconstructing the old one. On Zhuangzi's view, even if Derrida were unable to achieve this state himself, greater insight would allow Derrida to say of Zhuangzi (as Zhuangzi has Confucius say in the text) "Such men as they wander beyond the realm; men like me wander within it. Beyond and within can never meet" (Graham 1981, 83).

Both Zhuangzi and Derrida tear down edifices, but whereas for Derrida this leaves us playing in a sea of signifiers, for Zhuangzi this leaves us free to discover the nature of the Dao, and to connect up with it in such a way as to live free from worry and harm, moving skillfully and effortlessly through the world.

Notes

I am deeply indebted to P. J. Ivanhoe, Bernard Faure, Paul Kjellberg, Marjorie Perloff, Patricia Parker, and Laura Medin for their helpful comments.

1. For example, see Cheng 1990, 19–30; Chien 1990, 31–49; Xie and Chen 1992, 363–375; Yeh 1983, 95–126; and Zhang Longxi, *The Tao and the Logos: Literary Hermeneutics, East and West* (Durham: Duke University Press, 1992).

2. John Ellis, *Against Deconstruction* (Princeton: Princeton University Press, 1989), 83–4.

3. Roland Barthes, "Myth Today," in *A Barthes Reader*, Susan Sontag, ed., (New York: Hill and Wang, 1982), 93–149.

4. Christopher Norris, *Deconstruction: Theory and Practice* (New York: Routledge, 1991), 3.

5. Jacques Derrida, *Of Grammatology*, Gayatri Spivak, trans., (Baltimore: Johns Hopkins University Press, 1976), 79.

6. Derrida is not alone in this project. While "logocentrism" may define a large part of the early Western philosophical tradition, there are many others who worked to dismantle its foundation. Those such as Nietzsche and Wittgenstein had already exploded these simplistic myths about language and meaning.

7. Benjamin Schwartz, *The World of Thought in Ancient China* (Cambridge: Harvard University Press, 1985), 231.

8. Neither the *Daodejing* nor the *Zhuangzi* ever doubts the existence of a Dao—an ultimate reality, a deep, underlying pattern of the cosmos. They deny only that it can be expressed in *words*. As I will discuss below, the Dao is not a fixed, unchanging realm like that of the Platonic forms. It is more

like (and I venture forth tentatively here, bearing the Daoist caveats about language in mind) the pattern underlying the processes of continuous change in Nature. It is not a realm of Being or stable absolutes, but rather a realm of becoming, of continuous unfolding with which one can be harmoniously aligned or, conversely, opposed to and out of synch. While there are regularities (for example, the changing of seasons, the stages of a life), each individual manifestation and instantiation is unique, for the world is characterized by change. This is why awareness and context-sensitivity are so important for Zhuangzi; the mirrorlike mind always allows one to reflect the ever-changing situation without getting stuck, leading to natural, spontaneous, "echolike" responses. In fact, A. C. Graham characterizes Zhuangzi's ideal as "respond with awareness." See Graham in Mair 1983, 3–23.

9. This does not mean, as some would have it, that there are no bad interpretations or misinterpretations. Derrida often skillfully argues against a particular interpretation (often the standard or "received" interpretation) by drawing on textual elements that undermine it. An interpretation must be supported by the text; for Derrida, however, the text usually involves much more than most interpreters—including the author—recognize. Derrida has frequently pointed out how others have "misread" his own work (a point that he then uses to illustrate the instability of language and the omnipresent possibility of breakdowns in communication), and has used the texts in question in a rigorous way to make his point.

10. Stanley Fish, *Is There a Text in This Class?* (Cambridge, 1980), 340.

11. On the discussion of arbitrariness, see Ferdinand de Saussure, *Course in General Linguistics*, Roy Harris, trans. (La Salle: Open Court, 1991), 67–69.

12. In this infinite and circular process, Derrida would argue that we can never arrive at the final signified.

13. Even the division into degree units is "arbitrary."

14. In fact the differences are not purely linguistic, as they do correspond to some fact in the world (there *is* water and it *is* giving off a certain amount of heat). The arbitrariness lies in how this fact is categorized, labeled, and opposed to other concepts.

15. Jacques Derrida, *Limited Inc.* (Evanston: Northwestern University Press, 1988), 12.

16. Terry Eagleton, *Literary Theory: An Introduction* (Minneapolis: University of Minnesota Press, 1983), 132.

17. Jacques Derrida, *Positions*, Alan Bass, trans. (Chicago: University of Chicago Press, 1978), 9.

18. Barbara Johnson, in the introduction to her translation of Jacques Derrida, *Dissemination* (Chicago: University of Chicago Press, 1981), xvii.

19. While there is some movement of reversal occurring, Derrida's primary aim is to show how the attempted dichotomization of the elements breaks down due to the inherence in each side of the other. Authors who try to elevate one element by excluding its "other" will be haunted by a literary "return of the repressed," a movement that Derrida often illuminates. Christopher Norris writes that a deconstructive reading consists "not merely in *reversing* or *subverting* some established hierarchical order, but in showing how its terms are indissociably entwined in a strictly undecidable exchange of values and priorities" (Christopher Norris, *Derrida* (Cambridge: Harvard University Press, 1987), 56). This move is more like Zhuangzi's than it is like a position sometimes found in the *Daodejing* which elevates the traditionally "lower" or "weaker" side to primacy.

20. Laozi, *The Way of Lao Tzu* (*Tao-Te Ching*), Wing-Tsit Chan, trans. (New York: Bobbs-Merrill, 1963), 101. I follow P. J. Ivanhoe in preferring "and so" to Chan's translation of "therefore."

21. These comments on Wang Fuzhi are drawn largely from a guest lecture at Stanford by Ted Slingerland, May 18, 1992.

22. Wu Kuang-ming, *The Butterfly as Companion* (Albany: State University of New York Press, 1990), 6. A similar technique is used by the Madhyamika Buddhist philosopher Nāgārjuna, who negates all possible views in order to free one from attachment to any particular position. One achieves liberation with a view of "no view" and a position of "no position."*

23. The term "antirationalism" comes from A. C. Graham, and describes a position distinct from irrationalism. Irrationalism, which is a refusal to take into account facts that conflict with one's own subjective feelings, values, or desires, constitutes a rejection of reason; this might be rejected in favor of, as in the case of Western Romantics, heightened emotion. Antirationalism, however, is not antireason. It simply argues that reason alone is not sufficient to provide access to the deepest truths about the world. In antirationalist arguments, reason can serve a number of useful functions, many of them "negative," for example, when it demonstrates its own limits or undermines overreliance on it itself. For a discussion of these two positions, see sections 3.2 and 3.3 in A. C. Graham's *Reason and Spontaneity: A New Solution to the Problem of Fact and Value* (London: Curzon Press, 1985).

24. For a more extensive discussion of the religious use of apophatic language, see Mark Berkson, "Apophasis Pointing: Soteriology and the Transcendence of Language," unpublished paper.

---

*Compare Loy's contribution to this volume.—Eds.

25. I will argue that while apophatic language can neither refer nor rationally argue or convince, it can *affect* the reader or listener in a variety of ways; it can paint a certain impressionistic picture and can move the reader in a given direction. In other words, apophasis, in its own indirect way, can *point*.

26. These categories are employed by Michael Sells in "Apophasis in Plotinus: A Critical Approach" in *Harvard Theological Review* 78:1–2 (January/April 1985), 64–65.

27. Iris Murdoch, *Metaphysics as a Guide to Morals* (London: Chatto and Windus, 1992), 192.

28. Despite this emphasis on play, Derrida's methods are quite rigorous; he pays a great deal of close attention to meanings of words, context, and the inner logic of a text, drawing out elements that are usually marginalized or ignored in the "manifest meaning" or "standard interpretation." Derrida often undertakes a patient, exhaustive analysis of the language and logic of a text in order to highlight its blind spots or moments of self-betrayal. In a sense, one could say that Derrida tries to be truer to the "letter of the text" than other interpreters or even the author.

29. Jacques Derrida, *Writing and Difference*, Alan Bass, trans. (Chicago: University of Chicago Press, 1978), 280.

30. There is a tension inherent in this project, as it assumes that there can be any traditional reading to which the reader can apply deconstructive techniques. When Derrida undermines Rousseau's "intended" reading in "That Dangerous Supplement," he assumes he knows what Rousseau *meant*, and then proceeds to undermine it. Derrida seems to be aware of this when he discusses the idea of "dominant interpretation" (see Derrida 1988, 143), which involves the notion of "relative stability." He points out that although the notion of a dominant reading presupposes a relative stability (not, however, a univocal, eternal, or self-identical meaning), the very notion of stability itself involves in it the possibility of destabilization.

31. This idea of the active, creative reader is also seen in Barthes with the reader as a mythologist who exposes underlying, secondary meanings of myths trying to pass themselves off as "natural" by breaking open the forms.

32. For a discussion of this argument, see Zhang Longxi, "The *Tao* and the *Logos*: Notes on Derrida's Critique of Logocentrism," in *Critical Inquiry* 11 (March 1985).

33. Zhuangzi would surely avoid getting into the kind of "debate" that Derrida had with John Searle. See their original exchange in *Glyph*, vol. 1 (Baltimore: Johns Hopkins University Press, 1977), and Derrida 1988. Zhuangzi does not argue for positions using propositional language, so he is

an elusive target. The way to move freely through a constantly changing world is to avoid taking philosophical stands.

34. While there may not be any salvation, there is, in a sense, a transformative effect to Derrida's project. He calls for a new approach that overturns dominant ways of thinking in Western philosophy. The "unenlightened," then, continue to live in delusion, believing themselves to use, but actually being used by, language; they speak of truth and meaning, but really point to nothing at all. The deconstructionist, however, abandons such talk in favor of "play." The only "salvation," if there is any, is the awareness brought about by the Derridean method. Murdoch writes, "One may . . . presume that a certain proud 'authenticity' is to be achieved by those who are no longer duped by outmoded ideas" (Murdoch 1992, 200).

SIX

Cook Ding's Dao
and the Limits of Philosophy[1]

Robert Eno

[handwritten annotation: Practical Dao learning can be used for evil]

Introduction

A central challenge for *Zhuangzi* interpretation is the reconciliation of the text's skepticism with its apparently privileged knowledge of a natural and spiritual world invisible to the ordinary eye, and its various portraits of human excellence or perfection. Was Zhuangzi an epistemological relativist, arguing against the possibility of certain knowledge, or was he claiming that such knowledge existed, and that there were those, perhaps he himself, who had access to it?[2] Both options can be defended on the basis of the text, but they are contradictory, and neither seems to generate the decisive textual coherence that would mark it as Zhuangzi's fundamental position, regardless of occasional inconsistencies.

I propose here an alternative formulation of Zhuangzi's standpoint. I will argue that Zhuangzi identifies two types of knowing—practical or skill knowing and theoretical or fact knowing. He celebrates practical knowing, which he associates with the Dao and with learned skills of action, but asserts that its value and power are, in principle, vitiated by the development of theoretical knowing. Practical knowing is portrayed as dynamic, responsive, and improvisatory, providing access to a natural world that is similarly dynamic and free of fixed rules. Theoretical knowing, by contrast, is rigid, unresponsive, and limited by its own arbitrary rules: it blinds us to the world around us that is not structured in any way expressible by theory. Zhuangzi uses a relativistic critique to convey the unsoundness of theoretical knowing. His discussions of human perfection concern skill mastery, which may be subject to judgments of relative excellence, but which is viewed as a generically sound form of knowing.[3]

This portrait of Zhuangzi's ideas will proceed from an interpretation of the *Qiwu lun* 齊物論 "Essay on Equalizing Things," chapter, which, I will argue, is best seen as a theoretical prologue to the 養生主 *Yangsheng zhu,* "The Pivot of Nurturing Life," chapter. My model will picture *Yangsheng zhu* as the pivot of the Inner Chapters, and I will suggest how viewing this brief chapter in this way can make the sequence of the Inner Chapters appear more coherent.[4] A discussion of ways in which certain materials from the Outer Chapters enhance our appreciation of an epistemology of skill knowledge follows.

The analysis of knowing that I ascribe to Zhuangzi here brings into focus an aspect of the Chinese philosophical enterprise that I believe distinguishes it most essentially from Greek and subsequent Western traditions prior to the advent of pragmatist schools: the linkage of wisdom to habit and art.* A fundamental achievement of early Greek philosophy was the distinction between reason and other processes of understanding, and the exclusive privileging of reasoned knowing as grounded in objective reality and therefore philosophical. In early China perhaps the most fundamental of philosophical outcomes was the rejection of reason as privileged and the identification of practical knowing as the principal means of obtaining certain understanding of the world. In this essay, I read the *Qiwu lun* as the clearest articulation in early texts of the distinction between rational and practical knowing, and as the most thorough analytic defense of the valuation of practical knowing.

By steering Chinese thought in this direction, the *Zhuangzi* aligns itself with Confucianism in its valuation of skill knowledge and in its opposition to the rationalist tendencies implied by Mohism. Throughout the analysis that follows I will try to elucidate underlying structural similarities between the enterprises of the *Zhuangzi* and Confucianism. I will begin the discussion with a highly synoptic account of what I take to be relevant features of mainstream Western traditions.

Reason and Language in Greek Thought

The philosophical enterprise that grew from the work of the early Greek thinkers was overwhelmingly concerned with acquiring certain knowledge

---

*Compare Raphals, particularly pp. 41–42.—Eds.

of right theory. By the time of Plato the enterprise was itself legitimized by an implicit theory, which may be caricatured in this way: True wisdom is knowledge of the structure of the natural world, and humankind possesses the power to know this structure because it possesses the power of reason. "Reason" is discursive (linguistically representable) thinking guided by certain rules. The rules of reason, "logic," parallel the structures of the natural world, and so can illuminate the contours of what is real. Because these rules are intrinsic to *discursive* thinking, language, employed without distortions that may be elicited from its accidental properties, is the best "truth tool."[5] All of this was a displacement from the enterprise of mathematics, which provided the model for certainty and for the type of thinking—analysis from self-evident axioms—that could yield it.[6] In Greece the search for knowledge was a linguistic endeavor.[7] I suggest that in China, ideas of valid knowing derived in association with the notion of efficacious arts, or daos, and the central questions that lie behind the philosophical enterprise of early China concern control over action and events rather than understanding of the structures of the physical world and discursive thought. Speech was valued principally as a tool of action rather than of understanding; the keys to understanding lay in daos rather than in theories.[8] To support this claim, which will be central to my analysis of the *Qiwu lun*, I will outline a view of the relationship between the term dao and developments in philosophical thinking in China at the time of Zhuangzi.

Early Senses of the Word "Dao"

While we have little helpful prephilosophical evidence to give us insight into the meaning of the term dao, the graph form and early patterns of usage provide some clues. The graph for dao as it appears in Western Chou bronze inscriptions, is composed of three semantic elements: a foot, a crossroads, and an ornamented eye signifying a head.[9] Usage patterns in the bronze inscriptions and in the *Shijing* suggest that the word dao possessed four principal meanings during the prephilosophical period: as a noun, it meant "a path" or "an art"; as a verb, it meant either "to guide on a path" or "to say."[10] Together with the graphic form, these uses point toward an original sense of dao as *a formula of speech and step*.[11] If this is accurate, the word connoted from early on aspects of both discourse and skilled practice.

By the period of the philosophers the use of the term dao in the sense of a teaching or method is common. Used in this way, the term denoted a complex of skills, motor and verbal procedures for their transmission from teacher to student, and discursive doctrine that expressed the personal or social functionality of the dao and so asserted its value. Based on later usage, including that in the *Zhuangzi*, the term may have been applied broadly outside the area of philosophy to describe the skills, training procedures, and social cultures of various closed professions, such as divination, metallurgy, and music. Confucius and other teachers of refined arts may have initially appropriated the term in this sense.[12] The *Analects* portrays Confucius speaking of his teaching as "my dao," presumably one of many possible syllabi of art and doctrine (and, for Confucius, the only valid one). While much of Confucius's teaching was socially radical in its implications, the form of Confucius's dao was conservative, and in casting his search for human excellence in the form of a transmittable set of arts, Zhou ritual, Confucius's innovative role as a teacher of social and political virtuosity may not have departed fundamentally from the master-apprentice training model appropriate to many existing specialized professions.

But Confucius's aspirations for his dao were not prosaic; his goal was not merely to generate excellence in practice, but also to cultivate in his students a type of wisdom. I have argued elsewhere that Confucius and his followers believed that the comprehensive practical skills generated through mastery of the ritual syllabus would, in themselves, constitute the perfection of wisdom: sagehood.[13] For those who were not yet sages, however, this expectation required explanation and doctrinal support—the value of Confucian training would not have been self-evident. The *Analects* reflects this in its portrait of the disciples' labored questioning for meaning and in the body of doctrinal assertions attributed to Confucius, which came to provide a discursive structure grounding his ritual instruction.

Yet the text also alerts its readers to tensions between the practical and the doctrinal dimensions of the Confucian dao, and the "step" of Zhou ritual practice is given priority over the spoken formulas that rationalize its value.[14] The *Analects* is, on the whole, suspicious of speech; it links the celebrated virtue of *ren* to inarticulateness, and denigrates glib talkers who moralize as a pretext.[15] This tendency culminates in a passage probably composed late in the Warring States period wherein Confucius asserts that he would prefer to lead without words.[16] Even in the *Analects*, wisdom and speech may be at odds, and some, at least, of its authors seem to have felt that the insight generated by training in the Confucian ritual arts may have been undermined by an inauthentic type of wisdom reflected in some forms of Confucian discourse.

This tension between the practical elements of a dao and its intellectualization in speech lies at the heart of Zhuangzi's critique in the *Qiwu lun*. The hostility toward the discursive elements of a dao reaches even further in the *Daodejing*, where, as is well known, the word dao comes to denote a natural process from which human speech is specifically excluded, as if words alone have divided the universe into realms of authenticity and delusion.

The Discovery of Discursive Certainty

The circumstance that separates the inchoate suspicion of speech in the *Analects* from the radically logophobic position of the Daoist texts is, most probably, the advent of Mohist philosophy in the fifth century B.C.E. Although Mohists followed tradition in calling their teaching a dao, and may have resembled existing professional groups in their organization as corps of military engineers, Mohism was far more radical than Confucianism in innovating a new method of wisdom seeking. That method is congenial to Western readers because it resembles in essential respects the enterprise for knowledge acquisition characteristic of Greek philosophy. Mohists claimed that what is so could be discovered through argument, or through the processes of discursive thinking guided by rules that we call reason. Using argument, the Mohists constructed their set of basic doctrines, and for Mohism, it was these that constituted the core of their sect. Thus, for Mohism as for the Greeks, language was the essential medium of the enterprise of philosophy, in contrast to the Confucians, for whom it was ritual practice.

In the earliest Mohist texts we not only see arguments in near-syllogistic form (despite many confusions and flaws), we see an awareness of the *force* of reason: an appreciation of the link between logic and certainty. It is this discovery that forms a refrain concluding a succession of arguments in the third *Jian'ai* text: "I cannot imagine how people can fully hear of this doctrine of universal love and yet deny its validity."[17] Certainty could be acquired through words alone.

Confucianism was at core a dao-practice: the validity of its doctrines could be fully confirmed only through mastery of the ritual skills of sagehood. Mohism was not. Mohism was structured such that an appreciation of its arguments alone led to full understanding of the world with which it was concerned and its natural imperatives. The Mohist perspective could be attained without further skill training. Mastering the arts of defensive warfare might make one more effective socially, but it did not add to wisdom: that was fully attained by grasping the truth of Mohist arguments.

The Polemical Background to the Qiwu Lun

The advent of Mohism created two options for the development of systematic thinking in China. Mohist teachings made it possible for China to embark on a philosophical enterprise similar to that of the Greeks, one based on the connection between reason and certainty and taking theoretical knowing to be the basis for wisdom and behavioral excellence.[18] This contrasted sharply with the Confucian enterprise which sought the perfection of practical knowing through mastery of a set of skills, an enterprise that we may call "dao-learning," to distinguish it from philosophy in the Western sense.

Mohism attacked Confucian practice and the roughly sketched doctrines that Confucius had used to rationalize his teaching and lure students. Moreover, Mohism's commitment to argument allowed it to attack Confucianism through a coherent ethical theory far surpassing any of the ad hoc notions Confucianism had used to legitimize *li*, "ritual."

Confucianism responded to the Mohist challenge by attempting to defeat Mohist arguments and develop for itself doctrines equally compelling. Most probably, it is only after this response that Confucians begin to regard systematic doctrine as an indispensable feature of their dao, and to appreciate the problems inherent in this. Mencius, for example, professes his aversion to argument and explains his polemical style as a necessary response to Mohism and the teachings of Yang Zhu (*Mencius* 3B9).

Once Confucianism responds to Mohism in this way, the undertaking begun by Confucius—to transform individuals into sages through ritual training—becomes increasingly associated with the enterprise of developing well-argued doctrines to legitimize such a dao. As Confucianism becomes more philosophical it becomes less a dao-learning. By the fourth century B.C.E., Zhuangzi's era, the quest for skills to transform people had shifted to a debate concerning whose theory of human perfection was right.

The Qiwu Lun *Critique*

The *Qiwu lun* is a critique of this shift. The chapter analyzes the dichotomy of practice and speech, and claims that whereas practice can yield authentic knowledge, speech cannot. Speech may be a significant tool for living, but not for acquiring knowledge. The theme of the chapter is its linguistic skepticism, but it lays the groundwork for the link of skilled practice to valid understanding that lies at the center of the succeeding chapter, *Yangsheng zhu*, which celebrates Cook Ding's perfect control and immersion in the natural world. To illustrate how I am construing the *Qiwu lun*, I will comment on three passages, translated in light of my overall reading of the text. I begin with a section in which Zhuangzi attacks the Confucian-Mohist debate directly through a description of the way in which language becomes dysfunctional:[19]

> Pronounced sayings are not just puffs of wind—sayings consist of things said—it is only that what their words refer to has not been fixed.[20] Do they really say anything? Have they never said anything? We think our speech is different from the chirping of baby birds, but is there a real distinction, or is there none? How do daos come to be obscured, such that they are subject to judgments of 眞 *zhen*,

"authentic", or 僞 *wei*, "inauthentic"?[21] How do spoken words come to be obscured, such that they are subject to judgments of "true" or "false"?[22] How can a dao be walked and not really exist? How can words exist and be "unallowable?" It is that daos become obscured in minor perfections; words become obscured in flowery speech.[23] Thus it is that you have Confucians and Mohists, each with their own "this is it" and "this is not." What is "it" for the one is "not" for the other. If you would affirm their denials and deny their affirmations, view them in the light. (2/23–7)

In this section, by my reading, Zhuangzi sets up a clear distinction between authentic and inauthentic elements of a dao. A dao normatively described, consists only of arts developed to a high degree of perfection (not "minor accomplishment"). Initially, the role that speech plays in such a dao is limited to a harmless nonassertive one. Zhuangzi does not maintain that we should not speak, but that we should not abuse speech by using it to assert: that words should not be subject to judgments of true and false. A dao-teaching that employs language pragmatically through requests, orders, instructions, and so forth, may be a valid dao. But as daos come to compete, they use speech to make claims about themselves and the world; they elaborate a new type of "saying," doctrine, which is subject to judgments and which gradually vitiates the authentic element of a dao.

Zhuangzi makes his own assertion about the powers of skill knowing: it is, for him, the access route to understanding and full engagement in the natural world. "Things cannot have any 成 *cheng*, 'perfection,' or 毀 *hui*, 'imperfection.' All are in the final analysis comprehended as one. Only the person of full attainment knows how to comprehend them as one. He affirms no 'this is it.' His affirmation is lodged in 庸 *yong*, 'ordinary practice.' Ordinary practice means use; use is comprehension; to comprehend is to grasp—once you grasp it, you're nearly there! Reliance on assertion ends, and when it ends and you do not even know it is so—that is called dao" (2/35–36).[24]

My reading of this chapter turns on the centrality I give to the notion of "ordinary practice" here. The English phrase translates the Chinese word *yong*, which combines the senses of "common" and "use." The *Qiwu lun* sometimes employs, loosely, a verse/refrain type structure, the refrain including phrases such as, "The Sage views them in the light;" "The Sage proceeds from none of these, but throws them open to the light of Heaven;" and so forth. My interpretation selects one such phrase, "The Sage lodges his affirmation in ordinary practice," as a gloss on the others, appealing to the central issue of selecting skill knowing and discarding fact/theory knowing. The sage does not affirm through words, or doctrines, he affirms through practice, or the arts of ordinary experience, which is categorically different from linguistic assertion. The refrain of the following long section makes clear that this phrase (although not necessarily my interpretation of it) is, indeed, the proper gloss for "viewing things in the light." It is the culmination of a long description of the perfection to which a dao may reach, and the means by which it may destroy itself with words.

> The knowledge of the ancients reached the limit. What was the limit? There were those who believed that nothing had yet begun to be. The limit! Exhausted! Nothing to add! The next believed there was something, but there had not yet begun to be boundaries. The next believed there were boundaries, but there had not yet begun to be an affirmable "this" or deniable "that." It is in the patterns of affirmation and denial that Dao (or daos) becomes 虧 *kui*, "imperfect."[25] The source of this imperfection is what *cheng*, "brings to perfection," attachment. But after all, is there perfection and imperfection or is there not?
>
> Let us say that there is perfection and imperfection. This is like the master lute player Zhao Wen playing the lute. Let us say that there is truly neither perfection nor imperfection. This would be like the master lute player Zhao not playing the lute.[26] Zhao Wen playing the lute, music master Kuang beating the time, Hui Shi leaning on the *wutong* tree: the knowledge of these three men was close [to perfection].[27] It flourished in them, and they bore their knowledge to the end of their days. Only, different from others in their love of their knowledge, from love of their knowledge came a wish to enlighten others. But they enlightened others by means of that which was not the means of enlightenment, and thus Hui Shi ended with the darkness of logical disputations, and in the case of Zhao Wen, in the end his own son was left with merely the strings of the lute.[28] And so, in the end, these masters achieved no perfection after all. If what they achieved was perfection, then even I have perfection. And if such as they cannot be said to have achieved perfection, then neither have I nor has any thing.
>
> Thus the Sage sees by the glimmer of chaos and doubt. He does not affirm of anything: "this is it"; his affirmation is lodged in ordinary practice. This is to view things in the light. (2/40–47)

Zhuangzi's critique, then, is that with the coming of doctrinal rationalization, dao-practices lose their authenticity and become not only relativized, but based upon false views of the potential of language to reveal what is so. If this is the thrust of Zhuangzi's argument, then we can say that he is a thorough skeptic on the possibility of attaining fact or theory knowledge, that is, certain understanding based on the powers of language and reason. However, Zhuangzi would be proposing an alternative route to certainty based on the potential of ordinary skill knowing. This would be a knowledge that was unconnected to the assertion of propositions and that thus implied no fixed ontological axioms; it would be knowledge contributing to the virtuoso performance of ordinary life.[29]

In theory, Zhuangzi's critique stands in basic opposition to the Mohist enterprise, which is structured around the adequacy of reason and the potential of language, through argument, to reveal the contours of what is so. However, the critique of Confucianism, which was at root a dao-practice, is provisional. Were Confucianism to discard the rationalizations that its response to Mohism had fostered (and, in addition, any fundamental attachment to claims employed in persuasion and recruitment), it would return to its authentic form as a dao.[30]

Cook Ding's Ordinary Practice

The lengthy *Qiwu lun* is followed by *Yangsheng zhu*. Most of this brief chapter is given to the story of Cook Ding, whose virtuoso skills as a butcher take him to the heights of spirit-like spontaneity.[31] Cook Ding's story is one of a number of tales that Joseph Needham has labeled "knack-passages."[32] These passages illustrate the ideal of the person whose perfect skills have released him from the dualities of this and that, self and other, which are attacked as illusory in the *Qiwu lun*.

While the knack-passages are popular among readers of the *Zhuangzi*, they have not generally been seen as the center of the text. This may be because within the Inner Chapters, the story of Cook Ding stands as the sole representative of this group of passages. However, the location of Cook Ding within the Inner Chapters suggests a more pivotal role. Following as it does the destructive analysis of the *Qiwu lun*, the thrust of the Cook Ding tale stands as a positive counterpoint: a portrait of "ordinary practice" raised to the level of nonrelativized knowing.[33]

The text tells us that at Cook Ding's level of skill perfection, he no longer perceives the world through the mediate sense organs; his contact with the world is 神遇 *shen yu*, "a spirit-like encounter". When his skill is fully adequate to his task, Cook Ding's spontaneity or 神欲 *shen yu*, "spirit-like impulses," possess a type of congruence with his environment as it relates to his enterprise. His perfect motion is no longer governed by 官知 *guan zhi*, "the reflective awareness of his senses". These characteristics of his practice lead Cook Ding to declare that what he loves in his art lies beyond skill: it is its nature as a dao.*

Yet in contrast to protagonists in Outer Chapters knack-passages, Cook

---

*The reader may wish to compare this analysis of skill with Yearley's (p. 154), in particular Eno's "spirit-like encounter" with Yearley's "transcendent drives."—Eds.

Ding is not yet a perfect virtuoso. When he encounters interstices of ox bone wherein complexity supersedes his mastered skill he shifts into a state of conscious concentration, reengaging his sense organs to direct his movements. In its imperfection, Cook Ding's level of mastery bears a recognizable relationship to levels of human skill performance that we encounter in actual life, the skills of great athletes or performing artists. Borrowing terminology from Michael Polanyi's analyses of noncognitive knowing, we may say that in operation, such virtuoso skills operate "transparently" over a broad range of performance tasks; that is, they have been so deeply mastered that their motor execution requires no conscious attention, and the actor experiences a sense of unmediated interaction with the environment in which the tasks are performed. Where the challenges of the environment, in light of the task, supersede the degree to which the skills have become embodied, transparency gives way and attention is refocused on motor execution.[34]

The difficulties involved in skill performance cease to be of much interest in the more idealized portraits of knack-masters seen in the Outer Chapters (although we encounter discussions concerning distractions). However, this aspect does point toward a vital aspect of daos: despite the sense of *wuwei*, or nonstriving, which one may encounter in their operation, such effortlessness is cultivated through long and persistent effort. There is nothing spontaneous about the acquisition of skills, and if the celebratory tone of the *Zhuangzi*'s portrait of daos is interpreted as an imperative, we may conclude that the text not only passes a positive judgment concerning the value of skill knowing, but also takes the ethical position of advocating that people make a sustained effort to reform themselves through the acquisition of a dao. It is, in this regard, nonrelativistic in its value stance.

The dao-learning interests that govern the Cook Ding tale are entirely absent from the *Mozi*, which explores knowing and behavior solely in light of its faith in reasoning. However, there is considerable overlap with Confucian texts, both in terms of the Confucian interest in performance aesthetics (note that Cook Ding's carving rhythm is likened to a dance or musical performance), and in terms of the attainment of spontaneous assurance in action through repetitive practice.[35] Here again we see the *Zhuangzi*'s alignment with Confucianism as a single genre of enterprise, in distinction to Mohism's generic similarity to early Greek philosophy.

Cook Ding as a Model for Political Action

Cook Ding's story not only illustrates the implications of the *Qiwu lun*, it serves as a bridge to the fourth chapter, 人間世 *Renjian shi*, "The World of Man," which is principally concerned with issues of social behavior. In the three long anecdotes that comprise the first section of *Renjian shi*, Zhuangzi outlines a political ethic that combines elements of self-cultivation and perfect social responsiveness in the use of diplomatic skills for a political end. In each case, Zhuangzi's spokesman advises a potential political actor, who already possesses some degree of skill, by adopting the actor's political goals and designing an efficacious course for realizing them. These courses are modeled on Cook Ding's: the actor is advised to apply his existing skills by engaging an exhaustive focus on the object of his persuasions—in each case a dangerous ruler or prince. The object is analogous to Cook Ding's ox: the skill master's goal is not to impose his goals upon the object, but to detect the existing contours of the object—the ox's physiology or the royal disposition—and fully exploit these to obtain the desired goal. The outcome in *Renjian shi* is not sliced beef and an un-nicked knife; however, royal virtue and an uninjured diplomat or teacher are precise parallels.[36]

When viewed in this political context, we are able to see the connection between Cook Ding's mastery and the skilled virtue known in Confucianism as 時 *shi*, "timeliness". This skill grows from the *Analects'* formula for self-preservation: "When the Way prevails in the world, appear; when it does not, hide" (*Analects* 8.13, see Eno 1990, 50–52). The formula is quoted toward the close of the *Renjian shi* chapter in a tale of Confucius that the *Zhuangzi* shares with the *Analects* (4/87 and *Analects* 18.5). In Confucianism, the notion of timeliness develops much broader implications, and comes to signify the ability to transcend rules by cultivating comprehensive social skills that allow one to respond perfectly, in light of a goal, to all contingent circumstances.[37]

The doctrine of timeliness, in one form or another, seems to characterize most dao-learning texts, and is emblematic of the various visions of human perfection that such schools shared.[38] In texts of this nature we encounter in wide variety the ideal person so perfectly trained that in action his skills are transparent, requiring no attention for their perfect execution, thus allowing him to focus with full awareness on "the lay of the land" (often denoted by the term 勢 *shi*), and so exercise over his situation greater control than ordinary men. Analysis of such teachings would, in most cases, be best pursued by exploring how their particular daos of ritualism, militarism, quietism, and so forth are linked to the shared ideal of spontaneous perfection in action.[39] But the *Zhuangzi* is different. It seems to propose no dao: it would be perfectly cogent to suggest that Zhuangzi himself had no dao to pass on to disciples. The *Zhuangzi* is, instead, an analytic and literary defense and celebration of dao-practices and the perfection of timeliness. It champions non-analytic wisdom schools without being one, and attacks the adversary of these schools, Mohism, with its own weapon: analytic argument (but armed also with rhetorical tools the Mohists painfully lacked: humor and literary skill).

The Natural World of the Inner Chapters

An epistemology that takes skill mastery as the only valid form of knowing can entail no systematic ontology. An ontology is a theory, and the *Qiwu lun* not only rejects the possibility of valid theory-knowledge, it attacks assertion precisely because assertions necessarily imply ontologies: every "this is so, that is not" presumes an existential order in the world of things. The *Zhuangzi* prepares the ground for the *Qiwu lun*'s anti-ontology and advocacy of skill knowing by portraying a world that undermines notions of a universe furnished with stable entities and ordered by natural regularities characteristic of common sense views of reality and the structure of language itself.

The *Zhuangzi* foregrounds this issue in its first passage. When the text opens with the dramatic transformation of a world-size roe into sky-size bird it gives us more than a symbol for the Dao set in motion: it signals to readers that the natural universe of the text will not be governed by the regularities we expect from the nonhuman environment as we perceive it.[40] The 逍遙 游 *Xiaoyao you*, "Free and Easy Wandering," chapter reveals a world filled with talking animals, giant trees of incalculable age, huge gourds suitable as boats. It is a world for which the human habit of distinguishing persistent entities and assigning them functions is utterly unsuited, as Hui Shi, no more obtuse than the rest of us, discovers.

The shamanic universe of the *Zhuangzi* relentlessly reflects a fundamental duality between the empowered and the nonempowered: those whose focus allows them to manipulate this protean Nature and transcend the limits it initially seems to place on human life, and those who remain imprisoned within those limits. While the text offers examples of the preternaturally powerful—those who fly, live on air and dew, stroll through fire unburnt—it nowhere states in so many words how such miracle men achieve their focus and power. It may be this apparent silence that has led many commentators to claim that Zhuangzi was aware of some mystical type of knowledge, the product of communion with the transcendent Dao. But the logic of the text, from the first chapter through the third, points us instead to a prosaic form of knowing: skill mastery, or, perhaps, communion with *a* dao, without regard to what that dao may be.

The phenomenal field facing a dao-master undertaking his tasks is undifferentiated in its presentation as an appeal or challenge to his skills, something like the configurations of lights appearing in an action video game, that "exist as coherent entities" identically only as triggers to a series of skilled motor responses, and that may be transformed as arbitrarily as the *kun* fish. While we know—as Zhuangzi may well have known—that no skill perfection will enable people to fly or leap unhurt from high cliffs, it is also true that highly perfected skills can reveal material obstacles to be as illusory as video-game barriers, and allow people to overcome limits that to the unskilled may appear absolute. The interpretation of the Inner Chapters offered here takes Cook Ding's dao as the text's central model for how all of its sages obtain their powers. They see the world as it is: not as a fixed order of material entities, but as a field of flux that presents to them a changing array of opportunities to engage their powers for the ends they envision.

Once again, we find here an aspect of the *Zhuangzi* that is congenial to Confucianism. The ultimate ideal for the Confucian sage of timeliness is the cultivation of a perfect, error-free ability to read and respond to ethical action imperatives perceived in the context of unique situations. What one needs to "see" in such contexts is not an inventory of entities, but the contingent arrangement of phenomena within a field of meaning—a "situation"—characterized by its significant aspects in dependent relationship and in constant flux toward new arrangements. This is why the *Daxue* sets out the problem of learning by saying that "things have roots and branches [that is, significant essential aspects and nonsignificant aspects]; affairs end and begin again [that is, emerge in flux without natural boundaries]" (*Daxue* 1). We need to "know the before and after" of things—their relative importance within contexts and the way in which they succeed one another as new contexts emerge. This is a universe of emergent situations rather than a universe of entities located in time, space, and vector motion.[41] It is a world that eludes the theoretical certainties of reason, subject to be mastered by the ritual skills of the Confucian sage or the arcane skills of a *Zhuangzi* shaman.

The Order of the Inner Chapters: A Recapitulation

If we take the *Yangsheng zhu* chapter as the pivot of the Inner Chapters, there will appear to be a cogent sequential relationship among the first four chapters of the text as a core designed to discredit fact or theory knowledge and celebrate skill knowing.[42] The *Xiaoyao you* chapter anticipates the celebration of practical knowing by portraying a universe in flux, a natural world that is too protean to be known through theory-based assertions of what is so and what is not. The *Qiwu lun* demonstrates the incompetence of any form of discursive knowing, and affirms the linkage of ordinary practice, skill knowing, and sagehood. The *Yangsheng zhu* chapter elucidates the etiology and characteristics of skill knowing, and proclaims mastery to be the pivot of successful life. *Renjian shi* relates the features of Cook Ding's skill and focus to the most dramatically perilous aspects of the lives of its elite Warring States audience. The fifth and sixth chapters do not relate directly to the issue of skill knowing, and this would account for their location outside the four-chapter core. Chapter five, 德充符 *Dechong fu*, "The Sign of Full Power" (that is, physical mutilation or deformity), focuses on the lack of congruence between the appearance of the empowered person and accepted standards of excellence. In chapter six, 大宗師 *Dazong shi*, "The Ultimate Teacher" (that is, death), the *Zhuangzi* makes the protean character of its universe a vehicle to efface the greatest of all distinctions, that between life and death. With *Xiaoyao you*, it seems to bracket the *Inner Chapters*, and the final chapter, 應帝王 *Ying diwang*, "Fit for Emperors and Kings," which brings together brief passages on rulership, may be an appendix or late addition.[43]

Access to Nature and the Natural Through Daos: The Outer Chapters

The valuation of skill mastery in the Inner Chapters is developed in somewhat different directions in the Outer Chapters, although it is not a dominant theme among that group of texts. (The topic is rarely encountered at all in the Mixed Chapters.) These writings are particularly useful in helping us think through the relationship between dao-practices, the unmythologized natural world, and the notion of a transcendent Dao. Specifically, they elaborate on the *Zhuangzi*'s original interests to illustrate how the value of daos may lie in their power to provide us access to *the* Dao, or to Nature. It is through them, rather than through discursive thinking, that we know the actual world.

I wish to analyze three passages that share certain qualities: they are clearly nonrelativistic in their celebration of skill knowing; they portray excellence or perfection as within easy reach; they lay no stress on any elusive, metaphysical Dao; they focus on the quality of spontaneity.[44] The first is from the 秋水 *Qiushui*, "Autumn Floods," chapter, the latter two from 達生 *Da sheng*, "Mastering Life," wherein the greatest concentration of knack-passages appears

In *Qiushui*, we encounter a passage where the spontaneous qualities of natural species endowments is observed through personified animals (17/53–56).[45] First, a one-legged *kui*-beast marvels at the ability of a millepede to manipulate its many legs, then the millepede in turn marvels that a legless snake can outpace him. To the *kui* the millepede replies that what it does is nothing marvelous: "I [merely] place my 天 *tian*, 'natural,' mechanism in motion; I don't know how it works." The snake's remark is similar: "How can one alter the motion of one's natural mechanism?" The skills of these animals are spontaneously performed, like Cook Ding's, but they are not mastered: they represent the spontaneity characteristic of prehuman nature. Unmastered skills are not characteristic of the world of men, and it is precisely this lack of spontaneous skill that sets apart the human world and presents people with a natural imperative: the acquisition of spontaneity.

Conceiving the spontaneity of nature as a model for human beings does not seem to be a developed idea in the Inner Chapters—it is the *Daodejing* that makes the qualities of 自然 *ziran*, "Nature; what is so of itself; spontaneity," both a primal human state and a goal for humans corrupted by speech and values.[46] The *Zhuangzi*, especially the Inner Chapters, does not share the *Daodejing*'s interest in the biological world as it really exists. Nevertheless, the idea that through the repetitive practice of skill acquisition human beings can replicate the spontaneity of the non-human world fits well with the Inner Chapter's valuation of practical knowing, relativization of human norms, and cynicism about social pursuits.

In the *Dasheng* chapter, Confucius encounters a hunchback deep in the woods who exhibits perfect skill at catching cicadas on a sticky pole (19/17–21). The cicada catcher has mastered a cultivated dao, one intentionally selected and perfected through repetitive practice. Confucius says to him, "Are you [merely] clever, or do you have a dao?" The hunchback replies that he does have a dao, and goes on to describe it in terms of the method of study that he pursued to attain his skill perfection, much as Cook Ding described his dao. The product of this study, he tells us, is that when he exercises his skill, his perception of the world changes radically, and he perceives the natural world only in terms of its appeal to his skill: "I know only cicada wings." He himself marvelously resembles an element of the natural landscape: "I position my body like a crooked stump and hold my arm like a withered tree limb." Confucius characterizes this as "concentrating his *shen*, 'spirit.'" The tale of the hunchback illustrates how the spontaneity of nature can be cultivated in people, and suggests that it can form a conduit linking the individual to nature itself.

A final tale concerns a swimmer, whose preternatural abilities in swimming the Lüliang falls captures Confucius's attention (19/52–54). Confucius questions him as he did the hunchback, but the swimmer denies he has a dao. Instead, he cites his personal history as one who "grew up in the water." He attributes his skill to this long term engagement in a water environment, which gradually changed his 故 *gu*, "primitive endowment", into a different (second) 性 *xing*, "nature." He perceives the world of water only as an appeal to his skills; for him, whose universe is now the water, such imperatives appear as a determined 命 *ming*, "destiny." He exemplifies skill mastery acquired not through purposive study but through repetitive practice in response to environmental constraints.[47] Like the hunchback, however, the result is a changed view of nature as a phenomenal flux that is experienced as an appeal to skills that can be exercised with perfect spontaneity.[48]

The tales of the cicada catcher and the swimmer portray individuals who have used skill mastery to become immersed, so to speak, in the natural world. The hunchback has not only ceased to be aware of the world outside his skill-generated focus, his body itself replicates an object of nature apart from humanity. The swimmer, whose skills are free of purposive origins, has gone even further: his human endowment has been transformed and his destiny is governed solely by the natural motions of the waves (although his author-creator has preserved his human eloquence!). For these characters, a dao provides a conduit away from the human perspective and into a holistic engagement with nature.

Conclusion: The Ethical Implications of Zhuangzi's Dao-Learning

The *Zhuangzi*'s critique of theory knowledge and its powerful advocacy of dao-learning may have made an important contribution to the death of Mohist philosophy and to the continued proliferation of schools seeking human perfection through skill mastery. Clearly, though, the *Qiwu lun* failed to chasten the doctrinal spokesmen of these schools, who have left us texts marked with what Zhuangzi would regard as the pollution of theory and disputation, guaranteeing that the authenticity of their daos would be impaired. But we may wonder how without some form of theory one could actually go about establishing a dao-practice. What guides does the *Zhuangzi* offer to help us turn its theoretical advocacy into performance unhindered by discursive elements?

Zhuangzi's portrait of dao-mastery is pluralistic: any dao can perform the function of linking one to *the* Dao—if we understand that term to point toward the spontaneous flux of Nature. In this sense, Zhuangzi is relativistic. But he is clearly *not* a relativist concerning the status of the value that daos generate. The text's literary qualities conflict decisively with the ascription to it of a philosophical motive of thorough relativism. The description of Cook Ding is a celebration anchored in the analysis presented in the *Qiwu lun*: it is impossible to read the text and ignore its implicit claim that the value generated by dao-practice is a cardinal value, even if there is no cardinal dao. But in the Inner Chapters, it seems to me, the text resists any temptation to lay groundwork for a theory that would allow us to transform this valuation of skill mastery into a coherent ethical theory. Dao-practices can be adapted to any end: the dao of butchering people might provide much the same spiritual spontaneity as the dao of butchering oxen—as many a samurai might testify.[49] The *Zhuangzi*'s portrait of daos makes no selection among the goals to which it might apply.*[50]

This is, of course, where Confucianism and Daoism part company decisively. Like the *Zhuangzi*, the Confucians are absorbed in the power of dao-practices to create natural spontaneity and unmediated access to the environment, but for them, the environment where spontaneity belongs—for human

---

*On the question of the amorality of Zhuangzi's dao, compare Yearley (p. 176), Kupperman (p. 188), and Ivanhoe (p. 200–202).—Eds.

beings—is the social environment, and the skills that compose a human dao are social inventions.

The tendency of the *Zhuangzi*, if we consider the text as a whole, is to celebrate dao-practices, such as swimming and cicada catching, that are simple and personal, and which can be performed in a nonsocial context. Because, for Confucians, the social world is not nonnatural, but is rather the portion of nature most fitting to human beings, they celebrate daos such as poetic allusion, ritual choreography, and musical performance that rest on an intersubjective world of shared meaning and are received as history-generated givens, capable of modification, but not of invention by individuals.

Because Confucian skills are intersubjective, they function as media of communication, *grammars* rather than self-enclosed skills. To pursue the metaphor of language, the key feature of Confucian daos is that, like linguistic skills, shared mastery—a mastery that renders the skills themselves transparent when in operation—creates a medium of unmediated communication within the social world that underlies the utility of daos in pursuing goals: projects, games, life stories.[51] The status of such goal orientation is problematic for the *Zhuangzi*, which prefers daos free of social engagement and which pictures the human environment ahistorically, much like the nonhuman environment of plants and animals. Confucian daos, the components of the comprehensive, unified dao of the sages, are indeed constraints, as Zhuangzi claims. But Confucians claim that these are species constraints. They resemble the spontaneous "mechanisms" of the millepede and snake, but for human-kind, which must invent its own skills to attain the spontaneity of nature, such natural mechanisms evolve socially through history. From the Confucian perspective, the embodiment of these constraints *empowers* species members and frees them to pursue creative projects beyond the powers of an isolated human life.

But, of course, these are theories, and the analysis of the *Qiwu lun* would identify them as symptoms of a dao that has lost its authenticity—and, indeed, a survey of Confucian history might conclude that in later eras, laden with unending doctrines and texts, Confucians did lose sight of the original link between the ritual arts and wisdom. Yet if we wish to look to the *Zhuangzi* for ideals of human excellence that we may be moved to adopt in light of our own "spontaneous" (though cultivated) ethical dispositions, the implicit critique of Confucian theory—of Confucianism *as* philosophy—reveals the *Zhuangzi* as ethically inadequate. If Cook Ding's dao can help us see the limits of discursive, philosophical inquiry, philosophy can likewise illustrate the limits of the perfect vision engendered by Cook Ding's dao.

Notes

1. Portions of this essay reformulate ideas that originally appeared in my "Creating Nature: Ruist and Taoist Approaches," in Smith 1991, 3–28.

2. An example of two interpreters at opposite poles would be Robert E. Allinson, who views the text of the *Zhuangzi* itself as a vehicle designed to transform the reader's consciousness to an absolute level (Allinson 1989), and Chad Hansen (in Mair 1983). Hansen's interpretation rests on a recognition that the term dao in the *Qiwu lun* may be read as a generic term, a dao, or a practice. Although I do not follow Hansen in reading the term dao in the sense of "linguistic practice," I accept and rely on his insight concerning the generic use of the term.

3. Allinson has formulated a typology of approaches to Zhuangzi's relativism. Within his scheme, I believe my proposals here would fall under the category of "Both Relativism and NonRelativism" (Allinson 1989, 120–21), and will, I hope, make that category seem more coherent.

4. Rigorously speaking, my hope is to throw light on the epistemology of the Inner Chapters, rather than that of Zhuangzi as a thinker. Despite the fine textual work done by Graham, I am not prepared to subscribe to any existing theory of the text, nor do I have a well formulated alternative to offer. I am skeptical of all models that would relate the Inner Chapters to any one author. In this essay, when I refer to Zhuangzi, I am pointing to the mix of authorial and editorial hands that put the Inner Chapters into something like their present order, most likely during the late fourth century B.C.E.

5. Bernard Williams notes that discourse is an essential element of the prescriptive ideal of reason in his remark that the ideal, "requires in principle every decision to be based on grounds that can be discursively explained," in Williams, *Ethics and the Limits of Philosophy* (Cambridge: Harvard University Press, 1985), 18.

6. This model of knowledge was derived from speculation concerning the natural world. As Aristotle noted, quests for different forms of knowledge, such as the "practical" knowing of ethics, required different axioms and methods. Yet in the Western tradition, I believe it is valid to say that this lesson was not applied systematically, and ethical inquiry was modeled on the quest for knowledge of the natural world.

7. I hope it is evident that this brief attempt to capture a foundational aspect of the Greek philosophical enterprise is not meant to cover all thinkers with equal validity. Sophists, for example, would not fit this model well, though they used it as a foil, nor would Pythagorianism, to the degree that it

is mystical (although the example of Parmenides demonstrates that mysticism is not inconsistent with rational extremism).

8. This direction is consistent with the tendency for Chinese thinkers to analyze language as a regulative tool, as described by Chad Hansen in *Language and Logic in Ancient China* (Ann Arbor: University of Michigan Press, 1983), 59–61.

9. The head element, 首 *shou*, is almost certainly a phonetic component, but has traditionally been taken to make a semantic contribution as well; the *Shuowen jiezi* takes *shou* to be solely a semantic element (its phonetic contribution has been recognized since the commentary of Duan Yucai (see Ding Fubao, *Shuowen jiezi gulin*, 800b et seq.)). The likelihood that *shou* played a semantic role is suggested by its presence in the related word 馗 *kui*, a "crossroads joining all [nine] directions", although it could be argued that it appears there as an abbreviated form of dao.

10. No graph ancestral to dao has been identified in the Shang oracle texts. The sense of "path" is attested in several bronze inscriptions. The most reliable early instance of dao in the sense of "art" occurs in *Shijing*, "Sheng min" (245.5): "The agriculture of Hou Ji possessed the art of demarcation." The sense of "to guide" is found earliest in a bronze text at the turn of the first millennium B.C.E., 榖鼎 *Yu ding*; later orthography added a hand element, 寸 *cun*, for this usage (contrary to the *Shuowen*). The use of "to speak" is found in the *Shijing*, *Qiang you ci* (46.1). The sense of dao as "way," as in "the way of the former kings," does not occur in Western Chou bronzes; possible instances in the *Shijing* (see, for example, 261.1, 299.3) are more elegantly explained by the meaning of "path," while the sole possibilities in the Zhou sections of the *Shangshu* are either better taken to denote "speak" (*Kanggao* and *Guming*), to be a scribal variant (*Jun Shi*), or to be attributable to the late date of the text (*Hongfan: Kang Wang zhi gao*).

11. Given the later rhetorical power of the term dao, we might speculate on an original connection with the choreographed or processional liturgies of religious ritual. One candidate for an oracle text graph ancestral to dao would, in fact, conform to such a notion. This is the graph 徬. This character, the modern equivalent of which would be rendered 遵, supports such an interpretation in four respects. It functions regularly as a verb signifying a ritual activity. Its phonetic element may have served a semantic function, in which case its graph, a path and two mouths, would be consistent with the sense of processional liturgy. The reconstructed phonetic value of this element (**d'iôg*; using Karlgren's notation) is almost identical to that of the "head' element in dao (**śiôg*). Finally, the semantic contributions of the phonetic element may be shared with the later word 禱 *dao*, "to pray." (For

text instances of the graph and comparative usage, see Yao Xiaosui 姚孝遂 and Xiao Ding 肖丁 eds., *Yinxujiagu keci leicuan* 殷墟甲骨刻辭類纂 (Beijing: Zhonghua shuju, 1989), 872a; 305b–307a.) This suggestive evidence, however, falls well short of the standard necessary for a firm identification, the principal problem being the absence of independent instances of loan exchanges between the two phonetic graph forms involved.

12. This speculation is developed at greater length in my contribution to Smith 1991, 4–6.

13. See Robert Eno, *The Confucian Creation of Heaven* (Albany: SUNY Press, 1990), chapter two.

14. See, for example, the discussion of *Analects*, 5.13, in Eno 1990, 85.

15. Examples are numerous. In *Analects*, 12.3, Confucius characterizes the *ren*, "good," as slow of speech. In 11.23, we are shown his disgust at the disciple Zilu, who has quoted a saying of Confucius's back at him to justify behavior that, for Confucius, is clearly wrong. Confucius calls Zilu 佞 *ning*, "glib," a word that in graph and usage seems to have a root meaning as the antonym of *ren*. See Eno 1990, 232.

16. See the discussion of *Analects*, 17.17 and surrounding passages in Eno 1990, 86.

17. *Mozi*, 16.63, taking 皆 *jie* in the sense of "entirely," as context seems to demand. See also 16.21, 34, 45, 71.

18. Although the original philosophy of Mohism was devoted exclusively to ethics, unlike Greek thought, the later Mohist canons reveal an evolving interest in philosophy of language and physics (see A. C. Graham, *Later Mohist Logic, Ethics and Science* (Hong Kong: Chinese University of Hong Kong Press, 1978).) After the disappearance of Mohism, these avenues were not broadened.

19. My translations are indebted to the work of A. C. Graham. My understanding of the *Qiwu lun*'s central concern with the issue of assertion through speech is derived from Graham 1969–70, 137–59.

20. Taking the initial *yan* in the sense of an asserted teaching or aphorism (drawing on the interpretation Jeffrey Riegel gives the term in "Reflections on an Unmoved Mind," in *Studies in Chinese Classical Thought*, Henry Rosemont Jr. and Benjamin Schwartz, eds., *Journal of the American Academy of Religion Thematic Issue* XLVII.3S (September 1979), 439), I read the sentence as raising the distinction between words that do not seek to confirm a fixed ontology (such as imperatives) and propositions, which do imply the affirmation of a fixed ontology. The former do no damage, they are not undermined by the fact that "what their words refer to has not been fixed."

Only ontology-creating statements have an unprovisional stake in "fixing" their referents, and so overstep the valid use of language.

21. Taking dao to refer solely to the "arts" transmitted from teacher to disciple, excluding rationalizing doctrines. How can a skill be "fake?"

22. Taking *yan* here to refer to verbal forms used in transmitting arts (such as how-to imperatives), in contrast to statements (which are true or false), which are not intrinsic to a dao. How can an imperative be "true?" (I should note that my use of "true/false" is for convenience; I am not addressing the issues of "truth" in Chinese thought raised by Hansen in his "Chinese Language, Chinese Philosophy, and 'Truth'," *Journal of Asian Studies* 44.3.

23. That is, a dao-practice loses its authenticity when its core shifts from its arts to its rationalizing doctrines. The arts degenerate as statements proliferate. The word rendered as "perfection" is 成 *cheng*, and while the translation is strained here (it should denote skill accomplishment) I have employed it for consistency with uses of the term below, where it is an antonym for "imperfection" (or impaired perfection).

24. The two senses of "dao" (as a practice and as a holistic force) seem to be combined here in the final phrase.

25. Again, the two senses of dao work equally well here.

26. Traditional commentary suggests the distinction is between mastery as a dispositional quality and performance, which is subject to judgment.

27. Zhuangzi, by including Hui Shi, seems to place the mastered manipulation of cognitive skills on the same plane as mastery of motor skills. This accords with Ryle's strategies for ameliorating the categorical distinction between thinking and action.

28. The failure of all these masters lay in the means whereby they attempted to transmit their daos, which was through assertions rather than practical training. I am reading 非所明 *fei suo ming* by taking 所 *suo* to represent 所以 *suoyi* "the means by which."

29. There is an important piece of counterevidence. Mixed among the portions of the text that I have dealt with here is a discussion of the dependent relationship between assertions and their counterpart denials. That discussion includes the following passage: "Hence the sage proceeds through none of these, but throws all open to the light of heaven—and that too is to accord with an asserted view (因是 *yinshi*)" (2/29). The final phrase, which suggests that *all* knowing, including skill knowing, is dependent on worldviews generated through assertion, supports an interpretation of thorough relativism, rather than the position I am taking. There are three ways to respond to such counterevidence. In order of descending strength they are: to argue

that the final phrase is a commentarial insertion or a scribal transposition of four characters from a later portion of text (at 2/39); to claim that *yinshi* is used analogically to mean "relying on a *form of* assertion," where the form is generically distinct from linguistic assertion and so not unsound (perhaps related to the "reliance" of Cook Ding on the 固然 *guran*, "what is originally so"; to grant the counterevidence but claim that the overall coherence of the main argument can be assessed as more likely to reflect Zhuangzi's central point. While I feel that either of the first two responses may be valid, I do not have compelling arguments for them and so offer only the last.

30. Note that this picture of what is "authentic" in Confucianism does not necessarily match our portrait of what was *original* in Confucianism—Confucius may have employed doctrine from the outset, but it was not intrinsic to his mature dao.

31. I do not adopt the editorial revisions to *Yangsheng zhu* proposed by Graham in Graham 1981, 62–63. The evidence to support them seems to me inadequate for so radical a move. However, the passages that Graham inserts seem to me congenial to the ideas of this essay, and would also link the chapter more closely with the *Qiwu lun*.

32. Joseph Needham, *Science and Civilization in China*, vol. 2 (Cambridge: Cambridge University Press, 1956), 121. Graham has collected these in Graham 1981, 135–42.

33. A detailed exploration of the Cook Ding passage will reveal that it is not entirely consistent with the *Qiwu lun*: Cook Ding twice discusses his skill in terms of theory—once with reference to the metaphysical contours of nature, once in terms of the physical contours of oxen (both passages resonate with *Daodejing*, 11). My claim is not that *Yangsheng zhu* was uttered in one breath with the *Qiwu lun* nor even that they are by the same author, but that the logic that editorially located the Cook Ding story after the *Qiwu lun* accurately reflects their central concerns.

34. The terminology is borrowed from Polanyi, *The Tacit Dimension* (Garden City, NY: Anchor Books, 1966).

35. These issues are discussed at length in Eno 1990, esp. 171–80.

36. The self-cultivation components of these anecdotes focus on attitudinal adjustments in the actors rather than on skill training. This, it seems to me, is because the actors are already trained in the arts necessary for their tasks. The problem is that they are burdened with either doctrines (in the case of Yan Hui) or the distracter of danger (in the cases of Ye Gongzi Gao and Yan He), and their regimen involves eliminating these so as to allow the spontaneous application of their skills. The *Zhuangzi* was a written text, and its audience was thus principally cultivated men living among political actors.

The text addresses their predicaments, but we would not expect Zhuangzi to celebrate the daos associated with the elite. In his choice of the word *yong* to name the action of the sage, and his portrait of the sage as a kitchen servant, Zhuangzi accords with the *Daodejing* in linking illumination to rejection of cultural refinement.

37. For example, in *Mencius*, 5B 1, Confucius is idealized as "the sage of timeliness," who follows no rule other than to do what is appropriate. His accomplishments are deemed superior to those of lesser exemplars, who are praised for adherence to specific ethical rules. This virtue ethics, which resembles a situation ethics in employing rules-of-thumb in moral self-cultivation, contrasts with the Mohist effort to build an action ethics grounded in logically reasoned and inflexible rules.

38. This is a large claim, and one that I cannot defend in detail or nuance here. It is based on my reading of sage ideals in texts such as the quietist *Neiye* chapter of the *Guanzi*, the chapters of the legalist *Han Feizi* that seem to reflect the influence of Shen Buhai and Shen Dao, and sections of the militarist *Sunzi*, whose ideas I have come to understand better through the work of Kidder Smith. It is the tendencies of this broad trend in early Chinese thought that A. C. Graham has so interestingly used as a springboard in *Reason and Spontaneity* (Totowa, N.J.: Barnes and Noble, 1985), with *Zhuangzi* as his principal source.

39. This is because dao-learning is essentially a synthetic, rather than an analytic exercise. Daos aim to transform the perspective of the practitioner through practice. The validity of the doctrinal assertions associated with a dao would be a product of their systematic self-evidence from the viewpoint of the skilled adept, rather than analytic standards of truth to which individual claims may or may not conform. Our understanding of these schools and appreciation of the ways in which they may have been valid as dao-practices is often hampered by the fact that texts tend to reflect doctrinal elaboration rather than the practical teaching of each dao; keeping the handbook unpublished may have been a key to recruiting disciples. In some cases, of course, our extant texts may be little more than rhetoric, the products of authors imagining a dao-perspective without actually having relevant experiences of mastery.

40. This "cosmic egg" opening fits well with the models of Daoist mythology explored by Norman Girardot, who somehow overlooks its implications (he relates the passage to other issues; see *Myth and Meaning in Early Taoism* (Berkeley: University of California Press, 1983), 225). Note that the unity of the roe gives way to a bird whose name resonates with the notion of doubledness, perhaps an echo of the "one divides into two" creation image shared by the *Daodejing* and the *Great Appendix* of the *Yijing*.

41. Such a worldview would seem to be a good foundation for the reticular model of the universe associated with Han correlative cosmology (see Needham 1956, 279 et seq.). These ideas seem to me fully consistent with the outline of a Confucian "ontology of events" developed by David Hall and Roger Ames (see "Getting it Right: On Saving Confucianism from the Confucians," *Philosophy East & West* 34.1, 15).

42. Within each chapter there appear anecdotes or other passages that do not fit well in this model. The account summarized here attempts only to capture the dominant progression of the text: digressions may be due to the text's editorial history, literary imperatives, or, most likely, the richness of the *Zhuangzi*'s interests, which certainly go far beyond the single theme foregrounded in this essay.

43. Graham notes that the theme of rulership seems to be one that did not much interest the historical Zhuangzi, and that chapter seven repeats material from chapter two, which may suggest an independent editorial origin (Graham 1981, 94).

44. Because my discussion here is meant only to use the Outer Chapters to elucidate implications of the ideas of the Inner Chapters, my selection of materials entails no claim that they are representative of the Outer Chapters or that counterexamples may not be found.

45. I only deal here with this portion of the larger passage, whose message seems muddled by its final section (there are indications that the passage is a conflation).

46. Compare the five instances of the term *ziran* in the brief *Daodejing* with the seven instances in the entire text of the *Zhuangzi*.

47. The swimmer's statement that he has no dao tells us that for the author the term entailed the element of conscious study.

48. As in the earlier discussion of swimmers in the same chapter, this swimmer has "forgotten" the water (19/24)—swimming has become "transparent" for him; he does not attend to it.

49. Zhuangzi, of course, does not celebrate skilled killers: his exemplars are, from our point of view, benign, and it may be that Zhuangzi could have found a means to demonstrate that dao-mastery and evil were incommensurate, as I cannot. Nevertheless, it is very likely that by making his dao-master a member of what was surely a socially repellant trade, Zhuangzi was trying to emphasize the dissociation of skills and conventional values. In Warring States society, the brutality that disturbs our ethical dispositions was seen quite differently. Mencius, for example, describes how the master swordsman Bogong You has nurtured the "courage" to murder any who so

much as look at him cross-eyed, and his only comment is to compare his self-possession to that of Confucius' disciple Zixia (*Mencius* 2A 2). Zhuangzi may have celebrated a butcher rather than a serial killer like Bogong You in order to increase the shock value for his audience.

50. This is particularly clear in light of the outcome of the first anecdote in *Renjian shi*, where Confucius allows that his disciple Yan Hui can now proceed to serve at the court of Wei, even though he is not compelled to do so. The author thus allows his spokesman to affirm the activist political goals intrinsic to Yan Hui's original project—certainly not a Zhuangzi-like position. This suggests that for the Inner Chapters, at least, *wuwei*, which often seems well rendered as "non-goal oriented action," can actually be generated only through skills configured around a goal. This raises the issue of whether non-goal oriented action is, indeed, a coherent notion.

51. These features of the fully perfected Confucian dao make it resemble Pierre Bourdieu's concept of the social *habitus*. Only, for Bourdieu, the *habitus* is *essentially* transparent and excludes the prescriptive character of elite cultural norms (*Outline of a Theory of Practice*, (Cambridge: Cambridge University Press, 1977), 200, n. 26). For Confucianism in general, the *habitus*, like performance skills, is transparent only as features of it are engaged in performance. When not in performance, its features are attended to by all members of the community, who embellish it consciously to the degree that they are full social participants (arbitrary differentials in this last matter are the ethical Achilles heel of Confucianism's checkered history). Yet Confucianism does develop a theory linking uncultivated social practice to the dao: the notion, articulated in the *Daxue* and *Zhongyong*, that the dao of the sage kings is, at root, precisely the ordinary practice of common men and women.

SEVEN

Zhuangzi's Understanding of Skillfulness and the Ultimate Spiritual State

Lee H. Yearley

Introduction

Few books existing anywhere are both as compelling and as mysterious as is the *Zhuangzi*; it simultaneously draws one's attention and eludes one's grasp. Readers are swept along—at times almost swept away—by the book, and yet often feel that what moves them is difficult to grasp much less articulate. They sense that something ineffable is being presented or even thrust upon them. They realize that Zhuangzi strains, if gracefully, to present through language a vision he thinks is beyond language; they understand the book truly represents a raid on the inexpressible. Given this, any interpreter must worry that translating Zhuangzi's ideas into one's own prosaic world and pedestrian prose will deform what is crucial. Nevertheless, attempts at translation are necessary, if only to guide readers to the work and help orient them.[1]

Let us begin, then, but begin with a brief academic note. The book, the *Zhuangzi*, is surely the product of many different authors and their ideas, quality of mind, and depth of spirit differ considerably. But a persuasive (if not always fully convincing) argument can be made that at least the first seven of its thirty-three chapters are largely by one hand, and that aspects of that person's work appear elsewhere in the book. We will focus on the vision presented in those places and not examine the work's other visions, even though some of them are of considerable profundity. Numerous technical problems arise, however, even within this one strand of the *Zhuangzi*. Translation and textual difficulties abound, but perhaps most important, one must always worry whether any interpretation witnesses more to the ingenuity of the interpreter than to the actual message of the author.[2]

Nevertheless, we can describe with at least some confidence the spiritual vision of a writer whom we will call Zhuangzi. That Zhuangzi probably lived in the late fourth century B.C.E.; he may have been brought up a Confucian and then become a Yangist—a school that argued for the pursuit of private tranquillity rather than public service. Later events, however, such as a personal crisis, contact with Logicians, and his own ecstatic experiences seem to have led him to find his own highly distinctive way.[3]

Our examination will focus on Zhuangzi's depiction of the ultimate spiritual state. His more direct depictions of that state, as we will see, are very evocative. They are also often quite mysterious. Therefore we will fill them out by analyzing his more understandable portrayal of skillful activity. Such activity both reflects and points to the highest state, and examining it provides us with a reasonably accessible avenue into his often elusive ideas on spirituality.

Before beginning that inquiry, however, we need to examine briefly two relevant features of the context within which Zhuangzi's ideas on spirituality are set. One is his views on the self and the other his views on the character of human knowledge.

Zhuangzi's Notion of the Three Levels of the Self

Any reliance on a neatly defined model of the self will misrepresent significant aspects of Zhuangzi's thought, given his notions about the futility of normal kinds of analysis, his seeming commitment to the abolition of dichotomies, and his method of presenting ideas. If used with appropriate caution, however, such a model does help us to understand and sort out some important ideas in him.

In Zhuangzi's picture, permutations of which appear in many Chinese thinkers, the self can be moved by three kinds of "drives," three desires to act or impulses to move: dispositional drives, reflective drives, and transcendent drives.[4] Dispositional drives are those strong movements to action that are triggered by specific circumstances. Some of these drives arise from biological or "natural" sources—hunger, for example. Others arise from social conditioning, conditioning that may or may not be thought to develop those "natural" sources—deference to elders, for example. In both cases, if particular stimuli appear then specific responses are activated. The sight of food or of an elderly person produces in me a specific desire and action. I am disposed, then, to react without thinking to certain occurrences.

Reflective drives manifest the desire to have different drives than the dispositional ones that normally and easily operate. For example, my dispositional drives may make me prone either to anger quickly or to defer inappropriately. Yet I may, on reflection, desire to be a different sort of person: one whose anger comes only slowly and whose deference appears only when warranted.

Reflective drives will, then, introduce conflict into my life. My quick anger or easy deference, for instance, now produces a division within me. Part of me moves easily toward the action, but part of me is dissatisfied with that movement. Reflective drives may also, however, lead me to change my actions. They may lead me either to overrule the dispositional drive when it appears or to undertake a process of self-cultivation that results in my having different dispositional drives than I now have. That is, I may through sheer will power abort my overly quick anger or I may through cultivation reform myself so that, in time, that kind of anger rarely arises. Reflective drives, then, are characterized by the presence of conflict, struggle, and possible changes in action.

Transcendent drives generate activities that exceed the normal capacities of the self and seem to arise from beyond it. They produce abilities that surpass normal abilities and transform normal actions. When empowered by transcendent drives I find, for example, that I am so finely tuned to circumstances that my anger or deference appears, on reflection, always to be appropriate. Moreover, I find myself able to perform easily and well tasks that previously seemed to be far beyond my normal capabilities.*

Transcendent drives resemble dispositional drives in their strength, spontaneity, and lack of reliance on normal thought. Their content differs however, notably in how far the capabilities expressed surpass those found in dispositional drives. Furthermore, transcendent drives can operate only because reflective drives have led to fundamental changes in the self; those changes allow the drives to operate.

Transcendent drives may, then, resemble or draw on either of the other two kinds of drives. Finally, however, they dissolve both dispositional and reflective drives and thus cause the normal self to disappear. They allow powers such as the 神 *shen*, "daemonic",—powers we will examine later—to possess a person and therefore they help bring to a person the highest possible spiritual fulfillment.[5]

This tripartite division of dispositional drives, reflective drives, and transcendent drives illuminates, I think, both Zhuangzi's spiritual vision and the

---

* Compare Yearley's "transcendent drives" with Eno's "spirit-like impulses" (p. 135) and with Berkson's description of the dao as "acting through" the sage (p. 119).—Eds.

importance of skillful activity to him. It helps us see, for example, just how Zhuangzi differs from those Daoists who simply distinguish between a social self and a natural self. Those Daoists think the social self (the product of social training) is that from which one should escape and the natural self (one's "original" pure character) is that to which one should return.

Zhuangzi's position is, however, considerably more complicated than is this simple view, and this model helps us see the differences between them. Unlike the simple view, for example, Zhuangzi distinguishes between two kinds of social selves: the dispositional and the reflective. He tends to scoff (as would most Daoists and even some Confucians) at behavior generated by those dispositional drives that arise from social conditioning. But he often shows respect for actions that arise from reflective drives, although he can criticize the struggle that accompanies those actions. His respect is especially pronounced if, in his view, the person is fated to reach no higher level—a situation that, for him, Confucius exemplifies (79, 90; cf.128–134; also note 17).[6]

Even more important, this model helps us see that, unlike certain other Daoists (some of whose ideas appear in the *Zhuangzi*), Zhuangzi's spiritual fulfillment does not consist in the childlike gratification of "natural" or instinctive dispositional drives. Rather he wants people to be animated by transcendent drives. Zhuangzi is well aware, as his portraits of heedless rulers show, of the problems that can arise in lives controlled by instinctive dispositional drives (66–72; cf.200–217, 234–243). Furthermore, he understands well the difficulties in distinguishing accurately between the instinctive and the habitual. Finally, he does not think it makes philosophical or religious sense to rely on the notion of a simple, instinctual, nature contact with which can save one.

Zhuangzi's final goal, then, is to activate transcendent drives, and they can appear only after reflective drives have remade the self's dispositional drives. As we shall examine more fully later, the importance both of the training that underlies this remaking and of the state it produces clarifies why skillful activity points to the perfected spiritual state. That is, skills differ from dispositional drives because they arise from training and involve an attentive responsiveness to situations. They also, however, differ from reflective drives because they involve none of the division that arises from the mind adhering to ideals that conflict with simple drives.

Skills differ, then, both from the blind impulses manifested in dispositional drives and from the conflicts manifested in reflective drives. Therefore, examining skills can provide us with an illuminating way to understand Zhuangzi's spirituality, even if finally they can just point to the state that transcendent drives produce. Before turning to how Zhuangzi actually describes skills and that to which they point we need, however, to look briefly at the other subject that provides a general context for his ideas: the character of human knowledge.

Zhuangzi's Picture of Normal Ethical Knowledge and the Implications He Draws From It

Underlying Zhuangzi's picture of spirituality are his views on what constitutes normal human knowledge, especially ethical knowledge, and how that knowledge affects actions. We will treat here only certain aspects of this complicated and controversial subject and keep as simple as possible a necessarily somewhat technical discussion. Let us begin by recounting an old Chinese story, perhaps of Daoist origin, that captures well some of the flavor, purposes, and ideas in Zhuangzi's approach to knowledge.

The story concerns a poor farmer who lives near a village in north China.[7] One day a wild horse strays into his farm and is captured. The villagers rush to congratulate him on his improved situation, but the old man only replies, "How do I know if it is a good thing or if it is a bad thing?" The following week the horse escapes, and the villagers return to express their sorrow. The old man, however, only replies, "How do I know if it is a good thing or if it is a bad thing?" Within three weeks the horse returns accompanied now by a strong and beautiful stallion. Again the villagers appear and again they congratulate him on his improved circumstances. But his response remains as it was before.

The old man's only son, enamored of the new stallion, begins to ride it. One day, however, he is thrown and crippled. Lamenting the son's injury the villagers reappear, but the old man's reply can by now be predicted. Two months pass, and barbarian hordes invade the country. All the able bodied young men in the district are forced to join the army; only the old man's crippled son is excused. Fearful for the life of their sons, the villagers come again to the old man to declare how lucky he is that his son was thrown and is crippled. The old man, however, simply replies "How do I know if it is a good thing it or if it is a bad thing?"

Various points can be drawn from this story. Most important here is that the old man's confessions of ignorance rest on his sense that the evaluation of situations depends on the perspective employed. Such a viewpoint reflects Zhuangzi's belief that knowledge is "perspectival." That is, most important distinctions between the good and the bad arise from and depend upon the position, the perspective, from which a person views the world. Moreover, no fully objective way exists to decide which of the conflicting perspectives is correct because any decision is bound to reflect a perspective. (It will, for example, either just reflect one of several conflicting perspectives or introduce yet another; see especially 60.) Given this, people ought simply to confess ignorance, a confession that has, Zhuangzi thinks, massive implications because knowledge is what guides most action and forms most attitudes. The old man's attitudes and activities differ so much from those of the villagers, for instance, because he thinks he lacks knowledge.

Put one way, Zhuangzi's approach manifests a powerful incapacity to understand, a nurtured inability to understand what seems so evidently true to most people about how to live. That is, he has trained himself, and hopes to train us, to possess an incapacity to understand much of what is obvious to virtually everyone else. This incapacity is far from either naiveté or intellectual dullness, although it can seem like that to the uninitiated. Rather it involves the acuity and courage continually to query cherished beliefs about the seemingly obvious. Moreover, it can be developed only through a kind of intellectual asceticism, the voluntary surrender of the guidance knowledge gives us in order to be open to what better can replace it.

There are many technical issues, and some heated debates, surrounding both the philosophical and theoretical details of Zhuangzi's account. They are well analyzed in recent works, including pieces in this volume, and I will not attempt to engage those issues here. For our purposes what is crucial, and relatively uncontroversial, is Zhuangzi's idea that almost all ethical language encases a set of distinctions that produces attitudes that inform actions. Ethical language, then, helps to regulate behavior and emotional reactions. Moreover, different communities, or groups within communities, will often have different kinds of ethical languages and therefore will produce and validate different, even conflicting, kinds of actions and attitudes (48–61, 100–108).[8]

Such differences are likely to appear because these learned discourses, Zhuangzi emphasizes, build on dichotomies: they rest on oppositions, such as that between the beautiful and the ugly. This web of oppositions forms thought, attitude, and action and gives groups of people a distinctive identity. For example, one group's language declares tattoos beautiful and their lack ugly, and its members think, feel, and act accordingly. Those without tattoos are considered imperfect specimens of the human race and treated as such. Another group, however, employs the same general opposition—the beautiful and the ugly—but thinks tattoos ugly and behaves accordingly.

For Zhuangzi, then, ethical knowledge involves the application of distinctions that arise from a system of describing and evaluating that people are taught when they learn a language. These distinctions focus desires, engender goals, and develop attitudes: to be taught, for instance, that selfishness is bad and compassion is good leads people to feel bad when they are selfish and to pursue compassion. When people "know" in this realm, therefore, they make distinctions that engender attitudes that cause actions. What people pursue, fear, and hope for arises from the distinctions built into the discourse that a group gives to its members.

All this implies, Zhuangzi thinks, that 辯 *bian*, "disputes", between significantly different linguistic communities cannot be resolved, at least if they concern issues such as the character of selfishness or benevolence. Indeed, Zhuangzi does not even seem to think it worthwhile to consider those ways in which people might mediate such disputes. No nuanced discussion occurs, for example, about how people might either analyze the validity of arguments used or evaluate the evidence cited. All such disputes, for him, seem to be about those kind of differences that most of us would admit do not allow for any adjudication, or at least any easy adjudication. Examples would be differences either in taste—such as my predilection for bright colors or spicy foods—or in fundamental presuppositions about the character of the human good—such as my claim that just people can suffer no real harm no matter what may appear to befall them.

These ideas lead Zhuangzi to insist that in the ethical area one cannot possibly know with real certainty whether or not the normal knowledge that guides one's life is true. His position is not the simple and finally untenable "we know nothing." Rather it is the more complex and subtle, "we do not know if we do know or if we do not know." As Zhuangzi writes when considering the notion that life is better than death: "How do I know that to take pleasure in life is not a delusion? How do I know that we who hate death are not exiles since childhood who have forgotten the way home? . . . How do I know that the dead do not regret that ever they had an urge to life?" (58–59). He neither answers such questions nor thinks he can answer them; he simply does not know.[9]

Zhuangzi's position, as noted, contains strengths and weaknesses of a technical sort, but most important to us is how it produces the context for his depiction of a spiritual fulfillment that differs from what normal life provides.* A further feature of that context must be examined, however, before we turn to his actual depiction. A person might (as I think did some Confucians) accept most of Zhuangzi's ideas about ethical knowledge and still operate in a fairly normal manner. Such a position involves suspending one's judgments about the ultimate truthfulness of many ethical ideas but still choosing to live within the confines of a single community's discourse.

Reasons for adopting this position are many. They can range from theoretical judgments about what it is possible and necessary for humans to understand to practical judgments about the relative adequacy of a community's ideas. A crucial reason to adopt the position, however, rests on the judgment that humans have pressing problems, problems that demand some kind of solution. A person "solves" such problems by using whatever materials and procedures are available, helpful, and have plausible warrants.[10]

Zhuangzi rejects what could be called this "pragmatic approach" because he thinks both that normal life contains monumental problems and that a grand spiritual fulfillment is possible. This dialectic of great need and glowing

---

* See editors' note on page 76. Eds.

fulfillment places Zhuangzi's spirituality within what I will call a "discontinuous" or "nonameliorative" type of religion. Such a religious viewpoint is fundamentally discontinuous with normal life and expectations. It seeks far more than an amelioration of the problems ordinary life produces.

In an ameliorative or continuous religion people work within the framework provided by normal life, but in a nonameliorative or discontinuous religion they make a substantial break with normal life. The former aims to deepen and extend the best ethical and religious ideas people have. The latter is suspicious of any attempt only to build on or to fix what is already present, and therefore of any attempt to bring comfort to decent people, to make the world safe for well disposed people. The former applies bandages, if you will, to what is perceived as minor wounds, while the latter calls for major surgery. The former labels that kind of major surgery mutilation while the latter labels the application of bandages malpractice.

Zhuangzi is aware of possible problems in his approach. In a memorable passage that seems to reflect his ideas (as well as his notion that when you enter this way you lose all ways, and in a sense get lost), he speaks of what happens to the man who goes to Handan to learn their wonderful way of walking. He both fails to learn the Handan walk and forgets his own. The result is that he crawls home. Moreover, Zhuangzi unabashedly seems to accept one implication of this kind of view: the notion that a clear hierarchy of spiritual fulfillment exists and that some, even many, are fated never to reach the highest level. (See, for example, 78–79; 96–98; the hierarchy is not, of course, tied to normal standards of excellence.)

One crucial reason for Zhuangzi's position is his understanding of what occurs in normal life. The usual mood of Zhuangzi's writing is buoyant. His critique of normal life is never as prominent as in most forms of Buddhism or Christianity, two noteworthy examples of discontinuous or nonameliorative religions. Moreover, he never assumes that irresolvable conflicts between fate and human hope represent a tragedy (17, 23, 79). Nevertheless, for him, normal life often presents a panorama of futility. As he says: "Is it not sad how we and other things go on stroking or jostling each other, in a race ahead like a gallop which nothing can stop? How can we fail to regret that we labour all our lives without seeing success, wear ourselves out with toil in ignorance of where we shall end? What use is it for man to say that he will not die, since when the body dissolves the heart dissolves with it? How can we not call this our supreme regret? Is man's life really as stupid as this?" (51). Zhuangzi asks us to recognize the unhappiness that can haunt most people's lives. He asks us to see how our highest hopes crash on the rocks of our own ineptitude or the world's harsh realities; how our most gratifying relationships often die at our own hands through clumsiness or inattention; how our often trivial work sucks the vitality from us; how our goals, once attained, often turn out to be fragile or to taste bitter; how prey we are to having all we most treasure taken away from us against our will; and finally how our own and others' death can make all our hopes, fears, and loves seem senseless.

Such a recognition can, he thinks, help at least some people seek a different and better way. To the characteristics of that way we may now turn. We will analyze first his general but often cryptic presentation of it and then consider his portraits of skillful activity and that to which it points.

Zhuangzi's Figurative Depictions of the Ultimate Spiritual State

A few hints exist in Zhuangzi that the ultimate spiritual state involves a withdrawal into impassivity (see, for example, 95, 89–90). Nevertheless, he usually pictures it as a state of centered and adaptive responsiveness where the mind's normal movements are replaced by movements that arise from transcendent drives. Such a state differs radically from normal human responsiveness with its reliance on ordinary language's dichotomies and its utilization of dispositional or reflective drives.

The desired state is a form of intraworldly mysticism, and it differs from most Western and many South Asian forms of mysticism. Practitioners of intraworldly mysticism seek no union with an Ultimate Reality. Instead they seek a way through the world, a reorientation of perspective that allows them to see and act within the world.[11]

One of Zhuangzi's simpler, if also most brief and abstract, formulations of the desired spiritual state focuses on how it lacks the apparently normal essentials of being human. That is, the state lacks the "judging that's it, that's not" that arises from following the discriminating mind manifested in one's dispositional or reflective drives. As he says, "What I mean by being without essentials is that the man does not inwardly wound his person by likes and dislikes, that he constantly goes by the spontaneous and does not add anything to the process of life" (82). In such a state, people follow what is "so of itself," obtain a state of natural spontaneity that takes no unnatural action, and thus actualize the ability to perform successfully their specific function.

This brief, abstract picture of the ultimate spiritual state is filled out in fuller and more evocative depictions. In these portraits Zhuangzi employs metaphors or images rather than normal language because the ultimate state represents an alternative to the oppositions that underlie such language. Indeed, his most compelling images are brilliant attempts to create verbal pictures that pair apparently contradictory items: intruding and being at home; "it" and "other;" the mind's animation and a mirror's material character.

One especially evocative image characterizes the desired spiritual state as the axis at the center of a circle, the motionless center of a rotating wheel. The image builds from the idea that normal knowledge rests on dichotomies. Those dichotomies, such as that between the beautiful and the ugly, are noted in the passage as the "it" and the "other." "What is It is also Other, what is Other is also It. There they say 'That's it, that's not' from one point of view, here we say 'That's it, that's not' from another point of view. Are there really It and Other? Or really no It and Other? Where neither It nor Other finds its opposite is called the axis of the Way. When once the axis is found at the centre of the circle there is no limit to responding with either, on the one hand no limit to what is *it*, on the other no limit to what is not" (53). In this image, fixed dichotomies are replaced by something that moves continuously, adapts constantly to whatever occurs, and yet also responds from a center. Just as with the motionless center of a rotating wheel, the reactions noted here move from a steady center, but they fluidly and adaptively respond to whatever happens.

This state resembles, as it is put elsewhere, "the centre of the ring where becoming veers with circumstances." Such a state can, however, only be depicted adequately by piling apparent contradictions or paradoxes on each other. For example, to be in this state is to be in a situation where: "Other things and . . . [a person] had no end nor start, no 'How long'? and no time. To be transformed day by day with other things is to be untransformed once and for all. . . . [For such a one] there has never yet begun to be Heaven, never yet begun to be man, never yet begun to be a Beginning, never yet begun to be things" (110–11). Other images of the perfected state clarify at least somewhat these last paradoxes, even though they also attempt to move beyond the dichotomies found in normal language. One such image, which may refer both to the sage's mind and the Dao's action, depicts something that is "at home where it intrudes" and therefore manifests peace within strife or tranquillity within disturbance. "That which kills off the living does not die, that which gives birth to the living has never been born. As for the sort of thing it is, it is there to escort whatever departs, is here to welcome whatever comes, it ruins everything and bring everything about. Its name is 'At home where it intrudes.' What is 'at home where it intrudes' is that which comes about only where it intrudes into the place of something else" (87). At the highest spiritual level, for Zhuangzi, a process exists where apparent opposites such as coming and going or destroying and completing are combined. Strife, disturbance, and intrusion mix with tranquillity, peace, and "at homeness." All those oppositions that define normal life occur here, then, as complementary interactions defined by and contained within a more comprehensive reality.

The images noted so far attempt to describe, or point to, the actual process that occurs in the ultimate spiritual state. Another set of images are illuminating because the focus is less on the actual process and more on the conditions that make it possible. Especially prominent in these portraits is an emphasis on people freeing themselves from those pursuits that arise from normal knowledge's dichotomies. For example, it is said that one should keep oneself 虛 *xu*, "tenuous" and use the mind as a mirror. "The utmost man uses the 心 *xin*, 'heart', like a mirror; he does not escort things as they go or welcome them as they come, he responds and does not store" (98).[12] A mirror simply reflects whatever is presented. It applies no framework of interpretation, makes no judgments of appropriateness, and possesses no desire to pursue or grasp. Interpretations, judgments, and desires all rest on the dichotomies encased in normal language. Mirroring, which lacks all of them, can therefore point to the desired state. Moreover, mirroring also captures that 論 *lun*, "rational sorting", that, unlike other rational operations, Zhuangzi commends and thinks underlies genuine responsiveness. Sorting presents a coherent, objective picture of how things relate, but it does not grade, does not place things in terms of their relative values. (See 12, 48.)

The ability to mirror, as well as the other needed abilities, can be reached by the 心齋 *xin zhai*, "fasting of the mind". The usual reference of the character *zhai* "fasting" is to the voluntary surrender of physical nourishment that occurs before religious sacrifices; mental fasting, however, is described in the following way: "Unify your attention. Rather than listen with the ear, listen with the *xin* 'heart'. Rather than listen with the heart, listen with the 氣 *qi*, 'energies'. Listening stops at the ear, the heart at what tallies with the thought. As for 'energy', it is the *xu* 'tenuous', which waits to be roused by other things. Only the Way accumulates the tenuous. The attenuating is the fasting of the heart. . . . [When] the channels inward through eyes and ears are cleared, and you expel knowledge from the heart, the ghostly and *shen* 'daemonic' will come to dwell in you, not to mention all that is human" (68–69, cf. 71, 92). This practice is commended to Yan Hui, a person full of high-minded hopes and intricately conceived plans, who seeks to counsel an errant lord. He is advised that a process initiated mainly by the surrender of the mind's normal nourishment, its diet of distinctions and dichotomies, will enable him to go beyond the mind as a tallying and organizing faculty. That surrender, in turn activates "transcendent" *qi* "energy", the pool of energetic fluid out of which things condense and into which they dissolve, and also both the Dao Way and the *shen* "daemonic". When this occurs, Yan Hui will be moved by transcendent drives. He will reach a state where Heaven rather than he is the agent, and he will say the appropriate words as easily as a bird sings (69).[13]

Zhuangzi wants people, then, to surmount their usual reliance on normal discourse's dichotomies by a fasting of the mind that enables them to reach a higher state. Defined by its overcoming of contraries, this state resembles the motionless center of a rotating wheel that is at home where it intrudes, manifests a mirrorlike mind, and draws on transcendent drives. Qualities such as adaptive responsiveness, harmonious interaction, and reactive coordination characterize it.

The difference between this state and people's normal state is illuminated by Zhuangzi's use of two phrases that designate two possible approaches to thought and action: the *yinshi* "adaptive that's it" and the *weishi* "contrived that's it" (11, 25–26, 52–4, 104, 106–7, Graham 1969–70, 143–144, Graham 1982, 6–7). The adaptive approach, which resembles skillful activity, embodies the continuing adaptation of it and other. This approach relates feelings, judgments, and actions to changing circumstances. The contrived approach, in contrast, reflects the normal way of making and following distinctions. It acts according to those fixed principles that embody a specific group's sense of what is correct. The two approaches, then, differ fundamentally. To use the adaptive approach is to base responses on changing circumstances and to make relative judgments that accord with shifting conditions. To use the contrived approach is to act on inflexible principles and to remain unresponsive to varying, shifting circumstances.

Most people use the contrived approach; they act from dispositional or reflective drives. Accepting the rule that one should defer to elders, for example, their deference is motivated either by conscious choice or by inclinations that arise from socially formed dispositions that manifest the rule. Such actions rest on the learned dichotomies a cultural discourse incarnates: that is, the idea that deference to elders is good and therefore to be pursued, and that its opposite is bad and therefore to be avoided. Adaptive actions, however, rest neither on the choices nor on the dispositions that manifest such dichotomies. Rather, they effortlessly adapt to the external situation.[14]

Such perfected actions are designated by a set of abstract terms: they are spontaneous (自然 *ziran*, "natural action", "so of itself"), illustrate natural action (無爲 *wuwei*, "inaction" or "taking no unnatural action"), and manifest a contact with real power (德 *de*, "virtue"), the *shen* "daemonic", *Tian* "Heaven", and *Dao* the "Way". Some of these terms are given their most substantial depictions, depictions often fraught with metaphysical connotations, outside that part of the *Zhuangzi* we are examining. Nevertheless, all of them can be taken to refer to significant parts of Zhuangzi's spiritual vision.[15] We can best understand both the terms and the vision by turning now to probe Zhuangzi's presentation of skillful activity.

The "Skill Stories" in the Zhuangzi

A wide range of activities can be called skillful. Only some, such as playing chess, exemplify the category of skillfulness, however, while others barely fit into it, for example playing tic-tac-toe. Our concern is with the more exemplary cases as usually only they illuminate Zhuangzi's idea of spirituality.

Many stories about exemplary skills appear in the *Zhuangzi*: we read about, for example, a butcher, an archer, an engraver, a ferryman, a buckle maker, and even a catcher of cicadas. In these exemplary cases, people act skillfully when they can, at will, proficiently perform actions that have, at minimum, certain characteristics. That is, the actions reflect the mastering of techniques that overcome difficulties inherent in the activity. Moreover, they reflect the particular standards of excellence the activity exemplifies. Finally, they can be evaluated accurately only by people who have considerable experience with the activity. The skillful chess player, for example, can at will proficiently perform moves that manifest a mastery of techniques that overcome difficulties inherent in the game. Moreover, those moves reflect the game's specific standards of excellence, and their excellence is acknowledged by other experienced players.

Skillful activity has features, including those just noted, that imply much, and in virtually all the skill stories in the *Zhuangzi* those wider implications are made clear. The narratives in these stories either emphasize the described activity's more general meaning or explicitly state that the activity transcends what most people would identify as normal skillfulness (63–64, 135, 137).[16] Moreover, many images or ideas that appear in these stories are drawn from Zhuangzi's depiction of the ultimate spiritual state: for example, the axis at the center of a circle, the fasting of the mind, the acquisition of a mirrorlike mind, the utilization of *qi* "transcendent energy", and the attaining to the *shen* "daemonic".

Skillful activity, then, clearly points to the highest spiritual state. Given that let us discuss a few of the skill stories, saving for later a theoretical examination of exactly why skills help us to understand the highest state. A discussion of these stories is also helpful because it allows us to see how Zhuangzi actually portrays the idea of skill, as well as to taste the inimitable flavor of his presentation.

Probably the most famous of the skill stories, and the clearest one to appear in the first seven chapters, is the story of Cook Ding carving an ox:

> As his hand slapped, shoulder lunged, foot stamped, knee crooked, with a hiss! with a thud! the brandished blade as it sliced never missed the rhythm, now in time with the Mulberry Forest dance, now with an orchestra playing the Jingshou... [The watching Lord comments on the perfection of his skill but Cook Ding replies:] What your servant cares about is the Way, I have left skill behind me. When I first began to carve oxen, I saw nothing but oxen wherever I looked. Three years more and I never saw an ox as a whole. Nowadays, I am in touch through the *shen* "daemonic" in me, and do not look with the eye. With the senses I know where to

stop, the daemonic I desire to run its course. I rely on Heaven's structuring, cleave along the main seams, let myself be guided by the main cavities, go by what is inherently so. A ligament or tendon I never touch, not to mention solid bone. . . . [At a] joint there is an interval, and the chopper's edge has no thickness; if you insert what has no thickness where there is an interval, then, what more could you ask, of course there is ample room to move the edge about. That's why after nineteen years the edge of my chopper is as though it were fresh from the grindstone. However, whenever I come to something intricate, I see where it will be hard to handle and cautiously prepare myself, my gaze settles on it, action slows down for it, you scarcely see the flick of the chopper—and at one stroke the tangle has been unravelled as a clod crumbles to the ground. (63–64)

When Cook Ding cuts, the meat seems almost to part of itself. His rhythmic strokes, guided by the daemonic rather than normal perception, follow the natural makeup of the meat. This allows him to preserve his chopper's sharpness, find an easy solution to a complex task, and move in an aesthetically pleasing fashion. Moreover, his actions bring satisfaction to him, beauty and wonder to an observer's eye, and the completion of a difficult task in an effortless way. These actions reflect the eloquent plea, found in the story's probable preface, to imitate the motionless center of a rotating wheel and thereby to possess Heaven, its light, and the daemonic. Such a state, as Cook Ding's actions make clear, brings a far greater treasure than that brought by normal sight, hearing, and thought (see 11).

Various explicit or implicit aspects of this story are developed in other skill stories. (Some of those skill stories, however, contain developments that fail to reflect Zhuangzi's ideas, and therefore we will not discuss them.) [17] One aspect of the story about Cook Ding is developed in the story about the Wheelwright Pian. In order to show, among other things, the insignificance of books, the wheelwright describes the crucial and incommunicable "knack" truly skillful action involves; " If I chip at a wheel too slowly, the chisel slides and does not grip; if too fast, it jams and catches in the wood. Not too slow, not too fast; I feel it in the hand and respond from the heart, the mouth cannot put it into words, there is a knack in it somewhere which I cannot convey to my son and which my son cannot learn from me" (140). Such knacks are crucial in skills. Indeed, to have such a knack is to be at home where one intrudes; that is, to feel at home when the chisel intrudes into the wood. Moreover, this knack manifests well the distinctive kind of knowledge that is involved. The knowledge is defined by three elements: an adaptive responsiveness to change, a unification of the physical and the mental, and a resistance to being communicated by normal means.

To reach such a state of knowledge a person needs to possess a clear sighted and detached calm, a mirrorlike mind. Such a mind forgets the dichotomies that produce normal fears and hopes. An important aspect of this kind of calm is presented, in another story, when an inquirer asks whether he can learn to handle a boat like a ferryman who acts "as though he were daemonic." The questioner is told that:

> A good swimmer picks it up quickly because he forgets the water. As for a diver, he would handle a boat deftly even if he had never seen one before, because he looks at the depths as at dry land, at the capsizing of a boat as at his carriage sliding backwards. Though ten thousand prospects of capsizing or sliding go on spreading out before him, they cannot intrude into the place where he dwells. Why would he be ill at ease anywhere? Play for tiles, and you're skillful; play for belt-buckles, and you lose confidence; play for gold, and you're flustered. Your skill is the same as ever, but if you are attaching importance to something you are giving weight to what is outside you, and whoever gives weight to what is outside him is inwardly clumsy. (136–137)

The process for obtaining appropriate detachment from the hopes and fears that normally animate people, as well as the results of it, are described at greater length, and with more technical language, in the case of the Engraver Qing. When asked by the Lord what secret allows him to make a bell stand with a daemonic, ghostly quality, he replies:

> When I am going to make a bell stand I take care never to squander *qi* "energy" on it, I make sure to fast to still the *xin* "heart". After fasting three days, I do not care to keep in mind congratulation and reward, honours and salary. After fasting five days, I do not care to keep in mind your blame or praise, my skill or clumsiness. After fasting seven days, I am so intent that I forget that I have a body and four limbs.
> During this time my lord's court does not exist for me. The dexterity for it concentrates, outside distractions melt away, and only then do I go into the mountain forest and observe the nature of the wood as Heaven makes it grow. The aptitude of the body attains its peak; and only then do I have a complete vision of the bell stand. . . . So I join what is Heaven's to what is Heaven's. Would this be the reason why the instrument [the bell stand] seems daemonic? (135)

The process described here resembles the fasting of the mind that allows Yan Hui to obtain a quite different skill—the skill of counseling a lord and both making understood his message and preserving his life. Through such "fasting" he overcomes normal intentions and allows transcendent drives to possess him (66–69). In both cases the presence of transcendent drives allows a person to accomplish difficult tasks in a potentially hostile environment, the hierarchical world of courtly intrigue and the often brutal exercise of power.

This ability is evocatively displayed in the story of a man who swims beneath a three-hundred foot waterfall in the forty miles of turbulence the waterfall produces, turbulence that even fish do not inhabit. The story is perhaps the most obviously symbolic of all the skill stories, and it almost surely includes some terminology that carries more abstract, even metaphysical connotations than does virtually all of Zhuangzi's usual terminology. Nevertheless, the image is an especially striking one, swimming gracefully and easily through waters too rough for even fish. Moreover, the swimmer's answer to the question of how he can stay afloat is worth noting: "I enter with the inflow and emerge with the outflow, follow the Way of the water and do not impose my selfishness upon it. This is how I stay afloat in it. . . . It is so without me knowing why it is so—it's destined for me" (136). The swimmer's skill allows him to thrive in a realm that bring destruction to the nonskillful. Acting from higher forces rather than from normal human rules and dispositions, he moves spontaneously, harmonizes with a changing world, and is swept along by an inflow and outflow that manifests the higher Way.

Such a state resembles that commended to a Duke who, like Yan Hui, is about to begin a political mission. He is told to surrender his attachment to self-interest and morality and to follow instead the inevitable, the ordained; that is, to seek in any particular situation whatever single course perfectly fits it. "To let the heart roam with other things as its chariot, and by trusting to the inevitable nurture the center of you, is the farthest one can go. . . . The important thing is to fulfill what is ordained for you; and that is the most difficult of all" (71). To discover the inevitable in a situation, to be swept along by the flow of the ordained, is to be possessed by transcendent drives. Reaching that state is difficult however. It involves being unencumbered by the distinctions of normal ethical knowledge, and therefore remaining unmoved by ordinary dispositional and reflective drives. Skillful action both reflects such a state and points to its ultimate manifestation.

These skill stories point, then, toward the highest possible spiritual fulfillment. To grasp more fully both what skills are and why they can point to this higher state, we must investigate further the characteristics of normal skillful activity, and to that topic we may now turn.

The General Conception of Skillful Activity

To understand more fully the conception of skillful activity we will examine how such activity differs from most normal activity, especially how it manifests a distinctive kind of knowledge and sort of disposition. We can then analyze certain characteristics of skillful activity that point clearly to the spiritual state Zhuangzi commends.[18]

An important distinction can be made between two kinds of action. Let me put the distinction abstractly and sharply and then turn to concrete examples whose textured character introduces needed complexities. One kind of action, such as skillful actions, are "performances." Another kind, such as most normal actions, are "processes." (The distinction between performances and processes is drawn from the Aristotelian tradition; in Greek the distinction is between *kinesis* and *energia*, in Latin between *motus* and *operatio*.)[19]

A process is defined by the pursuit of a goal. The agent, that is, aims to progress toward a goal and fulfillment comes only when the goal is obtained. Moreover, the agent may obtain the goal by means other than those found in the process. Finally, the pleasure received involves the satisfaction, and other possible rewards, that occur when the agent finally possesses the goal sought. A performance, in contrast, is defined by the fact that each part of the activity is complete in itself, that each step has its own integrity. Fulfillment, then, is present at any stage. Moreover, the agent may obtain such fulfillment only by means of the performance. Indeed, the pleasure involved in the ongoing performance and the pleasure involved in reaching the goal of the activity are so intimately connected that one cannot describe one without describing the other. Finally, such pleasure is not characterized by passing, perhaps intense feelings. Rather it has certain very distinctive marks: for example, effortless concentration, lack of fatigue, quick passage of time, and a disinterest in doing anything other than what is now being done.

Building a rabbit hutch for my child's rabbit is a process; my pleasure is complete only when the hutch is complete. But listening to a symphony is a performance; my pleasure is complete at any particular moment. Moreover, I may decide to obtain the rabbit hutch by purchase rather than by construction, but no way exists to obtain what is involved in listening to a symphony other than by listening to it. With a performance, I feel fulfillment and a distinctive pleasure as I proceed and can obtain that particular fulfillment in no other way. With a process, however, only the project's successful completion brings fulfillment and that goal may be obtained by other means.

This abstract distinction clarifies, I think, important differences between two kinds of activities. Also important to us, however, is that the distinction clarifies the ways in which we can approach the same kind of activity; that is the differing attitudes we can have to it. Playing chess, for example, is a process if I aim simply to win, but it is a performance if involvement in the game is what basically animates me.

Put in a different if related way, my chess playing can be motivated either by internal goods or external goods. Playing well is an internal good, one that arises only from my actions, from my excellence as a practitioner of this specific kind of activity. Winning and what may come with it, such as money or praise, is an external good. Others give it to me because of the result of the game, a result that may be due to factors that have little to do with my own playing, factors such as my opponent's mistakes. Moreover, the pleasure I obtain differs considerably depending on which of the goods I aim at. The pleasure of receiving honor or money is far different from the pleasure of, say, effortless concentration and the full engagement of valuable human powers.

Zhuangzi never explicitly makes these distinctions, but they clarify his ideas about skill. That is, he thinks most normal actions are processes animated by the pursuit of external goals. Both skillful actions and spiritual actions, however, are performances animated by the possession of internal goods. Moreover, he also thinks that processes may become performances if people take the correct attitude to them.

Indeed, the possibility of people making such a change in the character of their action is at the heart of Zhuangzi's message. My construction of the rabbit hutch may become a performance when the goal of possessing a rabbit hutch becomes less important to me than the activity of building one or when the external good of winning a chess match is replaced by the internal good of playing chess well. Changing normal actions, which are processes with external goods, into skillful actions, which are performances with internal goods, is for Zhuangzi both possible and crucial to our spiritual development.

A further point that can be drawn from these distinctions also helps clarify Zhuangzi's general perspective. Skillful activity can arise only if social institutions provide the means necessary for people to obtain the techniques, attitudes, and opportunities that allow skills to be actualized. One can learn to play chess only if specific things are available, things ranging from chess pieces to an understanding of the traditions that convey the rules and ethos of the game. Institutions, however, usually also contain forces that make prominent the ideas that external goods are more important than internal goods, that processes rather than performances are crucial to human well being.

A clear if sad example of this is the institution of modern higher education. It makes possible the training that enables people to engage in acts that contain internal goods, performances such as reading the *Zhuangzi*. It also, however, generates a context in which external goods, and thus processes, are thought to be most important. Receiving a grade for the paper on Zhuangzi or a degree for the work done on various papers becomes the most acceptable way to think about one's education.

Social institutions, then, provide the nurture necessary for performances and for the possession of internal goods, but they also tend to guide people to think about them as processes defined by the external goods produced. Zhuangzi's ideas about how one should deal with social institutions, including motifs such as the "use of the useless" reflect, I think, his sense that such institutions are both crucial and dangerous. They are crucial because they make possible the training that underlies performances and the possession of internal goods. They are dangerous because they undermine what they make possible by emphasizing the significance of processes and external goods.

Other features of these distinctions between kinds of actions, the goods that accompany them, and the institutional settings they presuppose become even clearer when we discuss how skillful knowledge differs from normal knowledge and how skillful habits differ from normal habits. Our knowledge can be roughly divided into a "knowledge that" (normal knowledge) and a "knowledge how" (skillful knowledge). You may know that cars have spark plugs or that Zhuangzi said you should have a mind like a mirror. But you may also know how to replace your car's spark plugs or how to have a mind like a mirror. To know that something is so is to have information, to obtain it suddenly, and to judge its worth by the criterion of truth and falsity. To know how, on the other hand, is to possess an improved ability to do something, to obtain it gradually, and to evaluate your possession of it by whether you act deftly or clumsily. (See Ryle 1949, 25–61.)

We understand relatively well how we acquire knowledge that, but the acquisition of knowledge how is often a mysterious process. We do know the latter always involves a time consuming mastery of techniques in which initial attempts are awkward and require sustained effort while later ones are graceful and easy. Nevertheless, formulating exactly how we learn the skill or even exactly what we have learned is often virtually impossible. Books are usually of little help—as anyone can testify who attempts to acquire a skill such as tennis by reading. Moreover, too much conversation about the skill or reflection on it may even actually impede the attempt to master it.

We do, nevertheless, acquire such "knowledge how" and when we do, we acquire a disposition, a tendency to respond in specific ways when certain situations arise. We usually speak of all these acquired dispositions as habits, but significant distinctions exist among kinds of dispositions. Some of these distinctions we discussed earlier, but most important here is the difference between those dispositions properly called habitual and those properly called skillful.

Both are acquired, lead to spontaneous actions, and involve an intimate relationship between the mind and the body. Despite these similarities, however, the acquisition and the operation of the new abilities differ in important ways. A toddler acquires the habit of walking, but a rock climber acquires the skill of climbing. Both learn to move over the earth, but mindless repetition marks the toddler's acquisition, while the cultivation of intelligent awareness marks the climber's acquisition. Moreover, the climber's attentive and adaptive movements up a cliff differ from the toddler's heedless movements over the ground. Habits are acquired by conditioning, by a continuous repetition in which every performance virtually replicates every other performance. Furthermore, once conditioning is complete little attention is needed for correct performance. A skill, in contrast, arises from training not conditioning; it combines repetition with the stimulation of judgment by criticism. Furthermore, the activity involves constant alertness and the careful adaptation of acts to changing situations.

The ideas of pure habit and pure skill are abstractions that mark the two extremes of one continuum, and many activities will fit on neither extreme. For example, the toddler on rocky ground tends toward skill while the climber on an easy ascent tends toward habit. Indeed, the placement on the continuum of even apparently similar actions may depend on circumstances. When practicing basketball alone my jump shot from six feet is a habitual action. But that same shot taken in a game when I am closely guarded is a skillful action. Nevertheless, the distinction between skill and habits is revealing. Unlike habits, skills are acquired dispositions that arise from training and show attentiveness and adaptation.

Skillful actions, then, utilize "knowledge how" not "knowledge that" and operate from a distinctive kind of disposition. Moreover, they are activities not processes and manifest internal not external goods. These general features both distinguish skillful actions from other actions and point to the spiritual state that Zhuangzi commends.

These general features also underlie six more specific characteristics of skillful activity, and examining them can reveal much about the final spiritual state. Let us turn then to a description of each characteristic, using as examples two activities with which many may be familiar: one is physical, skillful tennis; the other is intellectual, skillful conversation. We will also, with each characteristic, refer to where it appears in the *Zhuangzi*.

The Six Characteristics of Perfected Skill Activities

One such characteristic is the kind of mental attentiveness that responds adaptively to changes in the outside world. This attentiveness produces very distinctive kinds of responses, and it is helpful to begin by enumerating what these responses are not. They are neither reflex actions—as when you react to touching a hot object—nor simple habitual actions—as when you tie your shoelaces. But they also do not resemble acts that arise from dispositional drives—as when hunger leads you to eat or a feeling of deference leads you to surrender a seat to an elderly person. Nor do they resemble acts that arise from consciously following rules—as when you fill out an income tax form or undertake any of the actions caused by reflective drives.

Instead, these skillful reactions manifest a special sensitivity to changing circumstances, an instantaneous responsiveness that accords with the general rules of an activity but is not simply guided by them. Skillful people, that is, see and move with changes, always adapting to them, never asserting themselves against them. For example, in a conversation you shift your approach as the other person's mood or argument changes, attentively adapting yourself to the contours of the ideas and feelings presented. Similarly, in tennis you quickly recognize and respond to your opponent's movements and shots without going through the normal processes of mental calculation (63–64, 138, 140).

Another characteristic of skillful actions is that although they are easier to produce than unskillful or normal actions, they reach their goals more effectively than do those kinds of action. That is, a notable gain in power and efficacy occurs but it occurs without the addition of effort. Skillful actions appear to tap a new source of power, one that generates a new flow of energy that exceeds what could be produced by either brute strength or willful application. For example, a skillful tennis serve expends little effort but produces speed and accuracy. In contrast, an unskillful serve arises from labored effort but generates little of value. Similarly, skillful conversation brings almost effortlessly obtained results, results that go far beyond what mere exertion could produce. Ease, power, and efficacy all combine, then, when a skill is in full flower (63–64, 106, 136, 137).

These two characteristics manifest still another attribute of skillful activity: the unification of the mental and the physical. Indeed, clear distinctions between the physical and the mental are extremely difficult to make when skills operate. Mind and body interact too subtly to see either one as an easily separable entity that commands or is commanded. Rather each is simply and easily informed by the other. In tennis, for example, the instantaneous strategic adjustments made as you feel the ball on the racquet or see your opponent change positions cannot adequately be divided into physical and mental activities; they appear to be one unified action. Similarly, in skillful conversation spoken words and bodily movements form too intimate a unity to allow one to speak easily of two distinct entities.

In instances like these, physical actions specify the mental's presence and mental actions are made manifest through physical movements. Each informs and signals the presence of the other. Moreover, this unification finds expression in, and may even also produce, the paranormal phenomena that appear in skill activities. A common example of such phenomena is the sense that the normal flow of time has stopped, that the speeding tennis ball, for instance, is virtually fixed in place (63–64, 81, 135–138, 140–141).

Skillful actions with these characteristics also both arise from and manifest a personal tranquillity. That is, one must effortlessly concentrate on the activity itself, and that involves forgetting normal concerns and goals as well as possessing a settled but active mind and a stable if vigorous physical state. For example, you play tennis badly if you worry too much about your everyday problems, your play's appearance, or even the possibility of victory. You must instead forget much of what usually animates you and obtain a settled simplicity that focuses only on correctly hitting the ball. Similarly, skillful discussion occurs when you focus on the play of conversation rather than on your normal concerns, whether they be the meeting of deadlines or the desire to be seen as a gifted conversationalist (134, 135, 136–37, 141, 142).

Skillful activity, then, manifests and even rests on equanimity. It also, however, feeds whatever tranquillity is present. If little is present, skillful activity will nurture it. If more is present the activity will deepen it. You may, for instance, begin your tennis game or conversation haunted by turbulent feelings or thoughts. Soon, however, the rhythm of playing or talking begins to triumph and a sense of stillness, peace, and effortlessness increases. Your stroke or conversation becomes more rhythmic, your mind more settled, and that in turn produces a general sense of tranquillity (136, 137).

Finally, skill activities, at least at their most refined, can make you feel part of the larger rhythm of some meaningful whole. This occurs in part because skills manifest in intensified form all those characteristics that distinguish activities from processes, characteristics such as the presence of fulfillment at any stage or the animation by internal not external goods. It also arises, however, from the attentive responsiveness and adaptation to change that characterizes skills. When two people are involved, as in a tennis game, this adaptive responsiveness creates a harmonious interaction where change begets change, and the participants create together a beautiful but shifting pattern that seems to reflect a more perfect and well-ordered reality. Similarly, a skillful conversation, even one that involves both important issues and considerable disagreement, can generate such a sense of harmonious interaction.

Perhaps even more revealing about this last characteristic of skill is the fact that the state just described can arise from doing some simple act, whether one is alone or with others. For example, when your tennis serve is truly skillful, a feeling can arise that your individual motions fit into the world's larger motions and your present world fits harmoniously into a more significant world. You think it perfectly right for you to be doing just what you are doing; you accept your place with total equanimity (136, 137, 141).

Skillful action is, then, a performance not a process, and one that manifests a distinctive kind of knowledge and sort of disposition. More specifically, it also contains those characteristics we just discussed: adaptive responses to external changes; gains in power and efficacy without additional effort; unification of the mental and the physical; generation and manifestation of tranquillity; and the sense of participation in a larger, more harmonious whole.

All these features of skillful activity point toward the spiritual state that Zhuangzi commends. I need, however, to stress again that the ultimate state transcends skillfulness. It involves, to use our earlier terminology, replacing both one's dispositional and reflective drives with transcendent drives; it involves being moved by forces and a wisdom that surpass the simply human. Moreover, crucial features of it can be understood only by examining, as we did earlier, those evocative but elusive figurative depictions Zhuangzi presents. Let us end by bringing together these various treatments in order to render, however inadequately, the ultimate spiritual state.

The Spiritual State Pointed to by Zhuangzi's Portraits of Skills and His Figurative Depictions

Understanding the state of ultimate spiritual perfection is made especially difficult by the fact that Zhuangzi never gives a clear account of the higher realm whose actions define that state. He is, in general, committed to over-turning, or at least questioning, dichotomies such as that between "higher and lower realms," or the normal self and its lord, or even "Heaven and human beings" (51, 84–85). Indeed, when describing the archer Yi's skill, he will even go so far as to declare: "The perfect man hates Heaven, hates what is from Heaven in man, and above all the question 'Is it in me from Heaven or from man?'" (106, cf. 111). Moreover, he employs—seemingly quite self-consciously—a wide variety of often mysterious formulations to point to the "higher." He speaks, for example, of returning to the root, trunk, seed, magic storehouse, ancestor from whom one is descended, or gate from which we emerge (51, 68, 84 ff., 109).

Given this, we can never hope to gain an adequate understanding of the full character of transcendent desires and the realm they manifest. Never-theless, we can at least proceed with what I earlier called a raid on the inexpressible because Zhuangzi does leave certain markers that point out a trail.

We have already examined many of those markers in analyzing both those figurative images that Zhuangzi uses to depict the ultimate spiritual state and those characteristics of skill that reflect and point to it. That account can be filled out by examining several other especially noteworthy passages and by returning again to some passages we have already examined.

Zhuangzi claims that the fully spiritual person lacks the normal person's "judging that's it, that's not," and therefore likes and dislikes; instead he or she "constantly goes by the spontaneous" (82). Nonetheless, only certain kinds of spontaneity manifest transcendent drives. The spontaneity shown in dispositional drives, for example, involves a surrender either to instinctive or socially conditioned desires. It disturbs or blurs a person's awareness of the changing features of the external world and impedes transcendent drives. A lucid, detached, impersonal calm must, then, underlie true spontaneity. That is, only a tenuousness born of the fasting of the mind and reflected in the possession of a mirrorlike mind provides a home for transcendent drives.

Attaining the perfected state involves a specific regimen of training, but the exact details of that regimen are unclear. We have seen at least hints of it, for example, in the process prescribed for Yan Hui and described by the Engraver Qing (68–69, 135). The regimen does seem clearly to involve discarding a person's normal reliance on language's dichotomies, on self interested plans of action (a "too easy path," Zhuangzi thinks), and on an inner allegiance to regnant manners and moral codes (68, 70, 79). Moreover, the cultivation of *qi* through breath control is surely one part of it. But other far more mysterious transformation disciplines seem also to be involved and of them we know virtually nothing.[20]

The result of this training is not simply to contact a nature that a person possesses from birth. Rather it is to allow transcendent drives to possess one. A sure sign of such possession is the development of a power, *de* "virtue", that is manifested, in part, by one's indifference to irreparable disasters and in one's detachment from normal concerns (see, for example, 76–83).

Perhaps most important, however, is another feature. The presence of transcendent drives is manifested in one's possession by the *shen* "daemonic" or, more accurately, in one's attainment of the state of "being daemonic." The daemonic is a force and "intelligence" that is higher than and alien to normal human thought, feeling, and effort. It fits, then, only uneasily into any of our normal categories of understanding. Indeed, it can be easily trivialized into the eerie or uncanny; falsely spiritualized into a moral sacred; inappropriately conjoined with our own contemporary overtones of restless anguish; and simply confused with the malignity of the demonic.

All such attempts to place the daemonic within accessible categories of understanding miss the reality to which Zhuangzi thinks he refers. For him, it represents that possession by a higher kind of ability that we saw mirrored, if imperfectly, in skill activities. To be more precise, the daemonic ought not be hypostatized, made into a substantial something; it is defined by its exercise, it does not just account for its exercise.[21]

Being possessed by the daemonic, becoming a daemonic person, is a distinctive characteristic of virtually all those who appear in Zhuangzi's skill stories, as well as of various other spiritual adepts he depicts. Daemonic aptitude and insight manifest, then, the realm of transcendent drives, the spontaneity of those vital processes that arise when we abandon normal knowledge, cultivate *qi*, and simply perceive and respond (63–64, 69, 105, 110, 135–138).

Such daemonic activity is amoral—if normal moral standards are the measure.* It can, however, involve the acceptance, when necessary, of certain fated duties such as love of parents or service to lords (70, 62, 66–72). Moreover, it need not involve the rejection of customary practices or moral codes if they are accepted simply as matters of practical convenience. In fact, accepting certain conventions can help one avoid fruitless conflicts that wear out the daemonic (54, 72–74, 78–79). Furthermore, Zhuangzi even hints that such activity produces a new kind of morality, one whose benefits extend to everyone, perhaps because such activity can heal others in mysterious ways, or, if followed by all, will allow people to interact as harmoniously as do those darting fish who never collide with each other. Nevertheless, the moral quality of this perfected state is usually of little interest to Zhuangzi, especially if morality is defined in a narrow or conventional way.[22]

Most important to us, however, is Zhuangzi's idea that people possessed by the daemonic cease to be normal agents, that is agents who manifest either dispositional or reflective drives. Instead, such people are empowered by higher forces, transformed by transcendent drives. People's normal deliberating selves, perceiving senses, and habitual or instinctual drives are replaced by an alien power and intelligence that creates a spontaneous and saving attunement to the changing facets of the world. This possession manifests all those characteristics we discussed in describing skillful activities, but their presence is intensified. Moreover, these characteristics now inform all of a person's actions. The person does more than just skillfully build bell stands, or cut meat, or give political advice; whatever skill a particular situation demands is instantly activated.

Possession by the daemonic allows one, then, to negotiate a way through the world in a fashion that resembles the easy movements of the swimmer who thrives in the turbulent foam below a waterfall. Moreover, all of one's actions manifest the characteristics that one sees only at times and imperfectly in even the most exemplary skill activities: tranquillity, easy movement; power without effort; attentive adaptation to changing externals; unification of the mental and physical; pleasurable fulfillment that is present at any moment; and harmonious joyful accommodation to the rhythms of a larger whole. This, then, is for Zhuangzi the ultimate spiritual state that at least some humans can achieve.

---

*On the question of the amorality of Zhuangzi's dao, see editors' note on page 142.
—Eds.

Notes

1. A situation that might well have pleased Zhuangzi informs the history of this piece. I initially wrote it almost fifteen years ago for a volume on Daoism, aimed at a general audience, that is yet to appear. The editors of this volume expressed interest in the piece, and with the approval of the other volume's editor, I accepted their offer. Much has, of course, happened both to me and to scholarship about Zhuangzi in the intervening time. Nevertheless, on rereading it I found that almost all of the piece still represents either my own view or a defensible position. (The distinction is one Zhuangzi might, I think, have relished.) I did find places in the text where infelicitous prose, evident lacunae or even errors, and problematic interpretations appeared and I have changed them. I have also added much material in the footnotes. Despite all these changes, the piece remains much as I originally wrote it, and the text itself surely remains aimed toward a general audience. This means the changes in me then and me now, and in the understandings of Zhuangzi then and now are, at times, only imperfectly reflected. Such a situation seems more fitting with this subject than with virtually any other I can imagine.

2. Good discussions about problems in both the text and the translation of the *Zhuangzi* occur in Graham 1979; Graham 1981, 27–33; Graham 1982; Roth 1991; and Mair 1994. Also note the general discussion of texts from this period found in E. Bruce Brooks, "Review Article: The Present State and Future Prospects of Pre-Han Text Studies," *Sino-Platonic Papers* 46 (July, 1994), 1–74.

3. See Graham 1981, 3–5 and 115–118. Ivanhoe 1991 inventories various interpretations of the so-called conversion experience and presents his own understanding.

4. Numerous questions, of course, surround any framework used to present a model of the self, perhaps especially one that applies to classical Chinese thought. I examine a number of them in my treatment of the self in *Mencius and Aquinas: Theories of Virtue and Conceptions of Courage* (Albany: State University of New York Press,1990), 95–111. Also see, however, my "Bourgeois Relativism and the Comparative Study of the Self," in J. Carman and S. Hopkins, eds., *Tracing Common Themes, Comparative Courses in the Study of Religion* (Atlanta: Scholars Press, 1991), 165–178, "Theories, Virtues, and the Comparative Philosophy of Human Flourishings: A Response to Professor Allan," *Philosophy East & West* 44.4 (1994), 711–721, and "Taoist Wandering and the Adventure of Religious Ethics," The William James Lecture, *Harvard Divinity Bulletin* 24.2 (1995), 11–15. Although none of my treatments examine explicitly the notion of transcendent drives, features of

it are analyzed in them. See, especially, the analysis of "empowerment" in Yearley 1990, particularly when the subject is the perfection of courage (pp.141–143 and 150–159); the general treatment of comparative issues when the self is the subject in Yearley 1991 and Yearley 1995; and the examination of the relationship between claims about human action and claims about ontology in Yearley 1994.

5. Graham's views on the problems in applying any Western ideas about the self to Zhuangzi surely have influenced my own views; see, for example, his "Reflections and Replies" in Rosemont 1991, 283–286. Nevertheless, the differences between us are often striking and I do think a more "rational" ordering of materials about the self is possible than he does. My acceptance of the general direction, if not always the details, of Taylor's analysis underlies many of these differences; see, especially, Charles Taylor, *Human Agency and Language: Philosophical Papers 1* (Cambridge: Cambridge University Press, 1985), 15–44. I do, however, think it important to take seriously the approach to Daoists' ideas of the self found in Norman J. Girardot, *Myth and Meaning in Early Taoism* (Berkeley: University of California Press, 1983); see, for example, 258ff. I find Wu's account less compelling, see Wu 1982, for example, 91–106. A last note: I use "drives" rather than "desires," despite the word's biological overtones and the awkwardness the term sometimes introduces, because it carries few connotations of consciousness and is not restricted to the human realm.

6. The Graham 1981 translation will be cited in the text by page numbers alone, as in the references that precede this footnote. That translation also contains an often plausible, if also usually controversial, reconstruction of the distinct parts of the text as well as an important commentary. Among the other translations, Watson 1968 and Mair 1994 are particularly noteworthy but also note Legge 1891 and Fung Yu-lan's translation of the first seven chapters, 1964.

7. The earliest Chinese version of the story appears in the *Huainanzi* (chapter 18), a collection of various essays organized around Daoist themes that was presented to Emperor Wu in 139 B.C.E. For an early and not altogether reliable partial translation of the text, see Evan Morgan, trans., *Tao the Great Luminant* (London: Paul, Trench, Trubner and Co., 1935); for a scholarly study of the history of the text, see Harold Roth, *The Textual History of the Huai-nan Tzu* (Ann Arbor: AAS Monograph Series, 1992).

8. For important treatments of these issues from different perspectives [apart from some excellent treatments in this volume], see Chad Hansen, *Language and Logic in Ancient China* (Ann Arbor: The University of Michigan Press Hansen, 1983), 55–65, 88–97; Graham 1969–70, 138–143; Graham, 1981, 9–14, 25–26; Graham 1989, 176–186, 199–202; Ivanhoe 1993; and

Kjellberg 1993. I focus here just on ethical language, conceived broadly as what involves judgments about the good, the bad, and the indifferent when the subject is human flourishing. It remains true, however, that Zhuangzi at times seems to refer to all language. Moreover, even when ethics is the focus the text contains a few passages at variance with my general portrait; see, for example, Graham 1981, 70.

Much of Zhuangzi's critique can be recast in terms of what today is called "behavioral nominalism" although he surely maintains a sturdy, even naive, realism about many things. This kind of critique is often powerful but, to my mind, many of its more dramatic results arise from adopting an observational rather than a deliberative posture toward ethical judgments. I share Hampshire's doubts about the adequacy of that posture; see Stuart Hampshire, *Innocence and Experience* (Cambridge, Mass.: Harvard University Press, 1989), 23–32, 38–41, 79–105, 109–110. Moreover, I now think identifying those weaknesses has significant implications for our understanding of thinkers like Zhuangzi, implications that I missed in some of my earlier work. For my revised view see Yearley 1994 and 1995.

9. Zhuangzi's ignorance also rests on his understanding of what has been called the problem of the criterion: Any criterion that establishes the truth of something will need still another criterion to establish the initial criterion's truthfulness, and that process results in an infinite regress (see Graham 1981, 58–59). Incidentally, throughout this discussion, I use "knowledge" rather than "belief" or "justified belief" for the sake of simplicity.

10. See Lee Yearley, "Toward a Typology of Religious Thought: A Chinese Example," *The Journal of Religion* 55.4 (1975), 426–443 and "Hsun Tzu on the Mind: His Attempted Synthesis of Confucianism and Taoism," *Journal of Asian Studies* XXXIX 3 (May, 1980) 465–480, but note Nivison's criticisms of this approach; see, especially, Graham 1981, 129–131, 138–142. For an examination of this position as a typical response to these problems, a position that I call "sophisticated parochialism," see Lee Yearley "New Religious Virtues and the Study of Religion," Fifteenth Annual University Lecture in Religion at Arizona State University, Distributed to members of the American Academy of Religion by the Department of Religious Studies, November, 1994, 20–21 (cited hereafter as Yearley 1994b).

11. See Lee Yearley, "Three Ways of Being Religious," *Philosophy East and West* 32.4 (1982), 439–451; also note Graham 1981, 20–21.

12. Compare Graham 1981, 259. Yearley in Mair 1983 contains an interpretation of Zhuangzi that relies in large part on developing ideas about detachment that arise from the notion of a mirrorlike mind. That interpretation is "experimental" and differs considerably from the one given here.

13. The concept of *qi* is both important and vexing; for a discussion of it

in Zhuangzi see Graham 1981, 8–19, 156–157. Yearley 1990, 232, footnote forty–seven, enumerates a number of different works that have examined the idea both in classical Chinese thought and as a paradigmatic example of the problems involved in the comparative analysis of crucial terms. For background to the issues involved see Lee Yearley, "A Comparison Between Classical Chinese Thought and Thomistic Christian Thought," *The Journal of the American Academy of Religion* LI.3 (1983), 427–458 and Yearley 1982.

14. Two important if general questions about this distinction need to be noted. First, does the distinction express the only available options? Second, even presuming the distinction is true, are the modes of action presented so dissimilar that a person could not move between them, using each at different times for different purposes? Put in another vocabulary, the issue concerns the place of rules or even injunctions in a framework that relies basically on the adaptiveness found in virtues; see my treatment of this subject in Yearley 1990, 44–51 and 98–100. My own view is that both modes need to be used; that Zhuangzi can, at times, be read as validating that view; and that many pictures of the self that draw on Zhuangzi, including Graham's, fail to consider fully that option. See note four for the background for my judgment.

15. Certain of these terms, notably *ziran* and *wuwei* are considerably more important in other parts of the *Zhuangzi*, or in other Daoist texts, than they are in that strand of the *Zhuangzi* we are examining. See Graham 1981, 16 and 32, Herrlee Creel, *What is Taoism? and Other Studies in Chinese Cultural History* (Chicago: University of Chicago Press, 1970), 48–78; Donald Munro, *The Concept of Man in Early China* (Stanford: Stanford University Press, 1969), 117–124, 136–138, 141–146; and Joseph Needham, *Science and Civilization in China: vol. 2 History of Scientific Thought* (Cambridge: Cambridge University Press, 1956), 46–56, 61–63, 68–70. Zhuangzi's views on *xing* "nature" and his insistence on both the frailty of metaphysical inquiry and the need to eliminate dichotomies account for many of these differences. On important aspects of this question, see Benjamin Schwartz, *The World of Thought in Ancient China* (Cambridge, Mass.: The Belknap Press of Harvard University Press, 1985), 229; and 234–235.

16. On the analysis of skillfulness in Zhuangzi see Graham 1989, 186–194 and Ivanhoe 1993. Eno's piece in this volume also covers this subject and is, I believe, very helpful to read in conjunction with mine.

17. A variety of technical questions exist about the relationship between the ideas contained in the first seven books and those stories about skill that appear elsewhere in the book and reappear in other Daoist works, such as the *Liezi*. (Graham 1981, 135–142, brings together the stories in the *Zhuangzi* in a section entitled "The Advantages of Spontaneity" and also notes where they appear in standard editions.) Certain notions or emphases

in these stories clearly represent different perspectives and others, at best, represent "developments" of Zhuangzi's ideas; see, for example, my later treatment of the skillful swimmer. I will not attempt here to defend my selections and interpretations, but I think a defense can be given.

18. For good analyses of the general conception of skillfulness see Gilbert Ryle, *The Concept of Mind* (London: Hutchinson and Co., 1949), 42–45; his "Teaching and Training" in R. S. Peters, ed., *The Concept of Education* (London: Routledge and Kegan Paul, 1967), 105–119; and James Wallace, *Virtues and Vices* (Ithaca, N.Y.: Cornell University Press, 1978), 43–52. MacIntyre's analysis of "practices" is also relevant here and in that analysis he develops well the Aristotelian distinction between internal and external goods; see Alasdair MacIntyre, *After Virtue, A Study in Moral Theory* (Notre Dame, Ind.: University of Notre Dame Press, 1981), 175–189. On the distinction between skills and virtues, see Yearley 1990, 117. Also note Lee Yearley "Conflicts Among Ideals of Human Flourishing," in J. Reeder and G. Outka, eds., *Prospects for a Common Morality* (Princeton: Princeton University Press, 1992), 238–243 and Yearley 1994b, 1–11.

19. On the idea of processes and performances in Aristotle, see J. O. Urmson, "Aristotle on Pleasure," in J. M. E. Moravcsik, ed., *Aristotle: A Collection of Critical Essays* (Garden City, N.Y.: Anchor Books, 1967), 323–33; he calls "performances" activities; also note the references to Aquinas and other people listed in Yearley 1990, 226, footnote five. We have, unfortunately, no technical terms in English that capture this distinction and therefore I must use these two often ambiguous terms. More important, the distinction involves some complicated questions—for example, the role of anticipation in listening to music—that we cannot examine here.

20. For apparent examples of these transformation disciplines see Graham 1981, 48, 84, 97; cf.96–98. On the vexing question of the exact character of these practices in especially early Daoism, see Needham 1956, 143–152; Kristofer Schipper, *The Taoist Body*, Karen Duval, trans. (Berkeley, Calif.: University of California Press, 1993), 196–215; Harold Roth, "Psychology and Self-Cultivation in Early Taoist Thought," *Harvard Journal of Asiatic Studies* 51.2 (cited hereafter as 1991b), 599–650; Victor Mair, trans., *Tao Te Ching, The Classic Book of Integrity and the Way, Lao Tzu* (New York: Bantam Books, 1990), 140–148, 155–161; and Victor Mair, trans., *Wandering on the Way, Early Taoist Tales and Parables of Chuang Tzu* (New York: Bantam Books, 1994), 371. Yoga-like practices are clearly involved, as Mair stresses, but I remain unsure either about how precisely we can specify them or about how close they may be to South Asian practices. Finally, note that Waley's work on this subject is still illuminating despite the problems we now see because of advances in scholarship; see Arthur Waley, *The Way and Its Power, A Study of the Tao Te Ching and Its Place in Chinese Thought* (London: George

Allen and Unwin Ltd., 1935), 43–53, 57–59, 116–120 and Waley 1939, 43–53, 66–68.

21. On the idea of the daimonic see Graham 1981, 18–19 and 35. Also note Waley 1935, 26–29. Roth has done meticulous historical work on the role and development of the idea of *shen*, translated by him as *numen*, in early Daoist thought; see Harold Roth, "The Early Taoist Concept of *Shen*: A Ghost in the Machine?" in Kidder Smith, Jr., ed., *Sagehood and Systematizing Thought in Warring States and Han China* (Brunswich, Maine: Asian Studies Program, Bowdoin College, 1990), 11–32, and Roth 1991b. Roth's work raises what is, to my mind, an important issue. Unlike later thinkers, Zhuangzi does not provide anything resembling a full account of what *shen* is and how it operates. This can be seen as a failure: that is, later thinkers developed the kind of theoretical account he should have had. To my mind, however, it is less a failure of Zhuangzi than a refusal, and a refusal based on solid philosophical ground. Zhuangzi can be said to refuse to become involved in the, for him, specious analyses that attempt to define *shen* as an entity and then relate it to other entities. He, therefore, never produces what Roth notes as a possible "ghost in the machine," and he has solid (and I think commendable reasons) for not doing so. For an analysis of some of the delicate philosophical issues that surround the analysis of something like *shen* see my treatment of the conception of dispositions in Yearley 1990, 106–108 and the interchange between myself and Martha Nussbaum on this point; see Martha Nussbaum, "Comparing Virtues," *The Journal of Religious Ethics* 21.2 (1993), 345–367 and my response, "'The Author Replies;' Book Discussion on *Mencius and Aquinas* by Lee H. Yearley," *The Journal of Religious Ethics* 21.2 (1993), 385–395.

22. On the possible new kind of morality, see Graham 1981, 77–79 and 90–91, cf. 140; also see Graham 1982, 26. The issue of Zhuangzi's relationship to normal ideas of ethics is far too complicated to discuss here. See, however, the treatment in Yearley 1995 and also note Crandell in Mair 1993, 101–124. My treatment of Mengzi's ideas of semblances of virtue and the village honest person (*xiangyuan*) in Yearley 1990, 67–72 is also relevant; on this subject at least Mengzi and Zhuangzi show some noteworthy similarities.

EIGHT

Spontaneity and Education of the Emotions in the Zhuangzi

Joel Kupperman

A working title of this paper had been "A Cicada Propounds Three Theses About Zhuangzi." This had been intended not only to be modest, but also to allude to the perspectivism with which the *Zhuangzi* opens. Part of the greatness of the *Zhuangzi* is that it is rewarding from so many perspectives. This is not accidental: The strongest vein of skepticism in the *Zhuangzi*, if I am right, is skepticism about meanings, including skepticism about interpretations of itself. It would go against the spirit of the work to pretend to supply a definitive or a "very best" interpretation. It also would do violence to the deliberate openness of many of the meanings. In what follows, I will point toward *a* reading of three major elements of the work. In each case, a brief statement of an interpretation will be followed by explanation and elaboration. The longest of the three sections will be the third, concerned with the project of educating the emotions, partly because it seems to me that the most difficult and contentious issues lie here.

I

The underlying project of the *Zhuangzi* is, as Robert Allinson says, self-transformation (Allinson, 1989). This must be qualified. The author's project in producing the Inner Chapters—his project for himself, that is—very probably is not what we would normally term self-transformation, at least if that phrase is taken to refer to a drastic change in what one is. We are to assume that the author already has been transformed, before producing the Inner Chapters. Of course there will be further changes: there is no suggestion of a static ideal. But it seems likely that the point of producing the work, for the author, had a great deal to do with a free play of spontaneous psychic forces, the sort of thing indeed that is celebrated in various forms throughout the book. In chapter one, the possible use of an unmarketable calabash is described in terms of floating away over the Yangtse and the Lakes (Graham 1981, 47). This is a good metaphor for the use to which the act of creating the *Zhuangzi* put an unmarketable wisdom.

What Allinson is right about is the nature of the project for us, the readers, that must be central to any plausible account of the meaning of the book. We are encouraged to see the attractiveness of styles of life of which we very probably have no personal experience. At the same time, the folly of styles of life in which we very probably participate is gently exposed. There is no sustained exhortation. But the implication clearly is that one would be better off if one approximated the free and spontaneous life that is presented as a possibility.

The word "approximate" is important here. There is no suggestion that there is a single version of the very good life to be followed. Perspectivism applies to styles of life. Not only is it the case that what is good for a loach or a gibbon would not be good for a human being, and vice versa (Graham 1981, 57), but also there is no suggestion that Cook Ding the daemonic carver could just as well have the psychological skills of Chu Boyu or that Chu Boyu could be a daemon carver (Graham 1981, 63–64 and 71–72). In chapter five, Confucius is made to say that (spiritual) Power can stand out without shaping the body (Graham 1981, 80–81). It is consonant with this that Power would not obliterate the various psychological leanings that are at the root of our individualities, and hence that Power could be expressed in a variety of styles of life as well as in a variety of physical forms.*

Also a wonderful style of life, like the wonderful dancing of a Margot Fonteyn or a Nureyev, is not adequately captured in words. Someone who studiously masters a description is not thereby in a good position to approximate the quality of the life. One reason for this (which will be explored in the next section) is that while nuance, generally speaking, does not have a major role in morality, it does have a crucial role in the nonmoral assessment of styles of life. As Camus points out, someone who takes a very impressive life as an example to be followed, risks having a life that is, in fact, ridiculous.[1]

---

*Compare Ivanhoe's notion of "ethical promiscuity."—Eds.

A digression on philosophical method is appropriate here, after the jarring note of quoting Camus in an explication of Zhuangzi. There is a dilemma inherent in comparative philosophy as practiced by Western academics attempting to understand and explicate Asian philosophies. On one hand, any approach that attempts to suggest that Asian philosopher X is really just like Western philosopher Y is almost certainly going to be too primitive, giving us a cartoonlike image of X and ignoring X's intellectual and cultural context. On the other hand, Western readers of comparative philosophy are likely to approach any Asian philosophy as something like a second (rather than a first) philosophical language, for which at least some rules of translation into familiar terms would be useful. A deeper problem is this. Experience suggests that one better understands any philosopher, Western or Asian, if one has been thinking independently about similar problems: this enables one better to see the point of various remarks, assumptions, and philosophical moves. If so, then an effective Western student of comparative philosophy will be functioning, in some small way, as a Western philosopher herself or himself. Use of an alien philosophical framework, thus, will facilitate interpretation of an Asian philosophy (which is something positive), while at the same time multiplying the risks of error and distortion (which is something negative).

These risks exist, of course, even with regard to texts that are, broadly speaking, within one's own philosophical tradition. At the root is the fact that interpretation of a text is itself an activity for which there can never be entirely strict rules, and that always calls for leaps of judgment. Because of this, many literary critics have argued in recent years that there can be no such thing as a definitive set of meanings of *any* text.[2]

If the writer of a text already believes this, or has intimations of it, there are a variety of ways in which she or he can react. Someone who is disturbed by the fluidity of interpretation can attempt to counteract it by thickening the content at key places, say by laborious definitions of key terms and articulations of central claims, or by elaborate notes that say, "What I really mean is." Someone who is resigned to the fluidity of interpretation may be far less strenuous in these matters. A writer who glories in the fluidity of interpretation, on the other hand, may act out a complicity with it, at key places saying, "Perhaps this is so; perhaps it is not," and by constantly suggesting the possibility of variations of perspective. This is the strategy of Zhuangzi.

This is one reason for the humor, the jokiness, that runs through the *Zhuangzi*. Another reason has to do with the project of transformation of the reader. If one were to want to change a group of people so that they become devotees of a religious or political cult, then it might seem appropriate to pull hard on their attitudes to life and to give them formulas for what they should be loyal to. Zhuangzi's ideal and project of transformation are of very different sorts.

A fuller characterization of these will be pursued in the last section of this paper, but for present purposes it is enough to dwell on Zhuangzi's emphasis on freedom and spontaneity. It most certainly would not be appropriate to pull people hard in the direction of such a good, or to give them formulas for what are in the last analysis qualities that people have to come to of themselves. One may nudge them in the right direction, and gently ridicule what they presently have. A strong pull would be counter-productive, and also would risk substituting a more virulent form of something unnatural for what people start out with.

II

The transformation at the heart of the *Zhuangzi* cannot be understood in terms of moral improvement. To move in the direction of being more like a sage may well not involve becoming a morally more virtuous person. But it will involve having a better life.

This may well seem confusing as it stands, and it has led to a lot of confused talk about relativism. P. J. Ivanhoe has done, it seems to me, an exemplary job of clearing away mistakes in this area (Ivanhoe 1993, 639–54). But it may be useful to look at the philosophical roots of the confusion. We can begin with a basic distinction, between morality and other aspects of a life that may be judged as better or worse. Failure to observe this has led to the worst mistakes.

The distinction in question is a modern Western one, which arguably reflects interest in morality as an instrument of social control—and perhaps even more strongly, reflects interest in carving out a territory (sometimes loosely identified with an area of privacy, or the part of life in which hypothetical imperatives alone govern) in which life can be better or worse which should *not* be viewed as subject to social control. It is often observed that no closely corresponding distinction occurs either in classical Greek or in classical Chinese philosophy, although this does not imply that we will be unable to find places in which an ancient Greek or Chinese philosopher treats certain matters in much the way in which we treat what we regard as moral matters. Arguably, for example, Confucian philosophy regards failure to mourn a dead parent for more than a few days much as we regard gross immorality.

One mark of what we consider to be immoral is, as John Stuart Mill observed, we think it deserving of punishment: if not actual legal punishment, then punishment from the force of society's condemnation or the internalized punishment of the malefactor's sense of guilt.[3] There are some forms of behavior that we dislike or think tasteless, to which a normal response is then distaste, contempt, and/or shunning; the judgment that something is immoral is more akin to impulses to hit out. We can add that much of traditional morality focuses on actions that directly harm others. (Mill's revisionary proposal, in *On Liberty*, was that we narrow the boundaries of morality so that it focus on nothing but these, thus preventing "the tyranny of the majority.") A morality can be most effective in discouraging such actions if it is able to be taught in the form of broad general rules that are able to be understood even by the very young and the very poorly educated. Nuances and subtleties thus cannot have a major role at the core of a viable morality. There is a contrast here with what a philosopher such as Aristotle or Camus can advise with regard to the most desirable kinds of life, in which the importance of nuances must be acknowledged and we cannot expect much show of precision.

P. F. Strawson has pointed out that there also is a great difference between the allegiance claimed by a social morality and that claimed by what he terms "individual ideals."[4] A social morality demands exclusive loyalty: one cannot make sense of the idea of a life genuinely governed by two conflicting moralities, whereas Strawson sees no comparable difficulty in the idea of a life governed by two conflicting ideals.

Most recent Western ethical thought has centered on the dialectical interplay between, on one hand, the society's control (legal, political, and moral) of the individual, and, on the other hand, the individual's right to preserves of independence. This has made it difficult for many philosophers to appreciate the distinction that has just been sketched: the temptation is to treat morality as the whole of ethics. But when, say, Aristotle argues that the contemplative life is the best for a human being, his thesis cannot be mapped onto what we think of as the territory of morality. There is nothing immoral, even in our terms, in a decision to lead an undemanding and humdrum life rather than to engage in the most desirable forms of human activity. (When we advise people not to drop out of college, we do not tell them that it would be morally wrong.) Similarly, it is impossible to get any sense of what is going on in the final chapter of G. E. Moore's *Principia Ethica* if one thinks that it is about morality.[5]

The *Zhuangzi* is, as far as I can see, not about morality. There is no clear suggestion that the sage either would violate, or would be sure not to violate, those socially sanctioned rules of conduct that most closely correspond to what the modern West thinks of as morality. There are, it is true, passages like the one in chapter six, in which Yan Hui is described as having "forgotten about Goodwill and Duty" (Graham 1981, 91). But this certainly cannot be construed as a decision to violate moral norms, and (for all that we are told) is compatible with a pattern of behaving in compliance with moral norms *but not as a result of thinking about the norms*. One reason for reading it as compatible is the passage earlier in the same chapter that observes that fish forget all about each other in the Yangtse and the Lakes, as men forget all about each other in the lore of the Way (Graham 1981, 90). The fish are not constantly bumping into each other, and it makes no sense to imagine the men as in anything like a Hobbesian state of nature.

The transformation at the heart of the *Zhuangzi*, then, is not necessarily or primarily a moral transformation. It is primarily a transformation in how one thinks and feels about the world, and in the behavior that expresses this. A key assumption is that even someone who loyally complies with all of the major recognized social norms, a "good" person, can have an inadequate and unsatisfying style of life, and should be motivated to transform herself or himself. There may be cases, of course, in which someone's inadequate and unsatisfying style of life includes what we would term immorality, and that enlightenment would have as one of its byproducts the elimination of the motivation for this immorality. This is not precluded by the *Zhuangzi*, but as far as I can see the work does not advertise increased moral virtue as one of the possible rewards of transformation.*

III

The transformation at the heart of the *Zhuangzi* concerns primarily one's emotions and also the connections between emotions, on one hand, and motivation and conduct on the other. We can approach this by way of examination of something that figures repeatedly in the *Zhuangzi*, and that has been treated as a puzzle by some Western philosophers: spontaneity. What is spontaneity?

There are two connected ideas here. On one hand, there is a spontaneity that (at least arguably) is necessarily a feature of all human thought and action, so that one must come to thoughts and actions spontaneously or grind to a halt. On the other hand, there is a sense (which is clearly uppermost in the *Zhuangzi)* in which some people are more spontaneous than others, and indeed some are so lacking in spontaneity that their lives are deeply flawed.

Let us look first at the thesis that we are, so to speak, condemned to spontaneity. A general form of this is the claim that no set of rules by itself univocally compels the next step (partly because of the openness of interpretation), which is a major theme of Wittgenstein's *Philosophical Investigations.* Less generally, we may look at three theses: (A) The next thought is not compelled, (B) Desire does not compel preference, and (C) The next action is not compelled. All three theses arguably can be found in Kant, and the interested reader can trace discussions of spontaneity in Henry Allison's *Kant's Theory of Freedom.*[6] But Kant is not the only Western philosopher with a strong interest in spontaneity, an interest that has led to some fissures in philosophical analysis.

---

*On the question of the amorality of Zhuangzi's dao, see editors' note on page 142. —Eds.

We may begin from the point that, even if there are constraints (related, say, to space, time, and the categories) on anyone's system of thoughts, these constraints do not in general govern the order of one's thoughts and they most certainly do not determine whether, at any particular moment, one has a thought at all (rather than having one's mind blank). In addition, if one looks at the actual functioning of people's minds, it is striking that the stream of thought very often includes seemingly random, unbidden thoughts. There is Mozart's famous remark, quoted by Daniel Dennett, about his musical ideas, that they come from one knows not where.[7] Remarks about the mysterious sources of ideas abound in the *Zhuangzi*. For example, "Pleasure in things and anger against them, sadness and joy, forethought and regret, change and immobility, idle influences that initiate our gestures—music coming out of emptiness . . . no one knows from what soil they spring" (Graham 1981, 50).

Some unbidden thoughts may be merely inconsequential; others may represent a hostility or a greed that is not one's dominant or considered attitude. There is a great temptation to say of the latter, as Mozart said of his musical ideas, that they are not my thoughts. This temptation is all the greater in that one repudiates such thoughts, and very probably would rather not have them.

This unwelcome spontaneity may impinge on one's sense of self. One major American philosopher of recent years, Harry Frankfurt, has devoted himself to resolving this tension. He has argued, with great skill and panache, that the self is formed as a result of higher order desires that have the effect of either incorporating or rejecting the first-order desires that one may happen to feel.[8] This leads to the image of a coherent self as an island in the larger sphere of one's mind: beyond the self, much of the mind may be ugly and/or chaotic.

I have argued elsewhere that this is too intellectualized a picture of how people arrive at a character or a nature of their selves, and that such factors as habit can play a major role.[9] But there is another objection that could be leveled equally at Frankfurt's and my accounts. It is that we are attempting to analyze and reconstruct something that verges on the pathological, a partitioning of the mind that easily can cut people off from the most interesting forms of spontaneity. In dreams and creative activities, it will be said, the boundary markers are down. Zhuangzi would surely concur with this objection. It is one of many reasons why dreams and transformations play such a role in suggesting the possibility of variations of perspective. This is the strategy of Zhuangzi.

We also can lead a coherent life without either cutting ourselves off from some of our desires or straightforwardly ratifying every one of them in our conduct. We may prefer not to act out a desire in any direct way, and neither our desires at the moment—nor our previous behavior—dictate what our next action will be. That neither preference nor action need be governed by desire is a major theme of many moralities, including Kant's. But it must be seen as the beginning, rather than the end, of a train of thought for Zhuangzi.

Here is an analogy that may help us to approach the problem of the relation between desire and preference. Commentators on the architecture of Sir Christopher Wren sometimes focus on the problem of the church steeple. This is round, before it tapers to a point, and is mounted on a square tower. The problem is in managing the transition from the square tower below to the roundness of the steeple without its seeming visually abrupt. This can be done through intervening (and visually intermediate) layers of construction between the squareness and the roundness. The steeple might be given an octagonal base, or one that is square but scalloped at the corners; the base might have more than one level, each one closer to round than the one below it. Wren, to the best of my recollection, never solved the problem twice in the same way, and his solutions are invariably both subtle and beautiful.

Similarly the transition from desire to preference should not be abrupt and jarring. Otherwise, as Zhuangzi makes Confucius remark in another context, the "tension might show in one's face" (Graham 1981, 67). One respect in which the analogy breaks down, though, is that the nature of one's desires, unlike the squareness of church towers, is not typically a given. Desires can be modified or eliminated, and by now, studies of Buddhism have made us used to the idea that the best solution to the problems of life is the elimination of desire. Might Zhuangzi's solution be, so to speak, a beautiful spire that is mounted on nothingness?

It is difficult to answer this with great confidence. But we should be cautious of imposing alien philosophical frameworks—Indian as well as Western—on Zhuangzi. We also need to be cautious in our handling of the English word "desire." It is often used (the word "cravings" running second) as an English translation for what Buddha recommended that one eliminate. It is also used in much recent analytic philosophy for motivational thrusts in general, so that "desires" is treated as roughly synonymous with "wants" or "would like." This reflects the crudity of a great deal of contemporary "philosophy of mind." Annette Baier has pointed out (to my mind convincingly, at least as regards the meaning "desire" *has* had) that the meaning of "desire" is more narrow and specialized.[10] The proper object of desire, she suggests, is "a thing or person in some future close relation to the desirer" (Baier 1986, 60 n.8). To this one might add that mild wishes are not likely to be called desires, and what gets translated as "desires" in Buddhist texts are at home in cases in which not getting what one would like is tantamount to suffering. The word can look out of place, conversely, in cases in which the response to not getting what one wanted is one of relative indifference.

Thus, even if it is true that Zhuangzi to some extent anticipated the advent in China of Buddhism, it would not follow that the spire of preference is mounted on nothingness. It can be mounted on wishes and urges that do not amount to desires. Indeed there is a passage that suggests that Zhuangzi's preferences, rather than resting on nothingness, rest on primal psychic chaos (Graham 1981, 97–98). (One may speak here of the shifting inclinations provided by one's *qi*, which may differ from conscious preferences in such a way that we risk frustration whether or not these conscious preferences are satisfied.[11]) We will return to psychic chaos shortly.

My immediate suggestion is that both the basic Buddhist injunctions regarding the management of emotions, and the respects in which Zhuangzi may have anticipated the advent of Buddhism, are easily lost in translation: The word "desire" has become so problematized that even recent writings in English that center on the word can be, as it were, lost in translation from English to English. It does look as if Zhuangzi wants us, at the very least, to lessen the urgency of our desires. Thus he remarks that "wherever desires and cravings are deep, the impulse which is from Heaven is shallow" (Graham 1981, 84). This is consonant with the suggestion that it is best that a man "does not inwardly wound his person by likes and dislikes, that he constantly goes by the spontaneous and does not add anything to the process of life" (Graham 1981, 82). This is spoken of as being without "the essentials of man," which strongly implies that it must be learned and that the learning will require effort. What is required is a "fasting of the heart," which paradoxically is a source of increased energy, in that one is put in touch with "the tenuous which waits to be aroused by other things" (Graham 1981, 68).

So much for Zhuangzi's view of desires. What of preferences? It might look as if his recommendation is that there be none. Graham translates one passage that way: Confucius is made to say appreciatively to Yan Hui that "you have no preferences . . . no norms" (Graham 1981, 72).[12] However the discussion of the Self might give one pause (Graham 1981, 51). Without self there is "no choosing one thing rather than another." Zhuangzi's view of the Self is not crystal clear; I think that one can read without irony his observation that "It seems that there is something genuinely in command, and the only trouble is that we cannot find a sign of it" (Graham 1981, 51). Hence I read him as holding that there is a self, and of course we choose one thing rather than another. In any event, the *Zhuangzi* is full of characters held up to our admiration who are doing what, in some sense, they prefer to do and are moving toward outcomes they prefer. One might, for starters, think of Cook Ding who clearly prefers not to wear out his chopper (Graham 1981, 63–64).

My interpretation of Confucius' appreciation of Yan Hui is that Yan Hui's choices are not governed by the rigid dictates of any code ("norms"), and that Yan Hui does not have preferences that are so strong that he is really disappointed if they are not fulfilled. In this sense he does not "wound his person by likes and dislikes" (Graham 1981, 82). The transition between desires (or wishes and urges), on one hand, and preferences on the other is made smooth first, by the fact that both elements are light rather than heavy, and secondly, that desires of any gross or antisocial sort (that might cause real trouble and tension if formed into preferences and acted out) have been lessened or transmuted by "fasting of the heart".

This still does not get us far. There is more to Zhuangzi's education of the emotions than fasting of the heart, and the account we have given thus far of the shaping of preferences does not explain the nature and importance of the spontaneity that is recommended. It is time to look at the puzzling series of semimagical presentations of self described in chapter seven, Second Series. Huzi presents himself to a demonic shaman first "as I am when I hold down the impulses of the Power," then as he was when "names and substances had not found a way in, but the impulses are coming up from my heels," then "the absolute emptiness where there is no foreboding of anything" (which Huzi achieves when he levels out the impulses of the breath), and finally himself as "it is before ever we come out of our Ancestor. . . I attenuated, wormed in and out, Unknowing who or what we were." The shaman is misled the first three times, and terrified the last (Graham 1981, 97).

One thing we might get from this sequence is that the psychic nature toward which the *Zhuangzi* points is both complex and fluid. We may be tempted, in general, to read any discussion that recommends what sort of person one should try to be in terms of a static picture of a soul, a sort of spiritual x-ray. This never entirely works: even the kind of harmony of psyche that is sketched in Plato's *Republic*, or the very different spiritual stability praised in Kierkegaard's *Fear and Trembling* has to be understood in terms of sequences in which checks and balances or appeals to what is highest come into play. My suggestion, though, is that it works even more badly for Zhuangzi than it does for Plato or Kierkegaard. Some of Huzi's self-transformations might seem to refer to earlier stages of spiritual transformation, but the point to bear in mind is that they are still present as part of what he is. He is still—as people say—"in touch with" the impulses of very early childhood, which worm in and out, with no essential connection with any sense of self. To be in touch with these impulses is to be aware of them, to accept them for what they are rather than attempting to squash them, and sometimes (but I think not always) to ratify them in one's preferences and to act on them.

There is a much later Zen story in which a Zen master, challenged to perform a miracle, says, "My miracle is that when I feel hungry I eat, and when I feel thirsty I drink."[13] I think that the *Zhuangzi* points in this direction. Education of the emotions here includes being aware of, and comfortable with, basic wishes and urges, including even those that a small child would have. It also includes one's sometimes acting on them, again easily and comfortably, even in some cases in which norms of good manners might seem to dictate otherwise. It should be emphasized that the Daoist sage is not someone who always acts on impulse or, in the vernacular of the 1960s, "lets it all hang out." But he or she will be someone whose preferences will not be at war with basic wishes or urges.*

This psychic connectedness with early and primitive levels of one's mind has been emphasized as a factor in artistic creativity by Anton Ehrenzweig, who links finished works of art with a "deceptive chaos in art's vast substructure."[14] In Ehrenzweig's view, both the artist and the scientist deal with apparent chaos, which they integrate through unconscious scanning (Ehrenzweig 1967, 5). One mark of the process of unconscious scanning may be a blank stare. (One is put in mind of the vacant stare that David Hume's friends, including D'Alembert, cautioned him about, and that made Rousseau especially edgy.[15]) Unconscious scanning "in contrast to conscious thought which needs closed gestalt patterns—can handle 'open' structures with blurred frontiers which will be drawn with proper precision only in the unknowable future" (Ehrenzweig 1967, 42).

Ehrenzweig draws a number of lessons from this for the education of artists. Students must be taught, he argues, "not to wait for their inspiration and rushes of spontaneity, but to work hard at being spontaneous through choosing tasks that cannot be controlled by analytic vision and reasoning alone." The objective constraints that are inherent in the tasks will trigger spontaneity (Ehrenzweig 1967, 146). This is, in fact, a perfect description of the work and professionalism of Cook Ding, who does not need a rush of creative inspiration to be spontaneous.

Anyone who reviews the literature referred to in this essay must be struck by the fact that no one attempts to provide a clear and direct explanation of what spontaneity is: not Zhuangzi, not Kant or Henry Allison, and not even Ehrenzweig. Here is such an attempt. Spontaneity, in the sense in which everyone has it, is the occurrence of a thought or an action, or the formation of a preference, in a descriptive and explanatory context in which it is anomalous. (I use the word "anomalous" in the sense it has in Donald Davidson's "anomalous monism."[16]) Spontaneity, in the sense in which some people are much more spontaneous than others, has to do with the relation between one's preferences and actions, on one hand, and the layers of one's mind (going back to childlike wishes and urges) on the other. For some people there is rather little relation: they are governed by norms of conduct and of what they should prefer, and may be hardly aware of psychic elements that run in different directions. Ehrenzweig sees this as characteristic of the kind of artist we would term "academic," who composes or paints by the rules. Someone who has a more easy and satisfying relation with these psy-

---

*See editors' note on page 90.—Eds.

chic elements, and is able to act in a way that is not only anomalous but also expressive and free from tension, is very spontaneous. For most of us it is not easy to be that kind of person. But Zhuangzi, who is not at all a relativist about values, clearly thinks that it is much better.[17]

Notes

1. Albert Camus, *The Myth of Sisyphus*, trans. Justin O'Brien (New York: Vintage Books, 1955), 50–51.

2. This is not to say that any interpretation is as good as any other. Some may be much more rewarding; some, on the other hand, may lack plausible connection with the text, the classic example being the interpretation of *Hamlet* that makes Claudius the victim of his crazy nephew. There can be, in short, critical standards even if there are not definitive interpretations. Analogous problems arise with regard to the objectivity of historical and social scientific accounts of sets of events, and I have discussed these in my "Precision in History," *Mind* 84 (1975). Alexander Nehamas has pointed out that issues of interpretation become serious only in the presence of competing interpretations, and furthermore, that it is not easy to say whether interpretations are competing, in that elements of two or more interpretations can be combined. See Alexander Nehamas, *Nietzsche: Life As Literature* (Cambridge, Mass.: Harvard University Press, 1985), 63.

3. John Stuart Mill, *Utilitarianism*, Chapter V, para. 14.

4. P. F. Strawson, "Social Morality and Individual Ideals," *Philosophy* 36 (1961).

5. The foregoing remarks about the internal structures of ethics have been kept brief. I have given a fuller treatment, especially concerning the boundaries of morality, in chapter one of my *Foundations of Morality* (London: George Allen & Unwin, 1983).

6. See Henry E. Allison, *Kant's Theory of Freedom* (Cambridge: Cambridge University Press, 1990). The sense in which someone's thoughts or actions are not compelled even though they fit a deterministic model of causation is a complex topic for Kant. It is related also to the question of whether causing something to happen is the same as what we think of as making it happen. It may be that Kant (for whom causation was a structural feature of phenomenal reality) associated causation more closely with predictable regularity than Hume in the last analysis did. See Galen Strawson, *The Secret Connexion: Causation, Realism, and David Hume* (Oxford: Clarendon Press, 1989).

7. Daniel Dennett, *Elbow Room* (Cambridge: MIT Press, 1984), 13.

8. Harry Frankfurt, *The Importance of What We Care About* (Cambridge: Cambridge University Press, 1988).

9. Joel Kupperman, *Character* (New York: Oxford University Press, 1991), chapter three.

10. Annette Baier, "The Ambiguous Limits of Desire," in Joel Marks, ed., *The Ways of Desire* (Chicago: Precedent Publishing, 1986).

11. I am indebted to the editors for this point.

12. Legge has "free from all likings" (Legge 1891, 257). Watson has, "You must have no more likes. If you've been transformed, you must have no more constancy!" (Watson 1968, 91).

13. *Zen Flesh, Zen Bones*, compiled Paul Reps (Tokyo: Charles Tuttle Co., 1957), 91.

14. Anton Ehrenzweig, *The Hidden Order of Art* (Berkeley and Los Angeles: University of California Press, 1967), xii.

15. See Ernest Campbell Mossner, *The Life of David Hume* (Oxford: Oxford University Press, 1970), 477.

16. See Donald Davidson, "Mental Events," in L. Foster and J. W. Swanson, eds., *Experience and Theory* (Amherst: University of Massachusetts Press, 1970).

17. Let me suggest that, on this topic at least, anyone who looks for a simple opposition between Confucians and Daoists will be disappointed. See my "Confucius and the Problem of Naturalness," *Philosophy East & West* 18 (1968). A charming example of Confucius' spontaneity is his deliberate rudeness in Book XVII chapter twenty of the *Analects*. See Arthur Waley, trans., *The Analects of Confucius* (New York: Vintage Books, 1938), 214. It may be also that spontaneity is one of the values pointed toward by Mencius' observation that "The great man is he who does not lose his child's-heart" (6B12). See James Legge, trans., *The Works of Mencius* (New York: Dover Books, 1970), 322. Lau has "retains the heart of a new-born babe." See D. C. Lau, trans., *Mencius* (Harmondsworth: Penguin Books, 1970), 130.

NINE

Was Zhuangzi a Relativist?

Philip J. Ivanhoe

Introduction

Chad Hansen and David B. Wong have offered interesting interpretations of the *Zhuangzi*,[1] both claiming that the text presents a view that is best described as a form of "relativism." This is not to say that they share a common understanding of the text; in fact they read it very differently. Hansen sees Zhuangzi as presenting a meta-ethical view that decisively undermines any attempt to ground ethical claims. Wong argues that it offers a refutation of rationally justified moralities and establishes an ethic of equal worth and universal compassion. In this essay, I describe their respective interpretations and endeavor to make clear the different senses of relativism they see in the *Zhuangzi*. I then present what I see as problems with their interpretations, both as readings of the text and as philosophical positions in their own right. I will argue that both interpretations suffer as plausible interpretations of the text because they do not provide any account of Zhuangzi's beliefs regarding the character of human nature. This omission in turn generates philosophical difficulties for their respective positions.

Hansen's Interpretation

Chad Hansen argues that Zhuangzi holds two related but distinct views. The first is that we never see the world "raw"—as it really is—but always under some description. As a consequence, we never have knowledge of things in themselves, but only as these are perceived through some conceptual scheme—what Hansen calls a dao—provided by language. This view can be understood as a form of "relativism" in the sense that it holds that knowledge is always relative to some frame of reference. Such a belief seems clearly true, and as I have described it, it is perfectly compatible with a common sense belief in truth and some forms of ethical realism. But Hansen sees Zhuangzi advancing a second claim that undermines any and all notions of truth about how the world really is and this leads him to a view that I will refer to as "strong relativism."[2] This second claim has two parts: (1) that these different ways of seeing the world, the different conceptual schemes embodied in different languages, are often incompatible with one another and (2) the differences between them are irresolvable since the only thing that makes a given view "right" is the fact that some person or group holds it.

As noted above, Hansen believes that the term dao simply refers to a linguistic scheme for carving up the world and guiding action; it never is used, as traditional interpretations would have it, to refer to the way the world really is. And so, Hansen concludes, one can talk about the various daos in the world but not the one Dao. This leads him to ascribe to Zhuangzi the view which I refer to as strong relativism: the belief that no account of the world is any more accurate or valuable than any other. In Hansen's own terms: There are many daos (that is, many ways of talking about the world) and all daos are equal. "Zhuangzi's dao is a linguistic rather than metaphysical object (roughly equivalent to prescriptive discourse) and . . . his doctrine is relativist rather than absolutist; that is, according to Zhuangzi there are many daos" (Hansen in Mair 1983, 24). Hansen claims that Zhuangzi holds these two views in regard to all kinds of knowledge: knowledge about things like pillars and posts as well as knowledge about values. He surely holds that Zhuangzi professes such a position in regard at least to values. I will focus exclusively on this aspect of Hansen's position, his claim that Zhuangzi espouses a strong form of moral relativity.

If, for the moment, we grant that this interpretation of the *Zhuangzi* is correct or at least close to right, how might one account for the many stories about skillful people, like the marvelous cook[3] in chapter three, that seem to describe Daoist exemplars and implicitly recommend that we somehow emulate such individuals? Hansen claims such passages provide no difficulty for his view, for these individuals have simply perfected one of the infinite number of possible daos available. Any judgments about how well they are doing or whether what they are doing is morally good or bad can only be made by criteria internal to the particular practice in which they are engaged. This is how we should interpret Zhuangzi's descriptions of skillful individuals.

When he talks about a butcher with extraordinary skill, we can understand this as a case of someone who has perfected a "particular dao/way until it has become spontaneous or second nature, not that there is some mystical insight anyone can adopt that will put her in harmony with 'The Dao' and thereby transform her into a perfect butcher (dancer, gardener, president, logician, boxer, Star Wars pilot)!" (Hansen in Mair 1983, 51).

We will return to this point later, but for now let us grant Hansen's interpretation of Zhuangzi's thought and examine some of its philosophical implications.[4] The first thing to note is that it provides no ethical guidance whatsoever. One might argue, though Hansen does not, that Zhuangzi's position is more honest or authentic than the views of his opponents, in that it more accurately reflects the true nature of the various daos in the world. After all, according to Hansen, Zhuangzi is aware and up front about the fact that his dao is simply one way of looking at the world. Zhuangzi's recognition of this fact distinguishes him from his opponents, who mistakenly believe that their dao is The Dao, the one that represents things as they really are.[5] Regardless of whether or not one reads Zhuangzi this way or what importance one thinks this holds, the fact remains that Hansen's interpretation provides no standards by which we might judge a given action as morally good or bad. I could agree with everything he says and still treat other people in a brutish, crudely exploitive, and self-serving manner. I could feel justified in doing so not because I believed that my actions are somehow grounded in some deeper truth about the way the world is but simply because this is the way I or my group does things. As Hansen says about judgments of right and wrong, "The appropriateness of any such assignment is internal— relative to a system of discourse" (Hansen in Mair 1983, 38). Even more simply, I can justify my actions in any given case on the grounds that I felt like acting in this way, "Any contrary inclinations—lusts, desires, doubts— are equally natural, equally given by heaven" (Hansen in Mair 1983, 40).[6] I would not have any deep justification that would allow me to advocate that others should also behave this way (although it would appear that I *could* do so if *that* happened to be my way), and I would make no complaint if they don't act as I do. Since there are no grounds to anyone's choice, anything goes and equally well. The ultimate warrant that justifies my action would seem to be—as Frank Sinatra tells us—that I did it *my way.*

While I believe that I understand and have faithfully described the general features of Hansen's position, I am not sure that I fully understand his use of the terms "relativism" and "skepticism."[7] And so, before proceeding, I wish to make clear how I believe he employs these terms. Hansen often contrasts relativism with "absolutism" and seems to mean by the latter any form of realism, in particular any form of ethical realism. It is clear that Hansen does not contrast "absolutism" with a kind of ethical pluralism; he means to contrast it with what I call strong relativism: the view that there is no valid basis for any ethical claim. As for skepticism, his position seems to be that Zhuangzi is skeptical about the possibility of language ever providing us with a true account of how things are because of the conventional nature of language. For example, he says, "This is a skepticism based on a view of the conventionality and function of *yan*/language" (Hansen in Mair 1983, 50).

I agree that Zhuangzi is a language or conceptual skeptic, but I believe that this is part of his greater distrust of the human intellect. Such skepticism is a special kind of epistemological skepticism, it does not entail any claim about how things are in the world nor does it in principle preclude other ways of knowing that might help us understand and accord with the things and events in the world (see Ivanhoe 1993). My understanding of Zhuangzi's view, unlike Hansen's, does not entail ascribing to Zhuangzi a complete distrust of language. To deny that language is adequate to the task of providing us with a full and faithful understanding of the world is not to say it is of no use in this task. (In fact, to do so would be to advocate the very type of dogmatic claim that Hansen rightly recognizes Zhuangzi consistently eschews.) Such an interpretation would also go against a good deal of textual evidence. Zhuangzi himself seems to walk a middle path in regard to language: "Saying is not blowing breath, saying says something" (Graham 1981, 52). At times, Zhuangzi seems to yearn for the right kind of conversation partner, "Where can I find a man who has forgotten words so that I can have a word with him?" (Watson 1968, 302). The very existence of the text would seem to present a problem for any absolute or dogmatic rejection of language.

I agree with Hansen's observation that Zhuangzi saw language as in some sense conventional, but I do not see how the kind of skepticism Hansen describes follows from this fact. Perspectivist arguments alone do not provide good grounds for moving from the conventional nature of language to strong relativism. I can (and do) grant that our language is conventional and that it only provides us with a limited and often incorrect grasp of the world and still hold that language helps us to understand the world and that there are better and worse attempts to do so. The understanding language provides often is inadequate and it is always relative to the perspective of human beings, but this is not to deny either that it provides part of an accurate account of the world or that it lacks criteria other than those internal to this particular (language) game. Language works when it helps us to navigate through the world, when it helps us to match up our natural desires, needs, tendencies, and capacities with the patterns and processes of nature. This is the external criteria for evaluating different ways of talking.

In order to make the case for the complete relativism of language one would have to show that the understanding language grants is ad hoc and *meaningless.* In the specific case of value judgments, one would have to show that the kinds of distinctions people tend to draw do not in any way reflect their own nature or the nature of the greater world in which they live. Such judgments would then be groundless, purely ad hoc and therefore meaningless. One way of arguing for such a conclusion is to insist that we evaluate our ethical judgments from a "god's eye" view of the world. If one ascends to such a height and contemplates human activity, our all-too-human view of the world does seem to shrink into insignificance. From the perspective of the infinite, the wholly objective "view from nowhere,"[8] what good could the Way, which allows you to "stay in one piece, keep yourself alive, look after your parents and live out your years," possibly have? (Watson 1968, 50)[9] Apart from the perspective of human beings, such issues clearly have no meaning.

In order to argue that our ethical judgments are groundless, Hansen "evaluates" them solely from such a completely "objective" point of view. At various points in his essay, Hansen—not Zhuangzi—appeals to "the point of view *of the universe*" and "the viewpoint *of nature*" in order to substantiate this position (Hansen in Mair 1983, 35 and 39). Only from such a point of view, can Hansen sustain his claims regarding Zhuangzi's purported skepticism and strong relativism. If one sees things "from nowhere," one will easily be convinced that nothing really matters and there is little to choose between one course of action rather than another. From such heights, the magnitude of our revulsion at the beating of Rodney King quickly diminishes in stature and loses all significance; as we approach the extreme, we cannot ask whether it was "right" or "wrong."

But is this Zhuangzi's position? Does he ever counsel us to abandon our human perspective and assume instead the god's-eye view of the world? There surely are places where Zhuangzi appeals to a Heavenly perspective to argue for the inherent value of every thing in the universe. For example, in chapter two he talks about the "piping of Heaven. . . Blowing on the ten thousand things in a different way, so that each can be itself" (Watson 1968, 37). Later in the same chapter we are told that the sage, "illuminates all in the light of Heaven" and "rests in Heaven the Equalizer" (Watson 1968, 40 and 41). These passages do recommend taking the Heavenly perspective into account, but they do not seem to recommend abandoning the human point of view for the Heavenly. Had Zhuangzi done this, he simply would have established the very kind of dogmatic position he always rejects. These passages, in which Zhuangzi argues for the Heavenly point of view, are better read as a form of therapy, designed to curb our terrible tendency toward self-aggrandizement.* They are to remind us that we are part of a greater pattern within which we are simply one small part.

---

* Compare the descriptions of Zhuangzi's project as "therapeutic" in Schwitzgebel (p. 90), and Berkson (p. 109) and Kupperman's idea of "educating" the emotions.—Eds.

The therapeutic use of the Heavenly point of view does not entail that human beings should view the world *only* from this perspective. One could believe (as I do) that from the perspective of nature all things *are* equal and at the same time still believe (again as I do) that there are better and worse ways for us—as human beings—to be. We each have particular roles to fulfill in the great scheme of Heaven, according to our differing natures and circumstances. We are not to abandon our individual roles but we must play them in light of an understanding of the greater natural pattern. I suggest that this is how Zhuangzi saw things. Consider the opening lines of chapter six: "To know what Heaven does and what humans do, this is ultimate! Those who know what Heaven does live lives engendered by Heaven. Those who know what humans do use what their wits know to nurture what their wits do not know. To live out the years Heaven has granted and not be cut off midway, this is the full flourishing of knowledge."[10]

Elsewhere I have argued that, at the very least, Zhuangzi implies that certain ways of being are contrary to our nature and the nature of the world in which we live (Ivanhoe 1993). If this is not the case, it seems impossible to explain the many criticisms he makes of other thinkers who recommended their own ways as right. Zhuangzi justifies both his criticisms of others and his own recommendations by appealing to the dao. If a given action or activity accords with Nature's pattern and processes then it is fitting and proper, it is in harmony with the dao. Hansen rejects such interpretations because he believes that the term dao means a "prescriptive discourse" and does not refer to the way the world naturally is. But one cannot make sense of the text without understanding that the term dao often refers to the way the world naturally is. *Pace* Hansen, the traditional view is in general correct: The dao is a metaphysical concept; it is the deep structure of the pattern and processes of the world. This is clear from passages such as the following, from chapter six: "The dao 'Way' has an essence and can be relied upon, but it does not act and has no fixed form. One can hand it down but one cannot receive it. One can grasp it but one cannot see it. It is its own root and its own trunk. Prior to Heaven and Earth, it has existed since ancient times. It divinized the ghosts and spirits and generated Heaven and earth. It goes before the highest point, yet is not high; lies below the six directions but is not deep. It arose before Heaven and earth yet is not old. It is elder to most venerable time yet is not aged" (6/23). Zhuangzi believed there are ways of living that are contrary to the way the world is: that is, which violate our nature and set us against the natural patterns and processes to be found in the world. Moreover, he further believed that there are ways of acting that enable us to accord with the nature of both ourselves as creatures—things among things in Nature's vast panorama—and Heaven's patterns and processes. People who act in such a way are paragons for human living. This, I submit, is the proper way to understand the stories of skillful individuals that are so much a part of this profound and wonderful text.

Earlier, I quoted a passage from Hansen in which he argues that his interpretation provides the most plausible reading of such cases, in particular of the case of the cook in chapter three. Hansen rejects the idea that this or the other skill stories provide any normative guidance. But I do not see how he can explain the fact that all of these stories concern benign activities.[11] In the specific case of the cook, I do not see how he can account for King Wenhui's final words. For after watching the cook's great skill and hearing him describe his art, the king is moved to exclaim, "Excellent! I have heard the words of a cook and learned how to care for life!" (Kjellberg 1993). If Hansen's interpretation were correct, the king could have "learned" how to "care for life" from watching *anyone*. Hansen might respond by insisting that he could have learned from anyone. But the fact is that *only* skillful people are presented as exemplars. Not only that, but there are no skillful people engaged in nasty or selfish activities. They are all quite benign. This leads me to conclude that Zhuangzi believed human nature is essentially benign and that the majority of our suffering comes from our tendency to subvert our inherent nature by overintellectualizing our lives. If we can guard against this and instead cleave to our intuitions and inclinations we can develop an inexpressible knack for according with and fitting into the great scheme of nature: the dao of which we ourselves are one small part.[12]

Hansen is correct to describe Zhuangzi as a skeptic regarding language, but as I have argued above, such a view does not entail strong relativism. In order to establish the strong relativism he attributes to Zhuangzi, Hansen must argue that Zhuangzi assumes a god's-eye view of the world, a perspective from which any claim of meaning recedes into insignificance. But there is no evidence in the text to support such an interpretation. Moreover, Hansen's interpretation cannot provide a plausible account of the skill stories that figure so prominently in the text. The fact that the skillful exemplars Zhuangzi extols all engage in benign activities shows that he believed people who have "forgotten" the deforming lessons of their socialization will prove to be quite benign by nature.

Such an interpretation of the *Zhuangzi* has the additional advantage of understanding the text as centrally concerned with the most heated philosophical debate of the time: the issue of the character of human nature.[13] Hansen's failure to recognize this aspect of Zhuangzi's thought weakens the plausibility of his interpretation and leaves him with an untenably strong form of relativism.

Wong's Interpretation

David Wong's understanding of Zhuangzi is very different from that of Hansen. One reason for this is that his interpretation is part of a much larger project on moral relativity. Wong's view of moral relativity is not what one might expect. While he claims that nothing normative follows from moral relativity alone, he argues that when combined with the liberal premise of not interfering with those to whom we could not rationally justify our inter- ference, moral relativity provides a prima facie reason for tolerance. Moreover, he attempts to combine moral relativity with a claim for the unalienable equal worth of individuals, arguing that moral relativity helps us to realize the implications of equal worth. Wong further believes that this recognition of equal worth entails that we should and will feel "compassion" or "deep love" for one another: "We should cultivate the part of us that spontaneously identifies with others, the state of consciousness in which the boundaries between self and others falls away. That state is *ci*, sometimes translated as 'compassion' or 'deep love'. *Ci* gives rise to unpremeditated aid to others when they are in distress, not aid given because it is a moral duty. The idea is that once we are able to suspend looking at people through our evaluative categories, we will be able to accept them for what they are, see them as beings like ourselves, and care for them as we care for ourselves" (Wong 1984, 208). Wong argues that such a compassionate attitude will result once people are led to abandon the attempt to ground ethics in some rational scheme. In other words, giving up the project of rationally justifying morality will lead us to see one another simply as human beings, and we will then adopt a feeling of compassion toward one another.

In his attack on the rational justification of morality, Wong proceeds in a way that is methodologically quite similar to Zhuangzi. In this part of his argument—what I will refer to as his negative project—Wong and Zhuangzi share a good deal (Ivanhoe 1993, 645–647). However, in his positive claims regarding the justification for equal worth and the attitude of compassion, Wong parts company with Zhuangzi. His attempt to show that Zhuangzi represents these aspects of his philosophical position is problematic. Wong provides no reliable textual evidence, and indeed there is none to be found, to support his claim that Zhuangzi shares these views. I will also argue that Wong's philosophical claims need further support on the issue of the purported compassionate character of human nature. I will conclude by suggesting that Wong's position would fare considerably better as an interpretation of the *Mencius* and that perhaps this text will provide some of what he needs to establish his view.

Wong's negative project is aimed at establishing what he calls "moral relativity," the claim that there is no legitimate rational justification for morality. What is distinctive about Wong's view is that he believes that accepting the fact of moral relativity will help us to recognize the equal worth of individuals (Wong 1984, 177–197).[14] The claim of equal worth is philosophical bedrock for a great deal of modern western ethical thinking and Wong considers several standard philosophical justifications for it that are worth reviewing.

First, Wong considers the standard Kantian argument for equal worth according to which people have worth beyond calculation because of their status as rational creatures. Rationality is the quality that makes us *sui generis*. Toward all those who possess this quality, we have a duty not to treat them merely as means, for to do so is to treat them as mere things and to act against our own characteristic rationality. The problem with such a view, according to Wong, is that rationality is difficult to define with much precision and whatever definition one might put forth there is the further problem that people possess this quality to profoundly varying degrees. It is not clear what minimum degree of whatever kind of rationality one might chose to promote entitles one to respect as a rational creature.

A related question about this approach, which Wong does not discuss, concerns its application to the ethical status of nonhuman animals.[15] Tom Regan[16] argues that most if not all mammals possess the minimum amount of rationality needed to qualify as what he calls moral patients and as such we have a duty to treat them with respect. To qualify as a moral patient a creature needs to be aware of its desires and beliefs and be capable of pursuing them in a deliberate fashion. This makes them, in Regan's terminology "subjects of a life." Most normal mammals of a year or more in age are such subjects of a life. However crudely, they seem to have desires and beliefs and act intentionally to achieve their ends. Those who want to defend the tradition against such a view designate a certain kind of self-referential reflectivity as the necessary minimal standard, and argue that most people have this, at least potentially, and no animals do. In addition, they claim that, different amounts of this quality *above the minimum* is of no consequence. Once on the bus, everyone enjoys an equal ride. But the claim that no animals possess this minimum level of reflectivity is controversial at best. And even if one were to grant that such reflectivity is uniquely and universally human, one can still question whether this is the best or only basis for granting a creature moral status.

One clear example of a thinker in the Kantian tradition is John Rawls.[17] He defines the minimal requirement for being a moral agent as a sense of one's own well being and a sense of justice. Rawls admits that different people have these senses to varying degrees but insists that all that matters is the fact that one has them, *how much* one has does not really make a difference. He also makes an empirical claim that all known people and cultures meet this minimum requirement. Even if one accepts Rawls' view and his empirical claim, there is still the problem that different individuals have different amounts of these qualities; this seems to imply that they should be treated differently. Alan Gewirth has tried to finesse this issue by proposing his own view of what constitutes the quality of rationality.[18]

Gewirth defines the minimum requirement in terms of one being a "prospective agent" who has purposes one wants to fulfill. He packs a good deal into the notion of being an agent and adds a number of qualifiers in terms of the need to have a fairly high level of awareness of the environment and one's alternatives, but the real innovation of his position is the idea of *prospective agency*. This allows him to include small children and to acknowledge that mentally deficient people *actually* will only realize such agency to a limited degree. He claims that such factors do not matter since they do not affect the prospective agency of such individuals. What he means by this is that wanting to be able to fulfill one's needs and desires is distinct from having the ability to fulfill them, and that only the former counts when we decide who has rights as a moral agent.

This seems convincing as far as it goes, but it does not seem to go very far. For one thing it ignores the importance of having or being able to have a clear idea of what it is one wants. Small children and mentally deficient people tend to lack the sophisticated and informed view of what they want that Gewirth requires. And if one loosens up this requirement, then it seems increasingly difficult to exclude at least some nonhuman animals. Another problem is that it is not at all clear how Gewirth's picture escapes the sliding scale problem we mentioned earlier; why doesn't it matter how clear one is about one's wants? People better informed and more reflective would seem to have clear warrants for having greater rights.

Wong turns to Joel Feinberg[19] as someone who offers what he describes as "a promising alternative: human worth is groundless and unconditional" (Wong 1984, 201–202). Feinberg holds that attributing equal worth to someone does not need to be grounded on some quality that they possess but is "a kind of ultimate attitude not itself justifiable in more ultimate terms" (Wong 1984, 202). To do this is to take what Bernard Williams calls the "human point of view" (Wong 1984, 202).

This condensed review of Wong's argument is needed in order to see the logic and force of his position and to enable us to appreciate those respects in which it resembles and those in which it differs from the views of Zhuangzi. I have already noted that I believe Wong's negative project is very much in the spirit of Zhuangzi's attacks on the moralists of his own day,[20] and I have learned a good deal from this aspect of Wong's analysis. However, what if any evidence is there that Zhuangzi shared Wong's positive project? From the quote with which I began my discussion, it is clear that Wong believes there is good evidence for this equation. Specifically, he claims that Zhuangzi believed that in the absence of any rational justification for morality, people should "cultivate the part of us that spontaneously identifies with others, the state of consciousness in which the boundaries between self and others falls away. That state is *ci*, sometimes translated as 'compassion' or 'deep love'."

Unfortunately, when we turn to the text of the *Zhuangzi* we find no justification for Wong's attribution. The character 慈 *ci* occurs a total of four times in the entire text of the *Zhuangzi*, never in the Inner Chapters that most recognize as the core of the authentic part of the text.[21] The word is used once negatively; twice it describes the basic Confucian attitude a parent has for its child and the final time it appears in chapter thirty-three, which we know was written long after Zhuangzi died. In this final case, it occurs in the opening part of the chapter, "To make benevolence his standard of kindness, righteousness his model of reason, ritual his guide to conduct, and music his source of harmony, serene in *ci* ('kindness') and benevolence— one who does this is called a gentleman." This is obviously not a reference to Zhuangzi or any form of Daoism. The fact is that in none of these cases is *ci* used as Wong claims it is used. Wong gives the impression that this is a central part of Zhuangzi's thought but unfortunately there is no evidence to support his case.[22]

Something like the feeling of cohumanity that Wong attributes to Zhuangzi is evident in the early Chinese tradition, but it is found in Mencius not Zhuangzi. At one point, Wong cites Gregory Vlastos' observation that recognizing the human worth of an individual is "like loving one's child" (Wong 1984, 199). This is almost verbatim what Confucians describe as the attitude cultivated people use as the basis for their treatment of others.[23] Wong goes on to say "we do not need to satisfy ourselves about the moral character of a drowning man before going to his aid." I assume Wong here means something like "wanting to go to his aid" for I do not think most people would, in fact, risk their lives to save another and they surely do not have a duty to do so. But if we take him to mean *feeling a desire* to aid the person, then this idea is well-represented by Mencius' famous parable of the baby at the well (*Mencius* 2A6).

Are there examples in the *Zhuangzi* of people going to the aid of or even feeling the desire to aid others in distress? I find no such examples.[24] There is no evidence in the text that Zhuangzi believed people by nature tend to have compassion for one another. (If there were such evidence it is hard to see what difference there would be between Zhuangzi and Mencius.) What we do find is evidence for the belief that in the absence of an overintellectualized view of the world people will tend to leave one another alone. And so I believe it is best to say that Zhuangzi thought people are by nature benign—not compassionate.

Wong offers an important contribution when he notes what one might call a notion of equal worth in the *Zhuangzi*. Zhuangzi did seek to broaden early Chinese views of what is worthy of respect and admiration. This is one of his greatest and most profound insights. By calling into question established notions about what constitutes the good and the worthy, he illuminated forgotten corners of human dignity. He insisted that one did not need to be a good Confucian or Mohist to be worthy of respect and admiration, the solitary person pursuing a craft with skill and in harmony with the world was in fact the one who had things right. Judging from certain passages, for example the extended discussion between Yan Hui and Confucius found in chapter four of the Inner Chapters, it would appear that he thought even a Confucian gentleman could pursue life with such an attitude. His way, it seems, was open to all, even those "punished by Heaven"—an expression Confucius uses to describe himself in contrast to Daoist sages (Watson 1968, 87). Zhuangzi ventured beyond even this broad view of human dignity, to see genuine value in other creatures and in the things of the world. All are part of the great dao and each has dignity and worth in itself. This is a sensibility lacking in many Confucians and most Mohists and it is terribly absent in our own age of crass selfishness and crude materialism. Zhuangzi's "relativity" is a call to consider the equality of all things as parts of nature and to see this as a source of wonder. At the same time, we must recognize that as creatures we each have our specific roles to fulfill and must carry on in our own sphere of activity. There is something like equal worth here, but Zhuangzi's view falls considerably short of the mutual human compassion that Wong ascribes to him. At the same time, Zhuangzi extends the notions of respect and worth beyond the realm of human beings.

I would now like to turn to what I take to be a critical aspect of Wong's philosophical position. He is strongly in favor of the ideal of equal worth primarily based upon a negative argument. That is, it is good to insure that people have equal worth because of the profoundly negative consequences of not doing so. There are important insights in this part of Wong's argument as well but there are also some problems. The important insight is something he picks up from John Rawls concerning the fundamental importance of self-respect. Rawls argues convincingly that without this basic good it seems inconceivable that people could muster the motivation to pursue any kind of worthwhile life. This is an important insight and it also seems true, as Wong argues, that our own society defines self-worth so strongly in terms of *material success* that it is no wonder so many people seem to lack the ability to enjoy and find satisfaction in their lives. Up to this point, I agree with the analysis, which is largely a diagnosis of the ills of contemporary capitalist Western liberal democracy.

At this point however, Wong begins to prescribe for this malaise in a way I find problematic. He calls for a general recognition of human dignity but claims, quoting Sennett and Cobb, that this is only or at least most easily attainable when we have an "image of human dignity without a face" (Wong 1984, 205). This view strikes me as implausible and even a bit unsettling. Instead of a faceless view of human dignity, what we need is a recognition of the dignity to be found in a myriad of human faces. We must learn to see the family resemblance that exists among a wide range of good human lives. In order to do this, we need to begin with a general conception of what kinds of things are good for human beings.

I do not see how one can regard another person as having worth in the absence of some notion concerning what things about human beings are worthwhile. Contrary to what Wong claims, there are ways of articulating such standards that do not necessarily lead to competitiveness or oppressively narrow visions of the good. We can identify a variety of traits of character and human activities that are widely recognized as constituents of or contributing to good human lives, in that they allow for the satisfaction of basic human needs, desires, and capacities. These excellences or virtues provide a solid basis for human worth. Here both Zhuangzi's broad-mindedness and Mencius' insights into the potential strength of our altruistic desires may have considerable contributions to make. Being an honest person, admiring the accomplishments and contributions of others regardless of their station in life, caring about others and being generous (in proportion to one's wealth) are just a few examples of such widely shared, egalitarian traits. Being a good husband or wife, spouse or significant other or a loving parent would be examples of such basic human activities. The well-to-do have no advantage in this regard and in fact no amount of wealth or power could make another woman a better mother to me than my own mother is. Nor do the rationally gifted appear to have any clear advantage in realizing such fundamental human virtues.

I am not suggesting that there is some set, well-defined and highly articulated conception of an essential human nature that must be realized fully in some specific version of the good life. As I have argued above, undermining such narrow and constricting ideals is one of Zhuangzi's greatest virtues. Zhuangzi shows us that there is a mad and wonderful variety of good human lives reflecting a range of highly contingent factors such as innate ability, environment, and the vicissitudes of fate. He shows us, in a compelling and vivid fashion, that our conception of the "good life" must move beyond pluralism to what we might call "ethical promiscuity."[25]

In calling for the recognition of the equal dignity of others, Wong urges us to esteem as equally valuable what others esteem, but he cannot mean by this that I should be able to esteem *everything* that some other person might happen to value, for some people are attracted to fairly despicable things. This is precisely what "moral relativity" normally is thought to entail, which is why many people (myself included) find it such an odious position. I do not think though that this is what Wong is advocating. Wong's moral relativity—like Zhuangzi's skepticism—is limited, it applies only to rationally-based philosophical systems. His position is not *really* what one normally thinks of as moral relativity; it is better thought of as what I call "ethical promiscuity." That is to say, it is the view that there are certain basic goods that all healthy, reflective, and well-informed people would agree are constituents of a good life. Nevertheless, there are many different and equally good ways of realizing these goods and many different configurations of them present equally valuable lives.[26]

Each of us is situated in a specific historical period and located in a given cultural setting and these factors clearly inform the ways we might realize a good human life. Moreover, even in a given time and place, we each can live only one life. And yet, we can recognize many of the paths not taken and many that we could not possibly have followed as leading to equally valuable lives. In these ways, we can appreciate other individual lives and many ways of life as equally worthy of esteem.

If this is how Wong in fact sees things, then, he needs to make clear what kinds of things he thinks define the range of possibilities for a good human life.[27] This will require him to propose at least a first, best approximation as to what human nature is.[28] Such an approximation will of course be open to emendation in light of our further and deeper understanding of ourselves as creatures and the world in which we live, but whatever picture one might argue for, it must be broad enough to accommodate the wide range of forms of life that most people can in fact accept as worthy of respect and esteem. As should be clear, I believe that Wong's failure to address the issue of the character of human nature lies behind the difficulties I see in both his attempt to offer an interpretation of the *Zhuangzi* and his constructive ethical theory. This is an issue where Zhuangzi, Mencius, and other early Chinese thinkers have considerable things to offer contemporary ethicists, for the character of human nature was a central concern in their ethical philosophies. I submit that it must be a central concern of ours as well.

Conclusion

I have described two important contemporary Western philosophical inter-pretations of the *Zhuangzi*. Both describe Zhuangzi as advocating a form of moral relativity. The view that Hansen ascribes to Zhuangzi is just what one expects from a thinker described as a moral relativist: He believes that Zhuangzi finds all ethical claims equally viable. According to Hansen, Zhuangzi's project is exclusively negative in the sense that his only claim is that no one can lay special claim: each and every point of view is "right" from its own unique perspective. As a result, Hansen reads Zhuangzi as a thoroughly amoral thinker.

I have argued that Hansen bases his interpretation on a mistaken and partial reading of the text. His reading is mistaken in that he takes Zhuangzi's occasional use of a god's-eye point of view as his definitive perspective. From such a point of reference it is true that all perspectives are equal and none can be said to be better than the next. I have argued that Zhuangzi only uses this perspective as a therapy to free us from the confines of our cramped and narrow perspective and give us a greater and more accurate appreciation of our true place in the world. His use of the Heavenly perspective is also part of his attempt to undermine what he regards as our overreliance upon the intellect. Zhuangzi believes that this will help to lead us back to our spontaneous inclinations and intuitions. Since he seems to believe that human beings are basically benign by nature, as long as they cleave to their spontaneous nature, they will lead lives largely if not fully free from mutual conflict and personal worry. Such ills arise only from their tendency to overintellectualize their lives and corrupt their basic nature.

Such an interpretation has the advantage of seeing Zhuangzi as deeply engaged in one of the central philosophical debates of his age, the character of human nature, and offering a distinctive view of his own. It also allows us to account for the many stories of skillful individuals that Zhuangzi offers as providing exemplars of proper living. These are important elements of the text for which Hansen's interpretation cannot provide an adequate account.

David Wong's interpretation of the *Zhuangzi* is part of his larger project on "moral relativity." His attacks on those philosophers who attempt to ground morality in some sort of rational appeal is quite similar in approach to Zhuangzi's own antirational approach.[29] In addition, his argument that this will lead to a greater awareness of moral worth resembles Zhuangzi's view that human flourishing can be achieved in a wide variety of activities, including many that were deemed low and demeaning in his own age.

However, Wong's claim that Zhuangzi believed that such an approach leads to a feeling of *ci* "compassion" finds no support in the text. While Zhuangzi seems to have believed that human nature was benign in character, this falls considerably short of "compassion". Moreover, in the absence of some account of the character of human nature, Wong's philosophical position appears quite vulnerable, for it is not at all clear what it would be like to respect and esteem someone in the absence of any and all criteria for what a good life might be.

This is not to say that Wong's position is without merit. Recent attempts to describe an Aristotelian-style ethic, when combined with a careful study of the various views offered by early Chinese thinkers appear to hold considerable promise. Since early Chinese thinkers tend to focus on more cooperative and primarily affective virtues, such as being a good family member or a generally caring person, they offer a way to temper the more competitive and intellectualist tendencies of the Aristotelian tradition. Wong's analysis of Zhuangzi's thought brings into focus several ideas that offer significant contributions to this larger, constructive effort. However, I have argued that such a position is not really a form of moral relativity and is best thought of as a form of what I call "ethical promiscuity."

In developing my responses to Hansen and Wong, I have come to appreciate more deeply and fully both Zhuangzi's philosophy and the Western philosophical problems these authors have used to analyze his thought. I have also come to a greater appreciation of the considerable resources within the early Chinese philosophical tradition for those seeking to develop a pluralistic ethic of human flourishing. Prominent among these are Confucian texts such as the *Mencius* and that most interesting of Daoist texts, the *Zhuangzi*.

Notes

I would like to thank Bryan W. Van Norden, Paul Kjellberg, and especially David B. Wong for helpful criticisms and suggestions on earlier versions of this essay.

1. For Hansen's view see his "A *Tao* of Tao in Chuang-tzu" in Mair 1983. Wong presents his interpretation of Zhuangzi as part of a larger project on moral relativism in his *Moral Relativity* (Berkeley: University of California Press, 1984).

2. I discuss Hansen's use of the terms "skepticism" and "relativism" in greater detail below. For discussions of skepticism and its relation to Zhuangzi's thought, see the essays by Kjellberg and Raphals in the present volume.

3. This figure is often referred to as "Cook Ding" but I agree with Paul Kjellberg that 丁 *ding* should be understood as an indication of rank, not as a proper name. See Kjellberg 1993, 34, note 1.

4. From what Hansen says in this essay as well as from what he has communicated in personal conversations, I believe that he accepts the ethical implications of his view as I describe them here. Robert Eno also seems to accept that the *Zhuangzi* presents a radically amoral philosophy. See his "Creating Nature: Juist and Taoist Approaches" in Smith 1991, 95. See also, Eno's contribution to the present volume.

5. Alexander Nehamas describes a similar strategy as one possible way of reading Nietzsche. See his *Nietzsche: Life as Literature* (Cambridge: Harvard University Press, 1985), 35. Iris Murdoch advances a similar account of Derrida in her essay, "Derrida and Structuralism" in *Metaphysics as a Guide to Morals* (New York: The Penguin Press, 1993), 185–216.

6. Among other things, this part of Hansen's position seems to be in clear opposition to Zhuangzi's repeated counsel to avoid excessive emotions and desires.

7. I have offered my own analysis of skepticism and relativism in relation to Zhuangzi in Ivanhoe 1993.

8. Thomas Nagel coined this expression and argues that along with our subjective and particular view of the world this objective perspective describes the irreducible and inescapable dual vision of which human beings are capable. See his, *The View From Nowhere* (Oxford: Oxford University Press, 1986).

9. This is just one of several passages where Zhuangzi points to clear and common goods. Compare Watson 1968, 66, where Crippled Shu is commended for being able to "finish out the years Heaven gave him." This is a good that Zhuangzi allegorically extends to plants as well. For example, consider the ancient tree who criticizes "useful trees" that are prematurely killed. Because of their usefulness, they are prevented from "finishing out the years Heaven gave them" (Watson 1968, 64).

10. My translation.

11. This is the case at least for those stories that appear in the Inner Chapters and those in other parts of the text that have been reasonably established as closely associated with this textual core.

12. I have discussed how Zhuangzi's notion of skill fits into the rest of his thought in Ivanhoe 1993. For different and insightful accounts of the notion of skill in the *Zhuangzi*, see Eno's and Yearley's contributions to the present volume.

13. Angus C. Graham has shown that the issue of the character of human nature was one of the most hotly disputed topics of the late Warring States period in China (Graham 1989). See also the discussion by Benjamin I. Schwartz in *The World of Thought in Ancient China* (Cambridge: The Belknap Press, 1985), 175–179.

14. Wong begins his chapter thirteen, where he presents his interpretation of Zhuangzi as a moral relativist, by saying, "A recognition of moral relativity can help us with the problem of making good on the principle of equal worth" (Wong 1984, 198).

15. This issue has a direct bearing on how one reads the Zhuangzi as well. For if we are to take the stories about the cook and others about wood carvers and carpenters as providing examples of how human beings should live their lives, then clearly things like oxen and trees are not "equal" in status to human beings. All are equal in having a place in the great dao but this does not entail that we treat each creature and thing in the world in the same way.

16. Tom Regan, *The Case for Animal Rights* (Berkeley: University of California Press, 1985).

17. Rawls has recently backed away from this position, but Wong is

interested in his views as expressed in his now classic work, A *Theory of Justice* (Cambridge: The Belknap Press, 1971).

18. Alan Gewirth, *Reason and Morality* (Chicago: University of Chicago Press, 1978).

19. Feinberg's views are put forth as part of his criticism of utilitarian positions, see his *Social Philosophy* (Englewood Cliffs: Prentice-Hall, 1973).

20. I would add that in addition to attacking those who tried to ground their ethical views with some rational appeal (for example, the Mohists), Zhuangzi was equally dedicated to attacking the traditionalist appeals of the Confucians.

21. 12/80, 29/39, 31/35, and 33/4. Watson 1968, 138, 328, 349, and 362.

22. Since writing this essay I have had the opportunity to discuss this issue briefly with Professor Wong. He now sees that he attributed this idea to Zhuangzi based upon instances of its appearance in the *Daodejing* and he agrees that Zhuangzi's view of human nature is better described as "benign."

23. In the *Kang gao* chapter of the *Book of History* the ideal ruler is said to treat his people, as if he "were taking care of an infant." See James Legge, *The Shoo King*, volume 3 of *The Chinese Classics* reprint (Hong Kong: University of Hong Kong Press, 1970), 389. This passage is quoted and discussed in *Mencius* 3A5.

24. In fact there are several passages where people seem to manifest a disturbing indifference to the suffering even of friends. See, for example, the case of the four friends in Watson 1968, 83–87.

25. Ethical promiscuity does not entail moral relativity, nor does it imply that one can blithely move from one form of the good life to another in quick succession. It is meant to emphasize that there is a remarkably wide variety of possible good human lives and good human communities. These good lives will share a kind of family resemblance and the people who live them will both be able to appreciate each other's lives and agree in ruling out absolutely certain kinds of practices. My view is strongly pluralistic without abandoning ethical realism. The term "ethical promiscuity" is inspired by John Dupre's notion of "promiscuous realism" in the philosophy of science. See his *The Disorder of Things: Metaphysical Foundations of the Disunity of Science* (Cambridge: Harvard University Press, 1993).

26. Stuart Hampshire captures both the open-ended nature and common core of this task. He writes, "Any conception of human potentialities has to represent a target which is not only always moving, but also moving in several dimensions. . . . The enterprise of the moralist . . . ought to be the

emendation and elaboration of those few well-argued conceptions of human powers which now actually influence people's lives and purposes" (*Innocence and Experience* (Cambridge: Harvard Unviversity Press, 1989), 32).

27. An example of such an attempt is Martha Nussbaum's "Non-Relative Virtues: An Aristotelian Approach," in Martha C. Nussbaum and Amartya Sen, eds., *The Quality of Life* (Oxford: Clarendon Press, 1993), 242–269.

28. In some of his more recent work, Wong indicates that he is perhaps coming around to this view himself. See "On Flourishing and Finding One's Identity in Community," *Midwest Studies in Philosophy Volume XIII*, Peter A. French, Theodore E. Uehling Jr., and Howard Wettstein, eds., (Notre Dame, Ind.: University of Notre Dame Press, 1988), 324–341 and "Coping with Moral Conflict and Ambiguity," *Ethics* 102.4 (July, 1992), 763–784.

29. I borrow the term from Angus C. Graham, who used it throughout many of his works. For his most clear and complete statements of this idea, see *Reason and Spontaneity* (London: Curzon Press, 1985) and *Unreason Within Reason: Essays on the Outskirts of Rationality* (La Salle, Ill.: Open Court, 1992). My use of this idea differs slightly from Graham's. He tends to focus on the role intensity of emotion plays in distinguishing antirationalists from irrationalists. While I agree that this criterion serves to distinguish types of antirationalists, I believe the critical difference separating all antirationalists from irrationalists is the degree to which one is willing to defend one's beliefs rationally.

Bibliography

This bibliography is intended to be a comprehensive survey of sources for Zhuangzi studies in Western languages. A complete account of the vast literature on Zhuangzi in Chinese, Japanese, and Korean would be far beyond the scope of this project; only major studies have been included, and readers are referred to the Asian-language bibliographies in the works of Wu Kuangming for further details (see below). Also omitted are most of the general studies of Chinese philosophy that are not specifically focused on Zhuangzi. With these limitations in mind, it is hoped that this collection of references will draw some attention to previously overlooked studies in non-English languages and prove a useful resource for scholars engaged in the study of the *Zhuangzi*. While we have used the Pinyin system throughout the rest of the volume, we have retained here the traditional Wade-Giles romanizations found in most card catalogues.

Akatzuka Tadashi 赤塚忠. 1974 *Soshi* 莊子. Tokyo: Shuei sha.

Allinson, Robert E. 1988. "A Logical Reconstruction of the Butterfly Dream: The Case for Internal Textual Transformation." *Journal of Chinese Philosophy* 15.3, 319–339.

———. 1988. "On the Origin of the Relativistic Thesis for Interpretations of the Chuang-tzu." *Han Hsüeh Yen Chiu* 漢學研究, 275–298.

———. 1989. *Chuang-tzu For Spiritual Transformation.* Albany: State University of New York Press. [Reviewed by Wayne Alt in *Asian Philosophy* 1.2 (1991), Burton Watson in *Journal of Chinese Philosophy* 20.1 (1993), Bryan Van Norden in *Journal of Asian Studies* 49.2 (1990), and W. Y. Li in *Journal of Religion* 71.2 (1991).]

———. 1989. "On the Question of Relativism in the *Chuang-tzu*." *Philosophy East and West* 39.1, 13–26.

Alt, Wayne E. 1991. "Logic and Language in the *Chuang-tzu.*" *Asian Philosophy* 1.1, 61–76.

Arendrup, Birthe. 1973. "The First Chapter of Guo Xiang's Commentary to Zhuang Zi: A Translation and Grammatical Analysis." *Acta Orientalia* 36.1–2, 311–416.

Boltz, William G. 1980. "The Structure and Interpretation of *Chuang-tzu*: Two Notes on *Hsiao Yao Yu*." *Bulletin of the School of Oriental and African Studies* 63.3, 532–543.

Buber, Martin. 1922. *Reden und Gleichnisse des Tschuang-tse; Deutsche Auswahl von Martin Buber*. Leipzig: Insel-Verlag.

———. 1991. *Chinese Tales: Zhuangzi, Sayings and Parables and Chinese Ghost and Love Stories*. (Translated by Alex Page; with an introduction by Irene Eber.) Atlantic Highlands, N.J.: Humanities Press International.

Burneko, Guy C. 1986. "Chuang-tzu's Existential Hermeneutics." *Journal of Chinese Philosophy* 13.4, 393–409.

Chang Mo-sheng 張默生. 1974. *Chuang-tzu Hsin Shih* 莊子新釋. Taipei: Shih tai shu chü.

Chang Ch'eng-ch'iu 張成秋. 1971. *Chuang-tzu P'ien Mu K'ao* 莊子篇目考. Taiwan: Chung hua shu chü.

Chang Chung-yuan. 1977. "The Philosophy of Taoism According to Chuang-tzu." *Philosophy East & West* 27.4, 409–422.

Chang Tsung-tung. 1982. *Metaphysik, Erkenntnis und Praktische Philosophie im Chuang-tzu—Zur Neu-Interpretation und Systematischen Darstellung der Klassischen Chinesischen Philosophie*. Frankfurt am Main: Vittorio Klosterman. [Reviewed by Cristoph Harbsmeier, *Bulletin of the School of Oriental and African Studies* 68.1 (1985), 167–8.]

Ch'en Ch'i-t'ien 陳啓天. 1978. *Chuang-tzu Ch'ien Shuo* 莊子淺說. Taipei: Chung hua shu chü.

Ch'en Ku-ying 陳鼓應. 1975. *Chuang-tzu Che-Hsüeh T'an-chiu* 莊子哲學探究. Taipei: Jih sheng yin chih ch'ang.

———. 1983. *Chuang-tzu Chin Chu Chin I* 莊子今註今譯. Peking: Chung-hua shu chu: Hsin hua shu tien Pei-ching fa hsing so fa hsing.

Ch'en Shou-ch'ang 陳壽昌. *Nan Hua Chen Ching Cheng I* 南華眞經正義. Taipei: Hsin t'ien ti shu chü.

Cheng Chung-ying. 1990. "A Taoist Interpretation of 'Differance' in Derrida." *Journal of Chinese Philosophy* 17.1, 19–30.

Chiang, Hsi-ch'ang 蔣錫昌. 1988. *Chuang-tzu Che Hsüeh* 莊子哲學. Cheng-tu: Chengtu ku chi shu tien fu chih: Ssu-chuan sheng hsin hua shu tien.

Chiao Hung 焦竑. 1970. *Chuang-tzu I* 莊子翼. Taipei: Kuang wen shu chü.

Chien Chi-hui. 1990. "'Theft's Way': A Comparative Study of Chuang-tzu's

Tao and Derridean 'Trace'." *Journal of Chinese Philosophy* 17.1, 31–49.

Ch'ien Mu 錢穆. 1951. *Chuang-tzu Ts'uan Chien* 莊子纂箋. Hong Kong: Tung nan yin wu ch'u pan she.

Chin, Chia-hsi 金嘉錫. 1986. *Chuang-tzu Yü Tzu Yen Chiu* 莊子寓子研究. Taipei: Hua cheng shu chü.

Chu Kuei-yao 朱桂曜. 1935. *Chuang-tzu Nei P'ien Cheng Pu* 莊子內篇證補. Taiwan: Shang wu yin shu kuan.

Chuang Tzu Yin Te 莊子引得. 1947. Peking: Yen-ching ta hsueh tu shu kuan yin te pien tsuan chü.

Chung, Tai 鍾泰. 1988. *Chuang-tzu Fa Wei* 莊子發微. Shanghai: Shang-hai ku chi chu pan she: Hsin hua shu tien Shang-hai fa hsing so.

Chung, Ying-mei 鍾應梅. 1981. *Tu Chuang-tzu* 讀莊子. Kowloon: Hsiang-kang neng jen shu yuan, Chung-kuo wen hsüeh yen chiu so.

Cleary, Thomas F. 1991. *The Essential Tao: An Initiation Into the Heart of Taoism Through the Authentic Tao Te Ching and the Inner Teachings of Chuang-tzu.* San Francisco: Harper.

Coxon, Anne Kogler. 1975. *Chinese Religious Thought: Mencius and Chuang-tzu.* Stanford: Stanford University Press.

Cua, Antonio S. 1977. "Forgetting Morality: Reflections on a Theme in Chuang-tzu." *Journal of Chinese Philosophy* 4.4, 305–328.

Elorduy, Carmelo. 1972. *Sesenta y Cuatro Conceptos de la Idealogia Taoista de Lao-tzu y Chuang-tzu.* Caracas: Universidad Catolica "Andres Bello," Instituto de Investigaciones Historicas, 1972.

Egerod, Sören. 1960. "Meng Tsi's and Chuang tsi's Parting Words." *Acta Orientalia* 25.1–2, 112–120.

Feng, Gia-fu and Jane English. 1974. *Chuang tsu; Inner Chapters.* New York: Vintage Books.

Forke, Alfred. 1927. "Tschuang-tse," in *Geshichte der Alten Chinesischen Philosophie.* Hamburg: L. Friederichsen & Co., 303–328.

Fukunaga, Mitsuji 複永光司. 1966. *Soshi* 莊子. Tokyo: Asahi shin bun sha.

———. 1969. "'No-Mind' in Chuang-tzu and Ch'an Buddhism." *Zinbun* 12, 9–41.

Fung, Yu-lan. 1964. *Chuang-tzu: a New Selected Translation with an Exposition of the Philosophy of Kuo Hsiang.* Paragon Book Reprint Corp. [Reviewed by Lionello Lanciotti, *Philosophy East & West* 15.3–4, 383.]

————. 1989. *A Taoist Classic: Chuang-tzu*. Beijing: Foreign Language Press, 1989.

Giles, Herbert A. 1926. *Chuang-tzu: Mystic, Moralist, and Social Reformer*. Shanghai: Kelley & Walsh.

————.1961. *Chuang-tzu: Taoist Philosopher and Chinese Mystic*. London, Allen & Unwin.

Giles, Lionel. 1920. *Musings of a Chinese Mystic: Selections from the Philosophy of Chuang-tzu*. London: J. Murray.

Girardot, N. J. 1978. "Chaotic 'Order' (*hun-tun*) and Benevolent 'Disorder' (*luan*) in the *Chuang-tzu*." *Philosophy East & West* 28.3, 299–321.

————. 1978. "'Returning to the Beginning' and the Arts of Mr. Hun-Tun in the *Chuang-tzu*." *Journal of Chinese Philosophy* 5.1, 21–69.

Goodman, Russell B. 1985. "Skepticism and Realism in the *Chuang-tzu*." *Philosophy East & West* 35.3, 231–7.

Graham, A. C. 1969–70. "*Chuang-tzu's* Essay on Seeing Things as Equal." *History of Religions* 9.2–3, 137–159. [Reprinted in Graham 1986.]

————. 1979. "How Much of *Chuang-tzu* Did Chuang-tzu Write?" *Journal of American Academy of Religion* 47.3, 459–502. [Reprinted in Graham 1986.]

————. 1981. *Chuang-tzu: the Inner Chapters*. London; Boston: Unwin Paperbacks.

————. 1982. *Chuang-tzu: Textual Notes to A Partial Translation*. London: School of Oriental and African Studies, University of London.

————. 1983. "Taoist Spontaneity and the Dichotomy of 'Is' and 'Ought'." In Mair, 1983, 2–23.

————. 1986. *Studies in Chinese Philosophy and Philosophical Literature*. Singapore: Institute for East Asian Philosophies.

————. 1989. "From Yangism to *Chuang-tzu's* Taoism: Reconciliation with Heaven by Return to Spontaneity," in *Disputers of the Tao*. La Salle, Ill.: Open Court.

Hall, David. 1984. "Nietzsche and Chuang-tzu—Resources for the Transcendence of Culture." *Journal of Chinese Philosophy* 11.2, 139–152.

Hansen, Chad. 1983. "A Tao of Tao in Chuang-tzu," in Mair, 1983, 24–55.

Hara, Wing-han. 1993. "Between Individuality and Universality: An Explication of Chuang-tzu's Thesis of *Chien-tu* 見獨 and *Ch'i-wu* 齊物." *Journal of Chinese Philosophy* 20.1, 87–99.

Ho Ching-ch'ün 何敬群. 1966. *Chuang-tzu I I* 莊子義繹. Hong Kong: Jen sheng ch'u pan she.

Hsiao Ch'un-po 蕭純佰. 1972. *Chuang-tzu Chih Yao* 莊子治要. Taipei: Shang wu yin shu kuan.

Hsieh, Hsiang-hao 謝祥皓. 1988. *Chuang-tzu Tao Tu* 莊子導讀. Chengtu: Pa shu shu she: Ssu-ch'uan sheng hsin hua shu tien ching hsiao.

Hsüan Ying 宣穎. 1977. *Chuang-tzu Nan Hua Ching Chieh* 莊子南華經解. Taipei: Hung yeh shu chü.

Huang Chin-hung 黃錦鈜. 1974. *Chuang-tzu chi Ch'i Wen Hsüeh* 莊子及其文學. Taipei: San min shu chü.

———. 1974. *Hsin I Chuang-tzu Tu Pen* 新譯莊子讀本. Taipei: San min shu chü.

———. 1982. "Chin San Shih Nien Lai chih Chuang-tzu Hsüeh." 近三十年來之莊子學. In *Taiwan Han Hsüeh Yen Chiu T'ong Hsün* 臺灣漢學研究通訊.

Ivanhoe, Philip J. 1991. "Zhuangzi's Conversion Experience." *Journal of Chinese Religions* 19, 13–25.

———. 1993. "Skepticism, Skill and the Ineffable Tao." *Journal of the American Academy of Religions* 61.4, 639-654.

Izutsu, Toshihiko. 1984. *Sufism and Taoism: a Comparative Study of Key Philosophical Concepts.* Berkeley: University of California Press.

Jablónski, Witold, et. al. 1953. *Czuang-tsy—Nan-Hua-Czen-King.* Warszawa: Panstwowe Wydawnicto Naukowe. [Reviewed by Derk Bodde, *Far Eastern Quarterly* 14.1 (1954),100.]

Kanaya, Osamu 金谷治. 1981. *Soshi* 莊子. Tokyo: Iwanami bunko.

Kao Heng 高享. 1973. *Chuang-tzu Chin Chien* 莊子今箋. Taiwan: Chung hua shu chü.

Karlgren, Bernhard. 1976. "Moot Words in Some *Chuang-tse* Chapters." *Museum of Far Eastern Antiquities* 48, 145–163.

Kjellberg, Paul. 1993. *Zhuangzi and Skepticism.* Ph.D. dissertation, Department of Philosophy, Stanford University, 1993.

———. 1994. "Skepticism, Truth and the Good Life: A Comparison of Zhuangzi and Sextus Empiricus." *Philosophy East & West* 44.1, 111–133.

Knaul, Livia. 1982. "Lost *Chuang Tzu* Passages." *Journal of Chinese Religions* 10, 53–79.

———. 1985. "Kuo Hsiang and the *Chuang Tzu*." *Journal of Chinese Philosophy* 12.4, 429–47.

———. 1986. "Chuang-tzu and the Chinese Ancestry of Ch'an Buddhism." *Journal of Chinese Philosophy* 13.4, 411–428.

Kuan Feng 關鋒. 1961. *Chuang-tzu Nei P'ien I Chieh ho P'i P'an* 莊子內篇譯解和批判. Peking: Chung hua shu chü.

Kuo Ch'ing-fan 郭慶蕃. 1988. *Chuang-tzu Chi Shih* 莊子集釋. Peking: Chung-kuo shu tien ying yin: Hsin hua shu tien shou tu fa hsing so fa hsing.

Kuo Hsiang 郭象. 1968. *Chuang-tzu Nan Hua Chen Ching* 莊子南華眞經. Taipei: I wen yin shu kuan.

Kupperman, Joel J. 1989. "Not in So Many Words: Chuang-tzu's Strategies of Communication." *Philosophy East & West* 39.3, 311–317.

Lang Ch'ing-hsiao 郎擎霄. 1974. *Chuang-tzu Hsüeh An* 莊子學案. Taipei: Ho lo t'u shu ch'u pan she.

Lee, Agnes Chwen-Jiuan. 1990. "The Philosophy of Liberation in Lao Tzu and Chuang Tzu [*wu wei* or non-striving]." *Ching Feng* 33, 191–204.

Legge, James. 1891. *The Writings of Kwang-Tze*, in *The Sacred Books of the East: vol. XXXIX The Texts of Taoism*. London: Oxford University Press.

Legge, Russel D. 1979. "Chuang-tzu and the Free Man." *Philosophy East & West* 29.1, 11–20.

Les Pères du Système Taoïste. 1984. Dyfed, Wales: Llanerch Enterprises, 1984. [Rendered into English by Derek Bryce as *Wisdom of the Daoist Masters*.]

Li, C.Y. 1993. "What Being: Chuang-tzu Versus Aristotle." *International Philosophical Quarterly* 33.3, 341–353.

Li Mien 李勉. 1973. *Chuang-tzu Tsung Lun Chi Fen P'ien P'ing Chu* 莊子總論及分篇評注. Taipei: Shang wu shu chu.

Lin Hsi-I 林希逸. 1971. *Chuang-tzu K'ou I* 莊子口義. Taiwan: Hung tao wen hua shih yeh yu hsien kung ssu.

Lin, S. F. 1988. "Confucius in the Inner Chapters of the *Chuang-tzu*." *Tamkang Review* 18.1–4, 311–317.

Lin Shu 林紓. 1923. *Chuang-tzu Ch'ien Shuo* 莊子箋說. Shanghai: Shang wu yin shu kuan.

Lin Yun-ming 林雲銘. 1968. *Tseng Chu Chuang-tzu Yin* 增註莊子因. Taipei: Kuang wen shu chü.

————. 1969. *Piao Chu Pu I Chuang-tzu Yin* 標注補義莊子因. Taipei: Lan t'ai shu chü.

Liou, Kia-hway. 1969. *L'oeuvre Complète de Tschouang-tzeu*. Paris: Gallimard. [Reviewed by M. Kaltenmark, *Revue de l'Histoire des Religion* 180.1, 92–93.]

Liu Hsiao-kan 劉笑敢. 1987. *Chuang-tzu Che Hsüeh chi Ch'i Yen Pien* 莊子哲學及其演變. Peking: Chung-kuo she hui ko hsüeh chu pan she.

————. 1992. "The Evolution of 3 Schools of Latter-Day Zhuang-Zi Philosophy." *Chinese Studies in Philosophy* 24.1, 3–54.

Liu Kuang-i 劉光義. 1986. *Chuang-tzu Hsüeh Li Ts'e* 莊子學蠡測. Taipei: Hsüeh sheng shu chü.

Liu Wen-tien 劉文典. 1947, 1980. *Chuang-tzu Pu Cheng* 莊子補正. K'unming: Yunnan jen min ch'u pan she.

Loewe, Michael, ed. 1993. *Early Chinese Texts: A Bibliographical Guide*. Berkeley, Calif.: The Society for the Study of Early China.

Ma Hsü-lun 馬敍倫. 1970. *Chuang-tzu I Cheng* 莊子義證. Taipei: Hung tao wen hua shih yeh yu hsien kung ssu.

Mair, Victor, ed. 1983. *Experimental Essays on Chuang-tzu*. Honolulu: Center for Asian and Pacific Studies, University of Hawaii.

————, tr. 1994. *Wandering on the Way: Early Taoist Tales and Parables of Chuang Tzu*. New York: Bantam Books.

————. 1994. "Introduction and Notes for a Complete Translation of the Chuang Tzu." *Sino-Platonic Papers* 48.

Major, John S. 1975. "The Efficacy of Uselessness: a Chuang Tzu Motif." *Philosophy East & West* 25.3, 265–280.

McPharlin, Paul. 1952. *Chinese Philosophy : Sayings of Confucius, Sayings of Mencius, Sayings of Lao Tzu, Sayings of Chuang Tzu and Lieh Tzu*. Mount Vernon, N.Y.: Peter Pauper Press.

Mei, Y. P. 1964. "Ancient Chinese Philosophy According to the *Chuang-tzu*, Chapter 33, the World of Thought, With an English Translation of the Chapter." *Ch'ing Hua Hsüeh Pao* 清華學報 4.2, 186–211.

Merton, Thomas. 1965. *The Way of Chuang-tzu*. New York: New Directions. [Reviewed by Cyrus Lee in *Chinese Culture* 24.2 (1983), 19–23 and 25.3 (1984), 31–42.]

Mikisaburo Mori. 1972. "Chuang-tzu and Buddhism." *The Eastern Buddhist* 5.2, 44–69.

Moritz, Ralf. 1985. "Der Chinesische Philosoph Zhuang-zi im Licht Neuer Forschungen." *Orientalistische Literaturzeitun* 80.2, 119–127.

Murohashi Tetsuji 諸橋轍次. 1972. *Soshi Heiwa* 莊子平話. Taiwan: Chuan hsin ch'i yeh yu hsien kung ssu [Chinese translation].

Nishida Saemon 西田左衛門. 1931. *Loshi, Soshi* 老子莊子. Tokyo: Si sei do.

Nivison, David S. "Hsün Tzu and Chuang Tzu," in Rosemont 1991.

Novaro, Mario. 1949. *Acque d'Autunno*. Bari: G. Laterza.

Ouyang Caiwei. 1987. "A Discourse on Zhuang Zi and Chan Buddhism." *Social Sciences in China* 8.1, 61–102.

Owens, Wayne D. 1990. "Radical Concrete Particularity: Heidegger, Lao-tzu and Chuang Tzu." *Journal of Chinese Philosophy* 7.2, 235–255.

Paper, Jordan. 1977. "Dating the *Chuang-tzu* by Analysis of Philosophical Terms." *Chinese Culture* 18.4, 33–40.

Parkes, Graham. 1983. "The Wandering Dance: Chuang Tzu and Zarathustra." *Philosophy East & West* 33.3, 235–250.

Pas, Julian F. 1981. "Chuang-tzu's Essays on 'Free Flight Into Transcendence' and 'Responsive Rulership' (Chapters One and Seven of *Chuang-tzu*)." *Journal of Chinese Philosophy* 8.4, 479–496.

Rosemont, Henry, Jr., ed. 1991. *Chinese Texts and Philosophical Contexts*. La Salle, Ill.: Open Court.

Roth, Harold. 1991. "Who Compiled the *Chuang-tzu?*" in Rosemont 1991.

———. "Chuang Tzu," in Loewe 1993. (Bibliography contains additional items of interest.)

Sakai Kanzo 坂井煥三. 1930. *Soshi Hsin Shaku* 莊子新釋. Tokyo: Ko do kan.

Sha Shao-hai 沙少海. 1987. *Chuang-tzu Chi Chu* 莊子集注. Kueiyang: Kueichou jen min ch'u pan she.

Shen Hung 沈洪. 1969. *Chuang-tzu* 莊子. Taipei: Shang wu yin shu kuan.

Slingerland, Edward. 1993. "Wang Fu-Chih's Chuang-tzu Explained." M.A. thesis, Department of East Asian Languages, U.C. Berkeley.

———. 1994. "Skepticism in Zhuangzi, Nietzsche and Foucault." Berkeley Preprint Series, Center for Chinese Studies, U.C. Berkeley.

Smith, Kidder, ed. 1991. *Chuang-tzu: Rationality: Interpretation*. Brunswick: Breckinridge Public Affairs Center.

Su Hsin-wu 蘇新鋈. 1980. *Kuo Hsiang Chuang Hsüeh P'ing I* 郭象莊學平議. Taiwan: Hsüeh sheng shu chü.

Sun, Siao-fang. 1953. "Chuang-tzu's Theory of Truth." *Philosophy East & West* 3.2, 137–146.

Suzuki Shuji 鈴木修次. 1974. *Soshi* 莊子. Tokyo: Shimizu sho in.

Thiel, P. Jos. 1969. "Das Erkenntnisproblem bei Chuang-tzu." *Sinologia* 11.1–2, 1–89.

Thomas, Léon. 1987. "Les États de Conscience Inhabituels dans le «Zhuang Zi»." *Revue de l'Histoire des Religion* 204.2, 129–149.

Tsao, Ch'u-chi 曹礎基. 1982. *Chuang-tzu Ch'ien Chu* 莊子淺註. Peking: Chung hua shu chu. Hsin hua shu tien Pei-ching fa hsing so fa hsing.

Waley, Arthur. 1939. *Three Ways of Thought in Ancient China*. London: G. Allen & Unwin.

Waltham, Clae. 1971. *Chuang-tzu: Genius of the Absurd* [Arranged from the Work of James Legge] New York: Ace Books.

Wang, Hsien-chien 王先謙. 1987. *Chuang-tzu Chi Chieh* 莊子集解. Peking: Chung-hua shu chü.

Wang Fu-chih 王夫之. 1961. *Chuang-tzu Chieh* 莊子解. Beijing: Chung hua shu chü.

———. 1962. *Chuang-tzu T'ung* 莊子通. Peking: Chung hua shu chü,

Wang Shih-shun 王世舜 et. al. 1984. *Chuang-tzu I Chu* 莊子議注. Chinan: Shang-tung chiao yu ch'u pan she.

Wang, Shu-min 王叔岷. 1978. *Chuang Hsüeh Kuan K'ui* 莊學管闚. Taiwan: I wen yin shu kuan.

———. 1988. *Chuang-tzu Chiao Ch'uan* 莊子校詮. Taipei: Chung yang yen chiu yuan li shih yu yen yen chiu so.

Ware, James R. 1963. *The Sayings of Chuang Chou*. New York: Mentor. [Reviewed by Dale Riepe, *Journal of Asian Studies* 24.2, 329–330, and Lionello Lanciotti, *Philosophy East & West* 15.1–2, 139.]

Watson, Burton. 1968. *The Complete Works of Chuang Tzu*. New York: Columbia University Press. [Reviewed by Richard Mather, *Journal of the American Oriental Society* 112.2, 334–6 and H. Klöster, *Sinologica* 12.3–4, 205–6.]

Wilhelm, Richard. 1920. *Das Wahre Buch vom Sudlichen Blütenland: Nan Hua Dschen Ging*. Jena: E. Diederich.

Woo, Peter K. Y. 1969. *Begriffsgeschichtlicher Vergleich Zwischen Tao, Hodos und Logos bei Chuang-tzu, Parmenides und Heraklit.* Taipei: 1969. [Reviewed by E. J. M. Kroker, *Sinologica*, 12.3–4, 227–9.]

Wu Kuang-ming 吳光明. 1982.*Chuang-tzu: World Philosopher at Play.* New York: Crossroad Publishing Company.

———. 1986. "Dream in Nietzsche and Chuang-tzu." *Journal of Chinese Philosophy* 13.4, 371–8.

———. 1988. "Goblet Words, Dwelling Words, Opalescent Words: Philosophical Methodology of *Chuang-tzu.*" *Journal of Chinese Philosophy* 15.1, 1–8.

———. 1990. *The Butterfly as Companion.* Albany: State University of New York Press. [Reviewed by Paul Kjellberg, *Philosophy East & West*, 43.1, 127–135, and B. Netto, *Journal of the Royal Asiatic Society* 1, 458–459; contains an excellent Asian language bibliography that has been partially incorporated here.]

———. 1991. "Non-World Making in *Chuang-tzu.*" *Journal of Chinese Philosophy* 18.1, 37–50. [Responded to by Jesse Fleming in the same issue, 51–52.]

———. 1992. *Chuang-tzu.* Taipei: Dongda Tushu Gongsi: Zongjing Hsiao Sanmin Shuju. [Includes bibliographical references (pp. 227–233).]

Wu I 吳怡. 1971. *Hsiao Yao te Chuang-tzu* 逍遙的莊子. Taipei: Hsin t'ien ti shu chü.

Wu, Laurence C. 1986. "Chuang-tzu and Wittgenstein on World-Making." *Journal of Chinese Philosophy* 13.4, 383–391.

Xie, S. B. and Chen, J. M. 1992. "Derrida, Jacque and Chuang-tzu, Some Analogies in Their Deconstructionist Discourse on Language and Truth." *Canadian Review of Comparative Literature–Revue Canadienne de Littérature Comparée* 19.3, 363–376.

Yang Dayong. 1992. "Yan Fu's Philosophy of Evolution and the Thought of Lao Zi and Zhuang Zi." *Chinese Studies in Philosophy* 24.1.

Yang Ju-pin 楊儒賓. 1987. *Hsien Ch'in Tao Chia "Tao" ti Kuan Nien ti Fa Chan.* 先秦道家道的觀念的發展 Taipei: Kuo li Tai-wan ta hsüeh ch'u pan wei yuan hui: Fa hsing che Kuo li Tai-wan ta hsueh wen hsueh yuan. [Series: Kuo li Tai-wan ta hsueh wen shih tsung kan; 77].

Ye Ch'eng-i 葉程義. 1979. *Chuang-tzu Yü Yen Yen Chiu* 莊子寓言研究. Taipei: Yi sheng ch'u pan she.

Yearley, Lee H. 1983. "The Perfected Person in the Radical Chuang-tzu." In Mair, 1983, 125–139.

Yeh, Michelle. 1983. "The Deconstructive Way: A Comparative Study of Derrida and Chuang-tzu." *Journal of Chinese Philosophy* 10.2, 95–126.

Yen Ling-feng 嚴靈峰, ed. 1961. *Lieh-tzu Chuang-tzu Chih Chien Shu Mu* 列子莊子知見書目. Hongkong: Wu chiu pei chai.

———. 1972. *Chuang-tzu Chi Ch'eng Ch'u P'ien* 莊子集成初篇. Taipei: Yi wen yin shu kuan.

———. 1974. *Chuang-tzu Chi Ch'eng Hsü P'ien* 莊子集成續篇. Taipei: Yi wen yin shu kuan.

Zen, P. J. 1949. "Le chapitre 33 du *Tschoang-tse*." *Série Bilangue "Textes et Documents," Bulletin de l'Université l' Aurore* 3.10, 104–136.

Zhou, Q. 1989. "A Survey of Recent Studies on the Thought of Laozi and Zhuangzi." *Chinese Studies in Philosophy* 20.3, 71–90.

Zia, Rosina C. 1966. "The Conception of 'Sage' in Lao-tze and Chuang-tze." *Ch'ung Chi Hsüeh-pao* 崇基學報, 5.2, 150–157.

Contributors

MARK BERKSON is a Ph.D. candidate in the Department of Religious Studies at Stanford University. He is specializing in Chinese religion and philosophy. He received his B.A. (1987) from Princeton University and his M.A. (1992) from the Center for East Asian Studies at Stanford. His interests include comparative religion and ethics, language and mysticism, and virtue theory.

ROBERT ENO studied at the University of Michigan and teaches Chinese language and culture at Indiana University. He has published numerous articles on a wide variety of subjects concerning classical Chinese thought. He is the author of *The Confucian Creation of Heaven: Philosophy and the Defense of Ritual Mastery* (SUNY Press, 1990).

PHILIP J. IVANHOE received his B.A. (1976) and his Ph.D. (1987) from Stanford University. His articles have appeared in such journals as the *Journal of the American Academy of Religion, The Journal of Religious Ethics, Philosophy East and West, The Journal of Chinese Philosophy* and the *International Philosophical Quarterly*. He is the author of *Ethics in the Confucian Tradition: The Thought of Mencius and Wang Yang-ming* (Scholars Press, 1990) and *Confucian Moral Self Cultivation* (Peter Lang, 1993). He is currently an Assistant Professor in Philosophy and Religious Studies at Stanford.

PAUL KJELLBERG is an Assistant Professor of Philosophy at Whittier College in Los Angeles. He has studied at Yale University (B.A., 1986), Tunghai University in Taichung, Taiwan (1986–7,) and Stanford University (Ph.D., 1993). His dissertation, entitled "Zhuangzi and Skepticism," is a historical review and philosophical analysis of Zhuangzi's skeptical philosophy. He is the author of reviews and articles that have appeared in *Philosophy East and West, China Review International*, and *Faultline*.

JOEL KUPPERMAN is a Professor of Philosophy at the University of Connecticut. He holds undergraduate degrees from the University of Chicago and a Ph.D. from Cambridge University (1963). He is author of *Ethical Knowledge* (George Allen and Unwin, 1970), *The Foundations of Morality* (George Allen and Unwin, 1983), and *Character* (Oxford University Press, 1991). His articles have appeared in *Philosophy East and West, Mind, The Proceedings of the Aristotelian Society, American Philosophical Quarterly*, and other journals.

DAVID LOY is Professor in the Faculty of International Studies, Bunkyo University, Chigasaki, Japan. He studied at Carleton College (B.A., 1969), the University of Hawaii (M.A., 1975) and the National University of Singapore (Ph.D., 1984). His papers have been published in such journals as: *Philosophy East and West, International Philosophical Quarterly, Man and World, International Studies in Philosophy, Journal of Indian Philosophy* and *Journal of Chinese Philosophy*. He is author of *Nonduality: a Study in Comparative Philosophy* (Yale, 1988) and *Lack and Transcendence: Death and Life in Psychotherapy, Existentialism and Buddhism* (Humanities Press, forthcoming).

LISA RAPHALS studied at Clark University (B.A. 1974), Boston College (M.A. 1976), Harvard, and the University of Chicago (Ph.D. 1989). She is the author of *Knowing Words: Wisdom and Cunning in the Classical Traditions of China and Greece* (Cornell 1992). She has published articles in *Philosophy East & West, Journal of Religions,* and *Journal of Chinese Religion*. She is currently Assistant Professor of Asian Studies and Social Studies at Bard College.

ERIC SCHWITZGEBEL received his B.A. (1991) from Stanford and is currently a candidate for a Ph.D. in philosophy at U.C. Berkeley. His interests include Chinese philosophy and developmental psychology. This is his first publication.

EDWARD G. SLINGERLAND is a Ph.D. candidate specializing in Chinese religious and philosophical thought at Stanford University. He received his B.A. in Chinese from Stanford in 1991 and his M.A. in Chinese from the Department of East Asian Languages at U.C. Berkeley in 1993. He is primarily interested in the treatment of epistemological and ethical problems in early Chinese thought and their relevance to issues in contemporary Western philosophy.

LEE H. YEARLEY is the Walter Y. Evans-Wentz Professor in, and Chair of, the Department of Religious Studies at Stanford University. His most recent book is *Mencius and Aquinas: Theories of Virtue and Conceptions of Courage* (SUNY, 1990). Other recent work includes the article "Conflicts among Ideals of Human Flourishing" in *Prospects for a Common Morality* (Princeton, 1993) and the 1994 William James Lecture at Harvard, "Taoist Wandering and the Adventure of Religious Ethics."

Name Index

Aenesidemus, 2
Alembert, Jean Le Rond D', 193
Allinson, Robert, xx, 29, 44, 45, 69, 92, 93, 95, 144, 183, 184
Allison, Henry, 188, 193, 194
Ames, Roger T., vii, 150
Appelles the painter, 7
Aquinas, 181
Arcesilaus, 6, 27, 35, 43, 47
Archer Yi, 174
Aristotle, 144, 181, 187. *See also* Aristotelianism

Baier, Annette, 190, 195
Barnes, Jonathan, 43, 44
Barthes, Roland, 99, 122, 125
Bass, Alan, 123, 125
Berkeley, Bishop George, 27, 36
Berkson, Mark, xvi, 124
Berthold-Bond, Daniel, 49
Bevan, Edwyn Robert, 43
Bogong You, 150–51
Bourdieu, Pierre, 151
Brooks, E. Bruce, 177
Buddha, 50, 52, 58, 62, 63, 64, 190. *See also* Buddhism, Śākyamuni Buddha
Burnyeat, Myles, 22, 23, 25, 42, 43, 44, 47, 48
Bury, R. G., 22, 43

Camus, Albert, 184–5, 187, 194
Candrakīrti, 65
Carman, John B., 177
Carneades, 6, 27, 43

Chan, Wing-tsit, 124
Chen, J. M., 98, 122
Cheng Chung-ying, 122
Cherniak, Susan, 49
Cherniss, H. J., 47
Chien Chi-hui, 122
Chomsky, Noam, 100
Chu Boyu, 184
cicada, xiii, 71, 183
cicada-catcher, 141, 143, 164
Cicero, 22, 35, 43, 46, 47
Clansman Tai, 90
Clare, L. A., 49
Cobb, Jonathan, 207
Confucius, 16, 25, 56, 64, 72, 73, 75, 93, 100, 122, 130, 132, 137, 141, 146, 148, 149, 151, 155, 184, 190, 191, 195, 207. *See also Analects*
Conze, Edward, 67
Cook (Cook Ding), xiv, xvi, 11, 16, 23–4, 75, 76, 89, 94, 117, 119–20, 132, 135–43, 148, 164–5, 184, 191, 193, 197, 202, 211, 212
Cooper John M., 47
Cornford, Francis Macdonald, 47
Coussin, Pierre, 25
Crandell, Michael M., 182
Creel, Herlee, 23, 70, 92, 180
Crippled Shu, 82, 212
Cua, Antonio, 93
Culler, Jonathon, 100

Davidson, Donald, 193, 195
Democritus, 44
Dennet, Daniel, 189, 195
Derrida, Jacques, xvi, 97–126, 211

Descartes, René, 27, 43, 85, 95
Ding Fubao, 145
Diogenes Laertius, 2, 22, 43, 47
dove, 17, 18, 71
Dretske, Fred, 95
Du Fu, 43
Duan Yucai, 145
Dupre, John, 213
Duval, Karen, 181

Eagleton, Terry, 106, 115, 116, 123
Ehrenzweig, Anton, 193, 195
Ellis, John, 98, 99, 104, 105, 113, 122
Engraver Qing. *See* Woodcarver Qing
Eno, Robert, xvi–xvii, 69, 93, 95, 137,
    146, 148, 180, 211, 212
Epictetus, 22
Etheridge, Sanford G., 22, 43
Everson, Stephen, 43

Faure, Bernard, 122
Feinberg, Joel, 205, 213
ferryman, 164, 166
Fish, Stanley, 103, 123
Fonteyn, Margot, 184
Forke, Alfred, 24
Foster, Lawrence, 195
Frankfurt, Harry, 189, 195
Freeman, Kathleen, 22
French, Peter A., 214
Freud, Sigmund, 43
Fung Yu-lan, 23, 178

Gable, Kirk, 92
Gaptooth. *See* Nie Que
Gewirth, Alan, 204–205, 213
Girardot, Norman, 149, 178
Graham, Angus Charles, xx, 24, 29,
    40, 42, 44, 45, 46, 48, 51, 60, 61,
    65, 66, 68, 69, 73, 87, 92, 93, 94,
    95, 103, 109, 119, 123,124, 144,
    146, 148, 149, 150, 155, 163, 177,
    178, 180, 182, 212, 214
Greene, Marjorie, 93
Groarke, Leo, 43

Guo Qingfan, 24, 25
Guo Xiang, 24

Hall, David, 150
Hallie, Phillip, 22, 23, 43, 45
Hampshire, Sir Stuart, 179, 213
Hansen, Chad, xviii, xx, 25, 29, 40,
    44, 45, 46, 49, 66, 68, 69, 79, 87,
    90, 92, 93, 94, 96, 100, 144, 145,
    147, 202, 209, 210, 211, 178, 179,
    196, 197–202, 209, 210, 211
Harbsmeier, Christoph, 45
Harris, Roy, 123
Hawkes, David, 43
Heraclitus, 21, 36, 38, 40, 41, 44, 46
Hobbes, Thomas, 187
Homer, 41
Hopkins, Steven P., 177
Huan, Duke, 74, 118
Hui Shi. *See* Huizi
Hui Neng, 66
Huizi, 10, 11, 14, 32, 33, 72, 75, 76,
    80, 81, 134, 138, 147
Hume, David, 27, 36, 43, 193, 194
Humphries, Rolfe, 22
Husserl, Edmund, 113
Huzi, 66, 192

Ivanhoe, Philip J., xviii, 25, 29, 44, 45,
    49, 66, 70, 87, 92, 93, 95, 117, 122,
    124, 177, 178, 180, 186, 199, 201,
    203, 211, 212

Jian Wu, 72
Jie Yu, 72
Johnson, Barbara, 107

Kant, Immanuel, 27, 188, 190, 193,
    194. *See also* Kantianism
Karlgren, Bernard, 145
Kempton, Kim, 92
Kierkegaard, Søren, 192
Kjellberg, Paul, xiv, xix, 23, 43, 70, 87,
    93, 94, 95, 96, 122, 179, 202, 211

kui beast, 25, 140,
Kun fish, 18, 71, 72, 81, 138
Kupperman, Joel, xvii–xviii, xix, 65, 194, 195

Lanson, Gustave, 99
Laozi, 46, 50, 119, 124
Lau, D. C., 195
Lee, Edward, 48
Legge, James, 178, 195, 213
Levett, M. J., 42
Levy-Bruhl, Lucien, 42, 49
Li, Lady, 8, 78
Li Bo, 43
Li Wai-Yee, 49
Lian Shu, 72
Liu Xiaogan, 24
Liu Xie, 48
Lloyd, G. E. R., 49
Long, Anthony, 22
Loy, David, xv, xix
Lucretius, 22

MacIntyre, Alasdair, 181
Magee, Bryan, 66
Mair, Victor, xx, 25, 44, 45, 46, 51, 59, 60, 66, 68, 69, 70, 79, 83, 87, 90, 93, 94, 95, 100, 123, 144, 177, 178, 179, 181, 182, 197, 198, 199, 200, 211
Mallarmé, Stéphane, 112
Maoqiang, 8, 78
Marcus Aurelius, 22
Marks, Joel, 195
Medin, Laura, 122
Mencius, 19, 23, 31, 32–33, 40, 41, 46, 100–101, 132, 150, 182, 195, 206, 208, 209. *See also Mencius*
Mengzi. *See* Mencius
Mill, John Stuart, 186, 194
monkey trainer, 10, 11
Moore, G. E., 187
Moravcsik, J. M. E., 181
Morgan, Evan, 178
Mossner, Ernest C., 195
Mourelatos, Alexander P. D., 48
Mozart, Wolfgang Amadeus, 189

Mozi. *See Mozi,* Mohism, Neo-Mohism
Munro, Donald, 180
Murdoch, Iris, 111, 125, 126, 211
Music Master Kuang, 134

Nāgārjuna, xv, 50–65, 110, 124. *See also Mūlamadhyamikākarikā*
Nagel, Thomas, 212
Nameless Man, 82
Needham, Joseph, 135, 148, 150, 180, 181
Nehamas, Alexander, 194, 211
Nie Que, 8, 23, 34, 41, 86, 87
Nietzsche, Friedrich, 122, 211
Nivison, David, 23, 24, 25, 177, 179
Norris, Christopher, 99, 100, 107, 113, 122, 124
Nureyev, Rudolph, 184
Nussbaum, Martha, 25, 182, 214

Obata Shigenyoshi, 43
Outka, Gene, 181
O'Brien, Justin, 194

Parker, Patricia, 122
Parmenides, 145
Patrick, Mary Mills, 22, 43
Peng bird, 18, 71, 72, 81, 138
Perfected Person. *See Zhi Ren*
Perloff, Marjore, 122
Peters, R. S., 181
Phaenarete, 39
Picasso, Pablo, 66
Pindar, 41
Plato, xv, 3, 21, 26, 27, 35–42, 44, 46, 47, 48, 99, 121, 129, 192. *See also* Platonism
Plotinus, 110
Plutarch, 47
Polanyi, Michael, 93, 136, 148
Price, A. F., 66, 67

Price, Richard, 36
Protagoras, 31, 36–37, 38, 40, 41, 44, 48

Pyrrho of Elis, 2, 27, 43. *See also*
Pyrrhonism

Raphals, Lisa, xv, 22, 45, 211
Rawls, John, 204, 207, 212
Reeder, John P., 181
Regan, Tom, 204
Reps, Paul, 195
Riegel, Jeffrey, 146
Riviere, Pierre, 49
Rorty, Richard M., 48
Rosemont, Henry, Jr., xx, 23, 25, 44,
    49, 146, 178
Roth, Harold, xx, 44, 46, 49, 177, 178,
    181, 182
Rousseau, Jean-Jacques, 107, 115, 193,
    125
Royal Relativity. *See* Wang Ni
Ryle, Gilbert, xvi, xx, 147, 170, 181

Śākyamuni Buddha, 50, 52, 62. *See
    also* Buddha, Buddhism
Saussure, Ferdinand de, xvi, 104–105,
    113, 123
Schipper, Kristopher, 181
Schofield, Malcolm, 25, 43, 44
Schwartz, Benjamin, 101, 122, 146,
    180, 212
Schwitzgebel, Eric, xv
Searle, John, 66, 125
Sedley, David, 22, 23
Sells, Michael, 110, 125
Sen, Amartya, 214
Sennett, Richard, 207
Sextus Empiricus, xiv, 1–21, 27, 28, 29,
    35, 38, 39, 43, 47, 86, 95. *See also
    Outlines of Pyrrhonism*, Pyrrhonism
Shen Dao, 33, 46, 149
Shen Buhai, 149
Shih, Vincent Yu-chung, 48
Shun, Emperor, 72, 93
Sinatra, Frank, 198
Sivin, Nathan, 49
Slingerland, Edward G., xix, 124
Smith, Kidder, 69, 144, 146, 149, 182,
    211

Socrates, 2, 26–28, 31, 35–39, 41, 42,
    44, 47
Song, Man of: bleaching silk, 10–11,
    12, 14; selling hats, 75
Sontag, Susan, 122
Spivak, Gayatri, 122,
Sprung, Mervyn, 65
Staniforth, Maxwell, 22
Strawson, P. F., 187, 194
Strawson, Galen, 194
Striker, Gisela, 22, 25, 28, 44, 48
Stroud, Barry, 95
Sūbhuti, 62, 64
Swanson, Joe William, 195
swimmer at Lüliang waterfall, 117,
    141, 150, 167, 176, 181

Taylor, Charles, 178
Theaetetus, 36
Tian Gen, 81
Timon of Athens, 2
True Man. *See Zhen Ren*

Uehling, Theodore E., 214
Unger, Peter, 96
Urmson, J. O., 181

Van Norden, Bryan W., 44, 49, 92, 211
Vlastos, Gregory, 28, 44, 47, 48, 206

Waley, Arthur, 23, 24, 69–70, 181,
    182, 195
Wallace, James, 181
Wang Liqi, 48
Wang Ni, 8, 9, 10, 23, 33, 78, 86, 94,
    96
Wang Fuzhi, 45, 46, 48, 109, 124
Watson, Burton, 23, 51, 59, 71
Weatherford, Margaret, vii
Wenhui, Lord, 11, 12, 23, 117, 202

Wettstein, Howard, 214
Wheelwright Pian, 15, 66, 74–75, 76,
    89, 94, 118, 119, 165

White, Nicholas P., 22, 48
Williams, Bernard, 144, 205
Wittgenstein, Ludwig, 110, 122, 188
Wong, David, xviii, 93, 196, 202–211,
   212, 213, 214
Woodcarver Qing, 14, 118, 119, 166,
   175
Woodruff, Paul, 27, 35, 38, 43, 44, 46,
   47
Woodworker Qing. *See* Woodcarver
   Qing
Wren, Sir Christopher, 190
Wu, Kwang-ming, xx, 40, 93, 94, 95,
   109, 124, 178

Xenophanes, 21
Xi Shi, 46
Xiao Ding, 146
Xie, S. B., 98, 122
Xu You, xiii

Xuan, King of Qi, 23
Xunzi, xiv, 1, 16–21, 25, 179. *See also*
   Xunzi

Yan Hui, 56, 148, 151, 162, 166–67,
   175, 187, 191, 207
Yan He, 148
Yang Zhu, 132. *See also* Yangism
Yao Xiaosui, 146
Yao, Emperor, 72, 93
Ye Gongzi Gao, 122, 148
Yearley, Lee H., xvii, xix, 70, 83, 95,
   178, 179, 180, 181, 182, 212
Yeh, Michelle, 98, 122
Zhang Wuzi, 81
Zhang Longxi, 121, 122, 125
Zhao Wen, 134
Zhen Ren, 10, 13, 66, 89
Zhi Ren, 8, 9–10, 59, 96
Zhuangzi, life of, 152
Ziqi of Nanguo, 30, 53

Subject Index

absolutism, 29, 45, 66, 101, 103, 104, 108, 114, 120, 123, 144, 197, 198–99

adaptive "that's it." *See yinshi*

alethia, 13

amoralism, xvii, xviii, 176, 209, 211

Analects, 130, 137, 146. *See also* Confucius

anātma, 52. *See also* self: non-existence of

anitya, 52

anti-rationalism, xv, xx, 29, 51, 65, 109–110, 124, 210, 214

Apology, 21, 47

apophasis, 109–112, 120, 121, 124, 125

appearances. *See phainomena*

apraxia, 48

Aristotelianism, 43, 168, 181, 210

Aṣṭasāhasrikā, 62, 64

ataraxia, xiv, 2, 4, 10, 12, 13, 16, 23, 28. *See also* peace, tranquility

authentic. *See zhen*

Autumn Floods. *See Qiushui*

axis of the Way, 61, 79, 161, 164

benevolence. *See ren*

bian 辯, 31, 32, 33, 34, 41, 157. *See also* dichotomies, discrimination, distinction, dualism, opposites

breath control, 66, 175. *See also* meditation

Buddhism, 50–65, 159, 190, 191. *See also* Buddha, Śākyamuni Buddha

Cartesianism, 43

cheng 成, 72, 118, 133, 134, 147

cheng xin 成心, 31, 32

Christianity, 159

ci 慈, 203, 205–206, 210

clarity. *See ming*

compassion. *See ci*

completion. *See cheng*

Confucianism, xvii, 14, 18, 25, 31, 32, 41, 45, 80, 93, 100, 101–103, 109, 128, 130–143, 146, 148, 150, 151, 153, 155, 156, 186, 195, 206, 207, 211, 213. *See also* Ruism

contrived "that's it." *See weishi*

courage, 150

criterion, 5, 9, 20, 31, 78, 170 179

cultivated heart-mind. *See cheng xin*

daemonic, 154, 162–6, 175–6, 184. *See also shen*

dao 道, etymology of, 129, 145

dao-practice, 131, 134, 135, 137, 140, 142, 143, 147, 149

dao-learning, xvii, 132, 136, 137, 142, 149

dao-master, 138, 142, 150

dao-teaching, 133

Daodejing 道德經, 46, 55, 102, 107, 122, 124, 130, 140, 141, 148, 149, 150, 213. *See also* Laozi

Daxue 大學, 139, 151

Dazongshi 大宗師, 140, 201

de 德, 39, 163, 175. *See also ming de*, power, virtue

death, xiii, xv, 8, 22, 34, 55, 64, 73, 83, 88, 89, 140, 158

Dechongfu 德充符, 139

deconstruction, xv, xvi, 51–54, 62, 98-122

deep love. See ci
dependent origination. See pratītya-
    samutpāda
destiny. See ming
Dialecticians, 100. See also Logicians,
    School of Names, Sophists
Diamond Sutra, 58, 62, 64, 66
dichotomies, 106, 153, 157, 160–63,
    166, 174, 175, 180. See also bian,
    discrimination, distinction, dualism,
    opposites
différance, 106, 114
dignity, 206
direct access to reality, 6, 97, 113, 121.
    See also immediate perception,
    prapañcopaśama, pure experience,
    unmediated access
discrimination, 33, 50, 55, 57, 62, 78,
    80, 105. See also bian, dichotomies,
    distinction, dualism, opposites
Discussion on Making All Things
    Equal. See Qiwulun
dispositional drives, xvii, 153, 154,
    155, 160, 163, 167, 171, 174, 175,
    176o
distinction, 30, 32, 33, 35, 79, 80, 86,
    102, 103, 104, 112, 132, 140, 156,
    157, 162, 163, 167. See also bian,
    dichotomies, discrimination,
    dualism, opposites
dogmatism, 2–3, 4, 5, 6, 20, 28, 35, 36,
    39, 43, 199, 200
dreaming: da meng 大夢 the "great" or
    "ultimate dream," 26, 34, 64, 85–86,
    95, 189; philosophical problem of,
    xv, 26, 27, 36–38, 52, 64–5, 95;
    Zhuangzi's of being a butterfly, 26,
    29, 34, 63–64, 86, 87, 89, 95
dualism, xv, xvi, 55, 56, 57, 59, 60, 65.
    See also bian, dichotomies, discrimi-
    nation, distinctions, opposites
duḥkha, 52, 53

education, 16, 18, 183, 192–93. See
    also training
elenchus "cross-examination," 28, 38,
    39, 40

emptiness. See śūnyatā
energy. See qi
Epicureanism, 22
epistēme, 27. See also knowledge
epistemology, 16, 20, 27, 31, 36, 44,
    127, 138, 144, 199
epochē, xiv, 2, 4, 6, 7, 28, 47. See
    also Suspension of judgment
Essay on Equalizing Things. See
    Qiwulun
ethical promiscuity, 208, 210, 213
eudaimonism, 23

fasting of the mind. See xin zhai
Fit for Emperors and Kings. See
    Yingdiwang
forgetting, 93, 159, 166, 172–73;
    morality, 73; one's body, 14; oneself,
    58–60, 65, 187; words, 117. See also
    wang xin, zuo wang
Free and Easy Wandering. See Xiaoyao-
    you

genuine. See zhen
glib. See ning
Great Learning. See Daxue
Greek philosophy, xiv, xv, 27, 41–42,
    127–29, 131, 136, 144, 146, 186
Greek skepticism, history of, 2, 43
guan zhi 宮知, 135
Guanzi 管子, 149
gymnosophs, 2

Hamlet, 194
Han Feizi 韓非子, 149
Handan Walk, 14–15, 159
Heart Sutra, 58, 65
heart-mind. See xin
Heaven, xix, 13, 30, 50, 58, 59, 60, 82,
    89, 101, 118, 119, 161, 162, 163,
    165, 166, 174, 198, 201, 207, 212.
    See also tian
Heaven's-eye view, 109, 200, 201, 210
History, Book of. See Shujing
Huainanzi 淮南子, 178

hui 毀, 133
human nature, xviii, xix, 18, 19, 100,
   196, 202, 203, 210, 212, 213
human, as opposed to natural, xvii, 13,
   19, 32, 76–7, 97, 108, 130, 138,
   140–42, 174. *See also ren* "human"
humor, xviii, 15, 24, 28, 32, 34, 39, 41,
   45, 110, 112, 116, 137, 185. *See also*
   irony, literary style

illumination, 30, 32, 39, 103, 149. *See*
   also ming
immediate perception, 38. *See also*
   direct access, *prapañcopaśama*, pure
   experience, unmediated access
imperfection. *See hui, kui*
impermanence. *See anitya*
impracticability. *See apraxia*
impressions. *See phantasia*
Inner Chapter, 20, 24, 44, 55, 59, 64,
   66, 71, 72, 73, 75, 78, 81, 82, 83,
   85, 87, 88, 91, 92, 128, 135, 138,
   139, 140, 141, 142, 144, 150, 151,
   184, 206, 207, 212
inquirers. *See skeptikoi*
irony, 23, 24, 28, 36, 38, 39, 48, 74,
   102, 191. *See also* humor, literary
   style
it/other. *See shi/bi*·

Kantianism, 204
karma, 52, 53
knack stories. *See* skill stories
knowledge: skill/fact, xvi, xvii, 45, 127,
   134, 143, 170; how/that, xvi, xx, 66,
   170; rational, linguistic/natural,
   intuitive, xx 15, 75–76, 139; real,
   true, xv, xvii, 27, 41, 89; great, 30,
   39, 40, 41, 61. *See also epistēme,*
   shi-fei, zhi
kui 虧, 134

language, xv, 1, 60, 68–126, 152, 197,
   199; role of in experience, xvi, 1, 32,
   35, 60, 54, 59, 66, 70, 72, 97, 128–

131, 197; problems with, xix, 13–15,
   40, 97–122, 128–132, 197; dualistic
   nature of, xv, xix, 31–5, 45, 46, 60–
   61, 74, 79, 104–109, 157, 160–62,
   175; skepticism concerning; xiv–xv,
   xix, 13–15, 32, 40, 44, 45, 72, 87,
   98, 101–104, 132, 199, 202; correct
   use of, 63, 81, 88, 109–122, 133,
   143. *See also* knowledge; linguistic
langue, 104, 114
Laozi 老子. *See Daodejing*
Later Mohism. *See* Neo-Mohism
lay of the land. *See shi*
li 禮, 100, 132
liang xing 兩行, 109
Liezi 列子, 57, 180
literary style, xviii–xiv, 16, 24, 41, 51,
   60, 137. *See also* humor, irony,
   poetry
Logicians, 69, 73, 153. *See also*
   Dialecticians, School of Names,
   Sophists
logocentrism, 99, 100, 121, 122

meditation, 52, 59. *See also* breath
   control, *xin zhai*
Mencius, 19, 23, 24, 45, 132, 149, 151,
   195, 203, 206, 211, 213. *See also*
   Mencius
metriopatheia, 4
mind. *See xin*
ming 明, xiii, 30, 32, 39, 41, 103, 147.
   See also clarity, illumination
ming 命 "destiny," 141
ming de 明德, 39
mirror, 58, 59, 119, 121, 123, 160–64,
   166, 170, 175, 179
Miscellaneous Chapters, 140
moderation of feeling. *See metriopatheia*
Mohism, xvii, 14, 31, 32, 35, 41, 45,
   55, 80, 84, 90, 93, 94, 101, 103, 109,
   128, 131–7, 142, 146, 149, 206, 207,
   213. *See also Mozi*, Neo-Mohism
Mozi 墨子, 136, 146
Mūlamadhyamikakārikā, 50, 51, 65. *See*
   also Nāgārjuna

mysticism, xvii, 9, 30, 31, 40, 42, 45,
46, 138, 145, 160, 198

naked philosophers. *See gymnosophs*
natural pattern. *See tian li*
natural mechanism. *See tian ji*
naturalism, 16, 19
Neo-Mohism, 20, 25, 29, 32, 33, 40,
41, 45, 46, 100
ning 佞, 146
nirvāṇa, 54, 62, 64
nonaction. *See wuwei*
nonduality, xv, 65

Odes, Book of. See Shijing
opposites, xv, 106-109, 115, 116, 120.
See also bian, dichotomies, discrimination, distinction, dualism
ordinary practice. *See yong*
otherness, 61, 107, 108, 124, 161. *See
also shi/bi*
Outer Chapters, 74, 82, 83, 128, 135,
136, 140, 150
Outlines of Pyrrhonism, 2–21, 28, 43,
44, 47. *See also* Pyrrhonism, Sextus
Empiricus

parole, 104
peace, xv, xvi, 2, 7, 10, 12, 21, 161,
173. *See also ataraxia*, tranquility
perfection. *See cheng*
performance/process, 168–173
perspectivity, 101, 156, 183, 184
phainomena, 2–6, 13, 43
phantasia, 13
phusei, 3–4, 13
pipes of heaven. *See tian lai*
Pivot of Nurturing Life. *See
Yangshengzhu*
Platonism, 27, 43, 99, 114, 121, 122
play, 51, 60, 81, 88, 103, 110–11, 121,
126, 184
poetry, 24, 40, 41, 45, 133. *See also*
literary style
postmodernism, xvi, 51

poststructuralism, 98, 99
power, 184, 192. *See also de*
prapañcopaśama, 58, 62
pratītya-samutpāda 59. *See also* direct
access, immediate perception, pure
experience, unmediated access
pratītya-samutpāda, 52, 54
propetes, 5
pure experience, 118. *See also* direct
access, immediate perception,
prapañcopaśama, unmediated access
Pyrrhonism, 2–8, 25, 27, 43
Pythagoreanism, 144

qi 氣, 162, 164, 166, 175, 176, 179, 191
Qiushui 秋水, 140
Qiwulun 齊物論, xv, 26, 27, 29, 33, 40,
44, 53, 68, 73, 77, 92, 127, 128, 129,
131, 135, 136, 138, 139, 143, 150

rash. *See propetes*
reason, xv, 5, 6, 29, 42, 51, 60, 97, 98,
110, 116, 119, 124, 127, 128, 129,
131, 134, 135, 139, 144; analytic
argument, 100, 137; analytic reason,
xvi, 41, 100, 128, 149, 193; rationality, 29, 40, 42, 44, 65, 119, 120,
128, 130, 132, 134, 135, 147, 204
reflective drives, xvii, 153–5, 160, 163,
167, 171, 174, 176
ren 仁 "benevolence," 34, 73, 130, 146
ren 人 "human," 13, 17
Renjianshi 人間世, 68, 136, 137, 139,
151, 207
ritual. *See li*
Ruism, 35, 144. *See also* Confucianism

sage, xviii, 18–19, 57, 58, 59, 61, 63,
66, 77, 78, 89, 101, 105, 108, 109,
117–19, 133, 134, 139, 147, 149,
151, 186–7, 193, 200, 207
saṁsāra, 62
School of Names, 94. *See also*
Dialecticians, Logicians, Sophists
self: nature of, xvii, 153, 177, 189–92;

non-existence of, 52, 53, 102, 118, 135, 154 *(see also anātma)*; relation to other, xv, 113, 203, 205 *(see also shi/bi)*; self-refutation, xv, 28, 33, 37, 40

senses, the, 4–7, 35–36, 38, 40, 44, 85, 86, 95, 135–6, 164, 176. *See also guan zhi*

shamanism, 81, 138, 139, 192

Shangshu, 145

shen 神, 135, 141, 154, 162–64, 175, 182. *See also* daemonic, spiritual

shi 時 "timeliness," 137

shi/fei 是非, 30–34, 40, 41, 45, 46, 55–56, 61, 79, 101, 102, 109, 133, 160–61, 174

shi 勢 "lay of the land," 137

shi/bi 是彼, 79, 108, 135, 160, 161

Shijing 詩經, 25, 129, 145

Shujing 書經, 213

Shuowen jiezi 說文解字, 145

Sign of Full Power. *See Dechongfu*

skandhas, 52

skepticism: typologies of, 9, 20, 28, 42, 70, 84–5; and relativism, xvi, 20, 69, 101. *See also* Greek skepticism, history of; pyrrhonism; language, skepticism of

skeptikoi, 6

skillful means. *See upāya*

skillfulness, 12, 13, 16, 66, 116, 120, 153, 155, 160, 171–4, 201; skill stories, xiv, 60, 74, 75, 117, 135, 163, 197

Sophists, 32, 33, 40, 55, 144. *See also* Dialecticians, Logicians, School of Names

Sorting which Evens Things Out. *See Qiwulun*

spiritual, 8, 12, 75, 87, 117–19, 135, 141, 142, 154, 201. *See also shen*

spontaneity, xvii, xviii, xix, 7, 18, 19, 48, 59, 116, 119, 120, 123, 135–37, 140–43, 148, 154, 160, 163, 167, 170, 174–6, 180, 183, 184, 186, 188, 190, 191–94, 195, 198, 203, 205. *See also ziran*

Stoicism, 20, 22

structuralism, 54, 99, 100, 106

style. *See* literary style

suffering. *See duḥkha*

śūnyatā, 58

Sunzi 孫子, 149

suspension of judgment, xiv, xv, 2, 4, 6, 7, 17, 21, 28, 38, 158, 203. *See also epochē*

Symposium, 3

"that's it"/"that's not." *See shi/fei*

"that's it" which deems. *See weishi*

"that's it" which goes by circumstance. *See yinshi*

Theaetetus, xv, 26–42

therapy, xvi, xix, 7, 20, 25, 69, 70, 91, 92, 93, 109, 117, 120, 200 201, 210

things, as self-existing and distinct, xv, 53–4, 55, 138–9

this/that. *See shi/bi*

tian 天, 23, 63; contrasted to ren "human," 13, 16. *See also* heaven

tian ji 天機, 15, 140, 143

tian li 天理, 12, 13

tian lai 天籟, 30, 108, 200

timeliness. *See shi*

training, xvii, 18, 130, 131, 132, 147, 148, 155, 171, 175. *See also* education

tranquility, 153, 161, 172, 173, 176. *See also ataraxia*

transcendent drives, xvii, 153, 154–5, 160, 162, 163, 166, 167, 174–77

tropes. *See tropoi*

tropoi, 4–7, 9

Ultimate Teacher. *See Dazongshi*

unmediated access to reality, xvii, 113, 116, 120, 136, 142, 143. *See also* direct access, immediate perception, *prapañcopaśama*, pure experience

upāya, 57

usefulness/uselessness, 10, 56, 68, 72, 73, 82, 83, 88, 89, 91, 170,

virtue, 39, 82, 137, 163, 175. *See also*
    de

walking with both things. *See liang xing*
wang xin 忘心, 59. *See also* forgetting
wei 偽, 19, 133. *See also weishi*
weishi 爲是, 46, 56, 60, 163
World of Man. *See Renjianshi*
wuwei 無爲, 59, 136, 151, 163, 180

Xiaoyaoyou 逍遙遊, 75, 138, 139, 140
xin , 58–9, 100, 101, 162, 166. *See also*
    chengxin, wangxin, xinzhai
xing 心, 141, 180
xinzhai 性, 14, 52, 53, 56, 75, 119, 121,
    162, 164, 166, 175, 191, 192. *See*
    also meditation
Xunzi 荀子, 16, 17, 19. *See also Xunzi*
Yangism, 93, 153

Yangshengzhu 養生主, 128, 132, 135,
    139, 148, 197, 202
Yijing 易經, 56, 149
yin/yang 陰陽, 56
Yingdiwang 應帝王, 140, 150
yinshi 因是, 46, 60, 147, 148, 163
yong 庸, 133, 149

Zen, 192
zhen 眞, 19, 132. *See also* Zhen Ren
zhi 知, 30, 41, 79, 89, 96. *See also*
    knowledge
Zhong Yong 中庸, 151
Zhuangzi 莊子: authorship of, xx, 24,
    45, 92, 144, 153; textual history of
    xx, 40
ziran 自然, 59, 141, 150, 163, 180. *See*
    also spontaneity
zuo wang 坐忘, 56, 121. *See also*
    forgetting